101

John Major, Tony Blair
and a conflict of leadership

MANCHESTER
UNIVERSITY PRESS

John Major, Tony Blair and a conflict of leadership

Collision course

MICHAEL FOLEY

Manchester University Press

MANCHESTER AND NEW YORK

distributed exclusively in the USA by Palgrave

Published by Manchester University Press
Oxford Road, Manchester M13 9NR, UK
and Room 400, 175 Fifth Avenue, New York, NY 10010, USA
www.manchesteruniversitypress.co.uk

Distributed exclusively in the USA by
Palgrave, 175 Fifth Avenue, New York, NY 10010, USA

Distributed exclusively in Canada by
UBC Press, University of British Columbia, 2029 West Mall,
Vancouver, BC, Canada v6t 1z2

British Library Cataloguing-in-Publication Data
A catalogue record for this book is available from the British Library

Library of Congress Cataloging-in-Publication Data applied for

ISBN 0 7190 6316 7 hardback
0 7190 6317 5 paperback

First published 2002
10 09 08 07 06 05 04 03 02   10 9 8 7 6 5 4 3 2 1

Typeset in Minion and Officina Sans
by Koinonia Ltd, Manchester
Printed in Great Britain
by Bookcraft (Bath) Ltd, Midsomer Norton

To the shining promise of boundless futures:

Jo and her mission
Nic and his vision
Lou and her calling

Contents

CONTENTS

List of figures and tables

Figures

Tables

Acknowledgements

I am grateful to those who provided me with background information, comments and observations during the course of this project. I am heavily indebted to them for their insights and guidance. On a more technical but no less important level, I would like to express my appreciation to the editorial and production staff at Manchester University Press. I am particularly indebted to Rachel Armstrong, Rachael Bolden, Richard Delahunty, Bobby Gainher and Tony Mason. MUP continue not only to excel in every aspect of design and production, but to maintain the highest standards of professionalism. I would also like to extend my thanks both to Jo Foley who applied her artistic skills to the tables and figures, and to Patricia Owens who devised the index with speed and efficiency. Lastly, I must express my gratitude to the Department of International Politics at the University of Wales, Aberystwyth. The research led nature of the organisation, together with the constant stimulus of my colleagues and students, has been a great source of encouragement and inspiration. The only area whose attribution cannot be shared is in the field of errors and omissions which of course remain all my own work.

Aberystwyth
June 2002

1 The leadership issue

Britain has traditionally had a highly ambiguous attitude towards political leadership. While leaders have clearly been a recognisable component of the British political system, their exact position and status have usually been left open to question, and very often to considerable suspicion. In many respects, political leadership has been regarded as superfluous to British governance. This outlook has been derived from a variety of sources. For example, it draws in a general way upon the norms of liberal democracy and the rule of law, which accentuate the value of individual rights and freedoms in the citizen's relationship to the state. The corollary of this political priority is a restriction in the room available for leaders to develop their claims to accumulate power and authority. Another source is Britain's constitutional understanding that political arrangements should not be abused by those seeking to exploit its areas of imprecision for political gain. Leaders, therefore, are persistently held in check by social as well as political restraints.

A further factor in Britain's habitual scepticism of leaders lies with its sense of national identity. 'Britishness' is closely associated to an absence of autocratic power. The faith in its institutions to prevent the accumulation of power in a single centre is combined with a normally critical disdain for political arrangements elsewhere which are almost invariably seen as inferior to the organisation of the British government. In the same way that the British system is thought not to lend itself to the claims and assumptions of political leaders, so British government is both characterised and celebrated for the absence of the kind of personalised executive force seen abroad. In this light, foreign governments are often depicted as objects of corruption, danger and derision. The usurpation of power by leaders is depicted in a variety of guises ranging from the imperial pretensions of a figure like Napoleon to the totalitarian extremes of Hitler and Stalin, and from the fascist violence of Mussolini or Franco, to the repression of leaders produced by the insecurities of weak or 'broken' states. The British reaction to such phenomena has been to reaffirm its attachment to liberal pragmatism over the mysticism and coercion of leader-centred systems. As a consequence, the predominant British view has been to associate high-profile political leadership either with the centralised character of continental states, or with the conditions of dangerously dysfunctional societies. Any domestic campaign to introduce a structure of personalised leadership and charismatic authority outside the parameters of wartime would provoke similar prejudices. A movement of this sort would be seen as an ill-fated attempt to import alien concepts and features into Britain (e.g. Oswald Mosley and the British Union of Fascists).

Notwithstanding these factors, the most significant source of Britain's characteristic disinterest in political leadership lies with the institutional arrangements of the political system itself. The framework of government is based upon the principle of a sovereign electorate transmuted into a parliament that in turn legitimises the formation and authority of the cabinet. The operational ethos of this set of arrangements is strongly collective in nature with very little discretionary licence allotted to individual leaders and their development. British government is distinguished by a high degree of institutionalisation, corporate activity and systemic continuity. These features are supported by the emphasis upon party discipline, collective responsibility and a professional civil service. Accordingly, party leaders are primarily leaders of parties within parliament and, therefore, are continuously dependent upon the support of their fellow MPs for their position.

By the same token, prime ministers are formally first among cabinet equals. Constitutionally, they are derivatives or expressions of their cabinets. Prime ministers have no department base with which to exert leverage. Their access to national authority and their usage of symbolic resources are confined by the monarchy's role as the head of state. They have only the same claim to democratic status as any of their cabinet colleagues or fellow MPs, and are constantly surrounded by leadership aspirants within their own party. It is conventional wisdom that in any cabinet there will be eight to ten ministers 'who were once leadership contenders, or who are either immediate threats to the existing leader or possible long-term future challengers'.[1] Just as the way to power in such a system is by a slow and graduated route of collective appraisal, so the exercise of power is cautious, sensitive and above all, collaborative in nature. Leadership in such conditions could almost be said to be a contradiction in terms – i.e. a leadership bound by the need to maintain party loyalty, cabinet unity and electoral support, and to comply with the moral code of constitutional conventions that always require government at the highest level to be a matter of consultation rather than direction.

These apparently imperturbable rhythms have occasionally been subjected to dramatic change when individual prime ministers have arisen to levels of extraordinary ascendancy. David Lloyd-George and Winston Churchill, for example, came to possess an individual authority resonated not only through government but throughout British society. Personal leadership on this scale, however, was largely attributable to the atypical conditions to World War I and

World War II. The nature of the emergency, the threat to the nation's security, the arousal of national solidarity and the driving imperative of wartime mobilisation permitted both Lloyd-George and Churchill to inaugurate periods of extensive and far-reaching leadership. These were marked by an accelerated centralisation of government and the creation of a command and control system of prime ministerial direction. The British system is, therefore, susceptible to intense episodes of strong leadership. At the same time, it is important to note that these periods have traditionally been confined to wartime. Following the emergencies, the system would quickly revert to the normal dynamics of adversarial party competition and leadership insecurity. While Lloyd-George's ascendancy did not survive the aftermath of World War I, Churchill was immediately voted out of office in 1945. Highly centralised government and highly personalised leadership have consequently become equated with the aberrational conditions of international conflict and total war. The appearance of such continental extravagance in leadership within the British system, therefore, can be counterbalanced by the recognition that it is merely an idiosyncratic function confined to national crisis. In this respect, the inflation in leadership can itself be seen as proof positive of the conditions requiring such an exceptional suspension of normal politics.

Given the case that in Britain 'weak government ... has been the norm and strong government the exception'[2] the study of leadership in British politics has generally languished in a state of conspicuous underdevelopment. Analysis has imitated constitutional tradition. The dearth of systematic studies of the premiership, or of the role of personal leadership within government, reflects the standard perspective that the prime minister has a minimalist position within the machinery of government. It is true that a prime minister performs a variety of roles and possesses considerable political leverage. However, the office has only a marginal constitutional presence; it is dependent upon the operation of conventions; it has no security of tenure; and it remains dependent upon the cabinet, the governing party and parliament. An individual prime minister may 'choose to give his or her government policy guidance or leadership, but there is no expectation that he or she will do so. The job does not have policy leadership as one of its positive requirements.'[3] In line with this classical perspective, the prime ministerial office is seen as a collection of partial and fragmented powers that are rarely fused into a cohesive aggregate. In a classic text on the subject, Bernard Donoughue points out that '[m]ost discussions of prime ministerial power are concerned with his or her positive capacity to influence and to execute policies.'[4] But as Donoughue reminds his readers, this is a deceptive prospectus:

> In fact, there are very severe limitations to that power ... A prime minister is a party politician who may not always be absolutely certain of his or her own

3

power base. The prime minister does not like to be too far apart from senior colleagues, some of whom are competing for the job at No. 10, perhaps waiting for the leader to become isolated and then make a mistake.[5]

Prime ministerial power is seen to be marginal and provisional in nature. As a result, opportunities for vigorous leadership appear to be strictly limited.

The customary perspective of prime ministers has been one in which they are expected to perform a set of functions related either to the government machine or to the party organisation. On both counts, the conventional understanding is that the prime minister attends to the roles afforded to the office through its linkage to larger and pre-existing structures. The British prime minister has traditionally been thought of as a given unit of authority, functioning within a system of disciplined parties and collective government. 'The very high degree of institutionalisation in British government' is widely regarded as the 'most powerful determinant of what a prime minister can and cannot do'.[6] Consequently, the 'person who walks for the first time through the door of Number 10 as prime minister does not create or re-create the prime ministership: the job, to a considerable extent, already exists'.[7] According to this traditional view of the premiership, the personal characteristics of a prime minister are not particularly relevant to an understanding of either the position, or of an individual's conduct within it. For example, in the opinion of Richard Rose,

> Personal style influences how a Prime Minister carries out the demands of office, but it does not determine what is done. The first priority of a Prime Minister is to do what is expected of him or her. How a Prime Minister meets these role expectations reflects not only his or her basic personality, whatever that may be, but even more what the incumbent has learned in a quarter century of socialization in Westminster and Whitehall.[8]

As a result of this view of the office, and of the orderly system that allegedly surrounds it, the role of personal leadership has often been dismissed as something of only peripheral significance in British political life. Apart from the most extreme conditions of wartime, prime ministerial leadership has been seen as mostly unnecessary, marginally unseemly, and largely non-existent. Accordingly, 'British political science has little or no literature on political leadership. In Britain we refer to the office of prime minister and his or her performance rather than national leadership or individual leaders.'[9]

Until recently, the apparently prosaic character of British political leadership had fostered a commensurately attenuated literature on the subject. However, attitudes began to change with the premiership of Margaret Thatcher. Even in a period of peacetime, Thatcher managed to exert an extraordinary level of influence within cabinet, across Whitehall and in the country as a whole. Thatcher's robust conception of politics and the radical nature of her policy objectives were refracted through the lens of her leadership style. The manner of Thatcher's leadership was dramatically different to that of her predecessors in that it was highly substantive in content and directly confrontational in approach. As she became more established in office, 'she was increasingly taken, at her own valuation as a prime minister who towered alike over colleagues and opponents'.[10] It was widely concluded that 'to an extent more than any other peacetime prime minister, Mrs Thatcher used power to further a personal conception of what needed to be done'[11] both within government and in society as a whole. As a consequence, government was increasingly seen as being personally motivated by Mrs Thatcher to serve her personal objectives.

In publicising her leadership and popularisng the value of leadership in an increasingly collectivist and anonymous era, Margaret Thatcher revived interest in the role of leadership within modern British politics. In effect, she made leadership into a normal, acceptable and even unavoidable subject of analysis and appraisal. She generated widespread inquiry into the nature of individual leadership and in its relationship to personality, history and government. Because individual leadership seemed so central and so salient to contemporary political development, Thatcher succeeded in eroding many of the barriers to considering the place of leadership in the conduct and analysis of British politics.

In addition to providing a model of strong leadership in British politics, Margaret Thatcher's period in office coincided with the emergence in this country of a highly advanced and sophisticated politics of national leadership. As a consequence of this competitive process, the British public has become increasingly exposed to, and conditioned by, a form of politics that thrives on the expectations of leadership, on the components of leadership, and on the attributes of individual leaders in performing a leadership role in British society. The importance of the mass media in leadership projection, the usage of opinion polling and market research to promote leaders, and the deployment of leaders by their respective parties into public settings of individual display and even spectacle have all contributed towards a leadership dimension in contemporary British politics. It is a dimension which not only draws ostensibly unrelated issues into its orbit, but which has established the meaning and value of leadership as a political issue in its own right. The attribution of leadership has become the measure of political effectiveness, an incessant theme in public discussion, and a key criterion of political evaluation. The net effect of these developments has been to transform leaders into public commodities that are continually probed, tested and evaluated for their leadership qualities. Leaders are in essence increasingly engaged in a highly publicised form of direct leadership competition. The intensity and reach of this competition has even prompted claims that British politics has been subject to a process of 'presidentialisation'.[12]

The purpose of this study is to provide an examination of the dynamics and processes of this matrix of leadership competition. By concentrating upon the position and interaction of leaders together with their respective roles, styles and objectives, the analysis intends to investigate the properties of political conflict at this level of engagement. The aim is to elicit the operational dimensions of leadership confrontation and to clarify the methods, strategies and protocols of leaders seeking to displace one another in terms of public and professional esteem. To survey and appraise the aggregate nature of contending leaderships constitutes a shift of emphasis in the standard analysis of British political leadership. It also marks something of a break with a tradition.

Conventional inquiry into leaders is almost invariably confined to individual practitioners operating within their own confined contexts. This is particularly so in the British parliamentary tradition where leaders at least until recently have usually been portrayed as party figureheads. As a consequence, despite the priority and the resources that are now given to the projection of leaders and leadership in contemporary British politics, very little sustained attention has been directed to the components and forces that are peculiar to the collective clash of individual leaderships. Even though the alternative prospectuses of leadership have come to dominate the medium and the terminology of political exchange, little analytical notice is taken of the process. Parties openly confront each other on the leadership issue. The capacity to provide leadership is widely accepted as a key criterion of governing. The calculations, strategies and expectations of each party are geared to protecting and enhancing their leaders in precise relation to an opposing leader. And yet, the actual relationship between leaders remains overlooked and under-researched. This absence of close analysis remains a conspicuous oversight. It has meant that individual leaders have tended to be dismissed as the secondary and derivative features of a wider universe of party exchange, political traditions, policy positions, electoral positioning and voting behaviour.

The aim of this work is to make a serious contribution to the study of contemporary British leadership by focusing on precisely that dimension which structures and animates the issue of leadership – namely the direct and competitive interplay between specific leaders. The object of such a study is to match the largely binary nature of leadership politics with an analytical device that is commensurately lateral in design. Contemporary leadership politics is one of mutual stimulus and response with each competing leader reacting to the other and being conditioned by the other. Individual leaders exert material pressures upon their competitors. Each in some way has the imprint of the other upon his or her leadership. In many ways, each becomes the measure of the other. Leaders do not merely coexist with one another. They largely define their leadership tasks and styles in relation to one another. In effectively shaping each other's worlds and opportunities, they generate a working environment that is mutually constitutive in nature.

As leaders calculate and manœuvre in relation to one another, so together they help both to define the nature and composition of the leadership issue and to shape the criteria of leadership upon which they are appraised as being effective or otherwise in their role as leaders. Leaders target each other. Their competitive dynamics draw on traditional notions of leadership. But the activities of leaders also continually develop and shape the medium of exchange and evaluation relating to leadership. It is by concentrating upon this common ground of interaction and mutual development that a study of this kind can bring to light an array of insights into the underlying dynamics of leadership competition within the structures and processes of British politics. While it is important to locate the selected pairing of two leaders within each of their respective personal and political contexts, the main thrust of such a bifocal analysis is to investigate how their leadership histories and predicaments become fused into a symbiosis of reciprocal influence and even mutual dependence. The intention of this study, therefore, is not to produce a segmented biography of parallel lives, but to show how two leaders can form a duality that generates a joint context for the exercise of their respective leaderships.

For the purposes of this study, the leaderships of John Major and Tony Blair have been selected to provide the analytical focus. This pairing was chosen for three main reasons. *First*, it provides a point of observation to examine the extraordinary pressures upon a sitting prime minister in emulating the achievements of his predecessor and in adjusting to the divisions and constraints generated by the manner of Margaret Thatcher's removal from the premiership. *Second*, Major's acute leadership problems with a party accustomed to leadership discipline coexisted with the transformation of the Labour party into a conspicuously leader-centred organisation. By tracking the rise of New Labour and of the enhanced status of leadership within its organisation and rationale, the paired nature of the study will be able to measure and assess the lengths to which a traditionally democratic party would go, in order to compete effectively in the politics of national leadership. *Third*, the conjunction of a Conservative hegemony under serious assault and the onset of the New Labour project geared to unprecedented leadership power offers an exceptional opportunity to apply close critical analysis of the role of leadership in structuring and characterising a regime change. Both the underlying developments and the specific properties of this sustained process of leadership enhancement were exemplified in this pivotal period by the methods and circumstances of the high exposure confrontation between John Major and Tony Blair.

In sum, the contention is that the confrontation between Major and Blair provides a unique vantage point from which to observe the primary elements at work within a deepening process of leadership-centred politics. Such a point of observation also permits the analysis to clarify how these developments have far-reaching consequences. During this period it became evident that the qualities, claims and imperatives of leadership were not simply the contemporary expressions of party political positioning. They had become motive forces in their own right. Moreover, the contingencies and calculations of leadership ramified well beyond the remit of Westminster and Whitehall. They also extended to alternative leaderships, and to alternative constructions of leadership, within parties as well as between them. The period witnessed the extent to which the leadership question had become a technique of political engagement, a standard of political evaluation, a discourse of political differentiation and an agency of change with considerable implications for the main parties, for the nature of political conduct and for the system of governance as a whole.

It is by concentrating primarily upon the relationship and interactions between these two contemporaneous leaders that it becomes possible to reach a deeper understanding of the common influences and developmental forces at work in the highly reactive dimension of political leadership in the British context. The focus upon twin leaderships allows for the analysis of the individual leaders set within the traditions and architectures of their respective parties. It also provides a framework for examining the interplay between the leaders and their effects upon each other. In doing so, the focus offers a point of analytical access that provides a strategic opportunity to (i) study the growing intensity and multiple subtleties of leadership politics; (ii) examine the implications and consequences of such a continuous process of personal interaction; and (iii) review the patterns of leadership symmetries and asymmetries within British politics.

The analytical framework is geared to the adoption and retention of an unusual stance – namely looking at the respective leaders in terms both of their own immediate environments and of the wider context of continuous leadership competition and outreach within which they had to operate. The analysis examines the contrasting predicaments and styles of John Major and Tony Blair. It situates both leaders within the broader context of leadership traditions, leadership predecessors and leadership rivals. The confrontation between the main protagonists occurred in an intense and critical period for both the main parties, which had undertaken extraordinary investments in their leaders. The battle for the premiership at this time generates a series of insights into the mutual responsiveness of different leaders within the field of British political leadership.

After tracing each leader's rise to prominence, together with the conditions and constraints under which they operated, the study then examines the nature of leadership conflict and the way leaders exert influence upon each other. The analysis surveys and assesses the factors and properties of leadership conflict within the largely non-ideological conditions of contemporary British politics. In doing so, the analysis reviews the contribution of leaders to the symbolic and substantive roles of leadership in the organisation of party conflict. It then proceeds to assess the significance of the leadership issue, and the ways it can be shaped and deployed not only by leaders and their support organisations, but also by the apparatus of news gathering and media comment. Finally, the study identifies and evaluates several key themes to have emerged from this period and whose consequences will be experienced far into the future. In particular, attention will be drawn not only to the issue of the capacity and utility of individual leadership within the British system but also to the implications for the governance of the United Kingdom of such an intensive and continuous competition for leadership authority.

Notes

1 Peter Riddell, *Honest Opportunism: The Rise of the Career Politician* (London: Hamish Hamilton, 1993), p. 227.
2 Peter Riddell, 'Old weaknesses regained', *The Times*, 15 February 1993.
3 Anthony King, 'The Prime Ministership in the Age of the Career Politician', *West European Politics*, vol. 14, no. 2 (April 1991), p. 34.
4 Bernard Donoughue, *Prime Minister: The Conduct of Policy under Harold Wilson and James Callaghan* (London: Jonathan Cape, 1987), p. 4.
5 Donoughue, *Prime Minister*, pp. 4, 35.
6 Richard Rose, 'British Government: The Job at the Top', in Richard Rose and Ezra N. Suleiman (eds), *Presidents and Prime Ministers* (Washington, DC: American Enterprise Institute, 1980), p. 44.
7 King, 'The Prime Ministership in the Age of the Career Politician', p. 31.
8 Rose, 'British Government: The Job at the Top', p. 44.
9 Dennis Kavanagh, *Thatcherism and British Politics: The End of Consensus?* 2nd edn (Oxford: Oxford University Press, 1990), p. 244.
10 Peter Clarke, 'Margaret Thatcher's Leadership in Historical Perspective', *Parliamentary Affairs*, 45, no. 1 (January 1992), p. 11.
11 Ronald Butt, 'The missionary in politics', *The Times*, 23 November 1990.
12 For example, see Sue Pryce, *Presidentializing the Premiership* (Houndmills: Macmillan, 1997); Michael Foley, *The British Presidency: Tony Blair and the Politics of Public Leadership* (Manchester: Manchester University Press, 2000); Anthony Mughan, *Media and the Presidentialization of Parliamentary Elections* (Houndmills: Palgrave, 2000).

2 John Major and the post-Thatcher honeymoon

Personal foundations of leadership

John Major was a social outsider and a political insider. These were neither marginal categories, nor unrelated conditions. Major had come from a genuinely deprived background. He had worked assiduously to remove himself from the insecurity of his past and to achieve a status that would allow him to be absorbed into the highest reaches of the Conservative party. His father may have been a failed businessman, but John Major became a recognised success story in the business of politics. His career appeared to nullify the impoverishment of his roots. And yet ironically, it was his past which served to promote his political career and to fashion a personal identity that would become a highly valued resource within his party. Ultimately, it would help rather than hinder his rapid rise to the party leadership.

John Major was born on 29 March 1943. His father had been sufficiently unconventional to warrant the distinction of notoriety. Tom Major's colourful life had taken him to the United States and South America where he worked in circuses and music halls. He had met Chief Sitting Bull, played in junior league baseball in Philadelphia, and been involved in an insurrection south of the border. By the time John was born, his father and mother were beyond the period of fanciful exertions. They were an elderly couple living in the Worcester Park suburb of south-west London, where Tom Major supported his family through a small manufacturing business specialising in garden ornaments. When this business failed, the family was forced to move to Coldharbour Lane in Brixton. The impact upon John was severe. His home was now a two-room flat with a gas stove on the landing at the top of the stairs. His mother and sister slept in one room. John and his father slept on bunks in the other. Although John progressed from Cheam Common Primary School to Rutlish Grammar School, he was not a conscientious pupil. Later he would acknowledge that he lacked motivation and bridled against school discipline. He was also concerned over the sacrifices that his parents had to make in order to maintain him at the school. Major recalls that while the school treated him well, his various resentments did not allow him to reciprocate: 'I think it was something to do with being bottom of the heap … [T]he fault was within me.'[1] He continued, 'I didn't like the regimentation of school life all that much. I didn't like the unthinking obedience that people wanted. I didn't always agree with decisions and didn't see why I shouldn't say so. I often did say so. I just felt generally disgruntled and no doubt was generally very disgruntling.'[2]

At the age of sixteen Major left school with only six O-Levels. He initially worked as a clerk but then opted for a succession of better-paid labouring jobs during which he developed an attachment to the basic fare of greasy spoon cafes. At nineteen, Major was unemployed for nine months until he managed to acquire a white collar at the London Electricity Board. This was to lay the foundation for his eventual entry into a position with the Standard Chartered Bank. During this period, Major joined the Conservative party and quickly secured a succession of positions, first in the Brixton branch of the Young Conservatives and then in the Brixton Conservative Association. In 1968, he won a seat on Lambeth Council. In 1970, Major became both chairman of the Conservative Association in Brixton and chairman of Lambeth Council's Housing Committee. His political progress coincided with advances in his career at the Standard Chartered Bank.

By the early 1970s, Major was enthusiastically pursuing a parliamentary seat. In the general elections of February and October 1974, Major fought un-successfully for the Labour stronghold of St Pancras. At this time he believed that his social origins were a handicap to being nominated to a winnable seat for the Conservative party. But in 1977, he was selected as prospective Conser-vative parliamentary candidate for the constituency of Huntingdon. He duly won the seat in the 1979 general election, which saw Margaret Thatcher replace the Callaghan government and institute a radical right agenda for a new Conservative administration. Major inclined to the view that he had reached his political limits because of the eroding force of his social background. Once again, he was proved wrong. This time he was touched by the patronage of Margaret Thatcher who in 1983 appointed him to the Whips' Office. It is widely acknowledged that Major immediately took to the collegiate ethos of the Conservative Whips' Office. He appreciated being at the centre of inform-ation on legislative proposals, government priorities, support levels and the requirements of political management. Whips are sensors whose job it is to predict and to prevent problems. They are negotiators who have to liaise between those with differing positions in order to reach practical accom-modations. They are also expected to be tough and to promote both the party's solidarity and the corporate integrity of the Whips' Office itself. John Major was thoroughly at ease in this environment. He quickly acquired a reputation for mastering legislative detail and for courteously engineering negotiated agreements on legislative enactments. His role as whip also appealed to his interest in the nature of politics and more especially in its potential for producing collective action. Within a year, Major had become the Treasury Whip and, therefore, an accepted member of the inner club along with its elevated links to the government machine and to government patronage.

With this background, Major moved almost seamlessly into government with his appointment as Parliamentary Under-Secretary to the Department of Social Security in 1985. By 1986, he had become a minister of state at the same department. Shortly afterwards, Major was being widely cited as future cabinet material. Once again, Major had impressed his peers by his conscientious attention to detail and by his conciliatory and personable conduct. These attributes dispelled doubts over the rapidity of his promotion. By successfully overcoming the emotive issue of the government's cold weather payments to pensioners, Major was thought to have been blooded as a high-profile politician: 'For the first time in his political life he had taken hard knocks, been accused of incompetence and indifference, and suffered personal ridicule.'[3] In the 1987 general election, Major often appeared at the high table of senior party figures in the morning press conferences. This was unusual for a minister of state. After the election, the discussions over the forthcoming cabinet reshuffle included the name of John Major. Margaret Thatcher was keen to bring him into the cabinet as Chief Whip but the Chancellor of the Exchequer, Nigel Lawson, wanted him for the post of Chief Secretary to the Treasury. Lawson had 'formed a high opinion of him'[4] when Major had been the Treasury Whip. His performance as a junior minister reaffirmed the Chancellor's earlier judgement:"[A]s Minister of State for Social Security, he had demonstrated an impressive grasp of the complexities of the Social Security rules and an ability to put the Government's case across in a firm, clear and agreeable way. This relatively unusual combination of mastery of detail and likeable manner would, I felt, make him an excellent Chief Secretary.'[5] Lawson won the argument and Major returned to Treasury business but this time within the Treasury itself.

The new Chief Secretary harboured some initial self-doubts over his capacity to take on the demanding role of controlling public expenditure. They were dispelled by the familiar formula of a prodigious work rate and an ability to lower the resistance of those around him through genial informality and expectations of mutual support. Even though his new responsibilities propelled him into every government department and implicated him in the sensitivities of budget allocations and priorities, Major managed to reach accommodations without rancour. His experience as a whip in being able to read the tidal patterns of political support and internal coalitions helped him to sense the possibilities of conciliation and the potential outlines of negotiated settlements. Major had always been adept at networking and at building relationships through the medium of politics. Now he used the same instrumental techniques at a higher level and for higher stakes. 'He was happiest …

sticking to the top man-management he was doing, and had always done very well. It was accomplished by knowing all the facts and then meeting ministers and forcing them into compliance by being nice to them ... [and] bringing up all those facts and details.'[6] It is true that the Chief Secretary works to a core job description of curtailing government expenditure and that this task is made easier when, as in 1987–88, the economy is not in recession. Nevertheless, even in these conditions departmental claims on the Treasury still have to be processed and successfully arbitrated. Major's was a bravura performance of individual bilateral negotiations that was sensitive both at the political level and at a personal level where he conveyed a 'wily understanding of how to present [the] harder strategies in a favourable light'.[7]

After a protracted period of strain between Margaret Thatcher and Geoffrey Howe, the prime minister decided in July 1989 that she wanted a new Foreign Secretary. She turned to John Major as a replacement. This was an astonishing promotion for a minister who had yet to run a department. The level of surprise was reflected in the response of the nervous recipient. The prime minister was aware of Major's reticence but described her decision in almost pedagogic terms:

> John Major was not at first very keen on becoming Foreign Secretary. A modest man, aware of his inexperience, he would probably have preferred a less grand appointment. But I knew that if he was to have a hope of becoming Party leader, it would be better if he had held one of the three great offices of state ... I had simply concluded that he must be given wider public recognition and greater experience if he was to compete with the talented self-publicists who would be among his rivals.[8]

In reality, the decision was probably induced more by Thatcher's desire to block the suspected Europhile, Douglas Hurd, from becoming Foreign Secretary. Like Geoffrey Howe, Hurd was thought to be an enthusiastic supporter of Britain's entry into the Exchange Rate Mechanism. The prime minister's ferocious antagonism towards such a policy and her chronic distrust of the Foreign and Commonwealth Office prompted her to opt for a minister who was known for his pragmatism. Such a politically motivated minister was more likely to acquiesce in the foreign policy interventions of a high-energy premier. John Major was very concerned about how the appointment would be perceived. In his autobiography, he recalls the conversation: '"Prime Minister I am very flattered but is this a good idea ... I'm not sure that it's a good idea from your point of view. People will assume I'm there just to carry out your bidding. That won't be good for either of us".'[9] The prime minister was unmoved precisely because she did want a minister in the Foreign Office that would be more amenable to her perspective: '"I'm very sure it's a good idea ... I want someone there who thinks as I do".'[10] The net effect of Margaret

Thatcher's flamboyant patronage and her related need for a senior trustee produced a Foreign Secretary with minimal experience of cabinet and less background in foreign affairs than any other holder of the position in the twentieth century.

Major was initially daunted by the scale and complexity of the issues which he was expected to confront. The new Foreign Secretary's recollection of the period was characteristically understated: 'Treasury briefs, which contain the hard facts of finance, came easily to me, since I have always had a facility for absorbing figures. Briefs at the Foreign Office were different. They were about themes, and were less precise than economic papers. I did not immediately find them as easy to absorb as those I had been used to.'[11] In fact, Major was at times overwhelmed by the steepness of the learning curve. Furthermore, he was confronted with the need to respond to the repercussions of the end of the cold war, to restrict the divisiveness of the European issue, and not least to adjust to the strains of a high-profile position that entailed striking a balance between restoring Mrs Thatcher's faith in Foreign Office advice, whilst forging his own independent identity as a senior minister. It was also a time when John Major's prodigious work rate and social charm would no longer allow him to pass unchallenged through the ranks of potential party leaders and their supporters: 'His appointment marked ... the point when Major ceased to be everyone's friend ... and began to arouse jealousy from elements in the Conservative party, and serious criticism in the press. The long honeymoon had come to an end.'[12]

It is thought likely that Margaret Thatcher planned to keep John Major at the Foreign and Commonwealth Office for three years before sending him back to the Treasury as Chancellor following the next general election in 1992. But a dispute between Nigel Lawson and Mrs Thatcher's economic advisor, Alan Walters, led to the dramatic resignation of the Chancellor of the Exchequer on 26 October 1989. After only ninety-four days as Foreign Secretary, Major was once again identified by the prime minister as her solution to a pressing problem. Lawson's abrupt departure once again forced the pace of Major's already accelerated political advance. Edward Pearce sums up the general perspective of John Major's extraordinary propulsion at the time:

> He had been moved to that job as to the Foreign Office, because the prime minister, ever more distant from colleagues, thought of him firstly as Not-somebody else, first Not-Howe then Not-Lawson, secondly, as the Thatcherite, which except in terms of personal esteem, he was not. She also hoped for an inexperienced, malleable Chancellor and someone who was far too young and short of accumulated office to be a threat to her.[13]

Major's defensive independence and disarming manner ensured that he would provide the prime minister with professional competence, while at the same time unobtrusively and even ambiguously enhancing his political status within the government. Major could not and, therefore refrained from, competing with the heady intellectualism and strategic thought of Nigel Lawson. Instead, he deployed his political skills for creating consensual agreements as discrete economic policies.

In appearance, Major was a middle-ranking minister in a senior position because of good fortune and a dependency upon an unpredictable patron who had a track record of breaking out of formal hierarchies of policy consultation and decision-making. Appearances, however, could be deceptive. Major's status and leverage as Chancellor were in fact extensive precisely because of the circumstances surrounding Lawson's abrupt resignation. This event underlined not only Thatcher's increasing isolation within government but also her declining power base inside the parliamentary party. She could ill afford to lose a second Chancellor, and especially a young Chancellor, so soon after Lawson's departure. Moreover, in addition to John Major at the Treasury, Margaret Thatcher also had to establish a relationship with a new Foreign Secretary – namely Douglas Hurd. Major and Hurd were quickly seen as a nexus and as an alternative power base to Thatcher within both the government and the Conservative party. Mrs Thatcher became increasingly besieged by the sustained opposition to the poll tax; by a severe economic downturn that entailed high interest rates and high inflation; by collapsing levels of public support; by evident signs of disruption as a result of government reform in the health and education sectors; and by growing strains within the party over the question of European integration. Within this context, John Major worked for stability, recovery and a modicum of invention (e.g. the introduction of the gift aid scheme, and Tax Exempt Special Saving Accounts or TESSAs).

The urgent need for the government to counter inflation prompted a widespread movement in government to reconsider Britain joining the Exchange Rate Mechanism (ERM). Nigel Lawson had advocated this policy as early as 1985, but Margaret Thatcher was resolutely opposed to it. She objected to it on political grounds that ERM membership would stimulate further European integration. She also rejected the ERM both on technical grounds that it would not necessarily stabilise the value of sterling and reduce inflation; and on doctrinal grounds that a floating pound and a free market in international capital flows remained preferable to structured interventions in order to give a currency an artificial immunity from market forces. The speculative ramifications surrounding the ERM and its links to European Monetary Union had led to large-scale strains within the government, which had culminated in the departure of Geoffrey Howe and Nigel Lawson from the Foreign Office and the Treasury. But by 1990, what had looked like a radical and iconoclastic policy was becoming an almost conventional piece of economic management and, in particular, a solution to Britain's need for exchange rate stability. By negotiating the decision to join the ERM past Mrs Thatcher's veto, John Major became personally associated with both the policy and with Britain's entry into the scheme in October 1990. It was seen at the time as an early sign of Margaret Thatcher's eroded dominance and an indication of divergent forces within the Conservative hegemony.

Context of leadership acquisition

After a prolonged period of eleven years in office, what had seemed the immoveable object of Margaret Thatcher's premiership suddenly turned into a resistible force. Within a matter of weeks, John Major was propelled into the joint position of Conservative leader and prime minister. The circumstances of this transition reflected both the internal strains of the party and the tensions over the roles and expectations of contemporary political leadership within the British system. John Major would experience the benefits but also the penalties of these discordant currents.

A general condition of political debilitation together with a set of particular triggers to dissent and defiance characterised the decline of Mrs Thatcher. In respect to the overall context of her third administration, Thatcher was confronted by at least four severe problems. First was the state of the economy. The indicators revealed an episode of 'stagflation' with inflation exceeding 10 per cent, unemployment rising by half a million in six months to 1.7 million, and a record trade deficit of £19 billion. At the same time, the government's policy of high interest rates, to correct an overheated economy, threatened to deepen the recession still further. Another dimension to the dispute over the economy was the widespread conviction that the recession had been induced by the prime minister's obstinate refusal to join the Exchange Rate Mechanism in the mid-1980s.

The second contextual element to Margaret Thatcher's decline was the controversy over the poll tax. The measure came to embody the methods and objectives of Mrs Thatcher's leadership style and governmental mission. To Mrs Thatcher, the old domestic rating system amounted to a restrictive practice. It compelled a minority of property owners to finance local government in a way that made it unaccountable and immune to pressures for improved management, or to any reordering of popular priorities. Apart from its asserted credentials as a device of democratisation, the community charge had an implicitly ideological character. It was seen as an instrument of assault upon the remaining enclaves of municipal socialism which, according to the government's perspective, remained dominated by public sector unions to the detriment of local economies. Mrs Thatcher had taken a high-profile position on this issue and was insistent upon its passage and application. In the face of violent street demonstrations, non-payment campaigns and a high level of political opposition that drew support away from the government and from Mrs Thatcher in particular, the prime minister remained adamant in her support for her showpiece reform.

The ructions over the future direction and nature of European integration constituted the third major issue that damaged the Thatcher premiership. Mrs Thatcher believed that her populist resentments over Europe were widely shared by the British people whom she assumed possessed the same Atlanticist prejudices as her own. She was certainly convinced that her jaundiced outlook represented a point of unity for the Conservative party and for the nation as a whole. Europe increasingly became the measure of her defiant style of conviction leadership. But the irritation engendered over her defiance was not confined to the leaders and officials of the European Community. Members of her cabinet became increasingly disturbed by the prime minister's outbursts and by her habit of making policy 'on the hoof' through unscheduled statements to the media. To many, the prime minister's treatment of the European issue not only underlined the divisions within the party but afforded a point of leverage for political opponents to criticise the government on the grounds of competence and direction. Every time the prime minister confounded her colleagues by disrupting the outcomes of protracted European negotiations, she added further substance to the image of a prime minister who was out of touch with her own cabinet, and arguably with the nature of political developments.

The fourth factor in the deterioration of the prime minister's position was the slump in her electoral position. In March 1990, the Labour party had a 20 per cent lead over the Conservatives. In the same month, Labour won the 'safe' Conservative seat of Mid-Staffordshire with a swing of 21.4 per cent. This was the largest swing from Conservative to Labour since 1935. By the end of the month, Labour had amassed an opinion poll lead of 28 points. While polling organisations were claiming that no government had ever recovered from such a deficit to win a general election, Mrs Thatcher was confident that the lack of support was nothing other than a mid-term hiatus. On previous occasions (e.g. 1981–82, 1987) she had always recovered from weak positions to be vindicated by general election victories. But this crisis was seen to be different. Labour was now a proficient electoral machine providing a credible alternative government. The political wear and tear of such a high-profile prime minister had generated a fatigue factor proportionate to the previous scale of exposure. Thatcher's position was further eroded by those MPs whose political careers had not fared well during the Thatcher years. By November 1990, 68 MPs had lost their front-bench positions, while 97 Conservative members had served 11 years on the backbenches without being considered for promotion. The presence of such injured ambition, together with the brooding dissent of those who had either never been supporters of the Thatcherite persuasion, or who were facing political defeat in the rising column of marginal seats, cultivated speculation on the future of the Conservative party without Margaret Thatcher.[14] The time when even she would have to consider stepping down was thought to be more imminent than ever before. The atmosphere within the parliamentary Conservative party during this period was described by John Major as one in which 'a sense of exasperation with the leadership was palpable'.[15]

In spite of the severity of her position, Mrs Thatcher showed no sign of resigning. She gave no indication of a prospective successor. By the same token, none of the possible contenders for the leadership wished to risk giving the appearance of disloyalty to the prime minister. A further Conservative victory was essential to all the complex calculations and permutations of their leadership ambitions, but none was prepared to will the means to achieve the initial end of that fourth consecutive victory. 'As the Labour lead stabilised for month after month of opinion polls, and as the government suffered further by-election reversals, Mrs Thatcher began to look like a lame duck premier who was insisting upon running in the next election. She would either lose and stand down, or try to win by persuading the electorate to place its trust in a leader who, in all likelihood, would stand down after the election in favour of an unknown successor.'[16] Whether it was timidity over organising a serious challenge to the prime minister, or complacency in relying upon a Conservative hegemony to secure yet another election win, the prospect of any party action being taken against Thatcher was minimal.

This background of political and electoral deterioration would not have been transformed into the open turmoil that erupted in November 1990, had it not been for a succession of events that created the conditions for a leadership crisis. In the main, the crisis was precipitated by the resignation of the deputy prime minister, Sir Geoffrey Howe, in reaction to the prime minister's intemperate report on the European Council meeting in Rome at the end of October. In that report to the House of Commons, the prime minister not only deviated from the prepared statement but completely undermined it. She had agreed to a brief prepared by the Treasury and the Foreign Office which incorporated John Major's compromise position accepting a 'hard ecu' common European currency alongside existing national currencies. This device retained the pound in its central position, but held out the option of a single currency in the future, should Britain and the rest of Europe wish to make such a choice. Although the Chancellor had made considerable efforts to arouse European interest in the hard ecu idea, Mrs Thatcher undid much of his work by her unguarded remark that it was unlikely the ecu would become widely used throughout the Community. John Major was astounded: 'I nearly fell off the bench. With this single sentence she wrecked months of work and preparation.'[17]

The prime minister used this report to Parliament to make a number of other inflammatory remarks on the whole project of European integration. She reaffirmed her position as one of intransigent defiance against any further devices of creeping European federalism. Sir Geoffrey Howe resigned in protest the next day. His letter of resignation made references to the threat that the country faced in its isolationist stance towards Europe and the need to find common ground on the European issue. His resignation speech to the House of Commons on 13 November 1990 was far less coded in style and content. It was in effect a devastating indictment of the prime minister in terms of both policy and attitude. He was quite explicit in his accusation that Mrs Thatcher was running the risk of becoming a liability even to those causes which she herself espoused. More seriously, she publicly undermined the consensus building work of her senior colleagues like John Major. Howe recalled the way that the 'hard ecu' policy had been damaged by her stated disbelief that the ecu would ever become a common currency let alone a single one. Howe exclaimed: 'How on earth are the chancellor and the governor of the Bank of England, commending the hard ecu as they strive to do, to be taken as serious participants in the debate against that kind of background noise?'[18] Howe concluded that Mrs Thatcher's position on Europe posed a serious risk to the future of the country. It amounted to a 'very real tragedy'[19] not least to the prime minister herself. He believed that the conflict of loyalties he had experienced could only be resolved by leaving the government. He concluded his critique by calling on 'others to consider their response to the tragic conflict of loyalty with which I have myself wrestled for perhaps too long'.[20]

The manner of Geoffrey Howe's departure, in conjunction with the earlier resignation of the Chancellor of the Exchequer, Nigel Lawson, provided the catalyst for Michael Heseltine to challenge Margaret Thatcher for the leadership. The declaration of his candidacy represented the culmination of a prolonged period during which he had cultivated the status of a prospective party leader. Since his own ill-tempered resignation from the cabinet during the Westland crisis in 1986, Michael Heseltine had stalked his prey in the guise of one committed to the party. In a party that placed a high value on loyalty and hierarchy, his strategy was to establish himself in the position of an heir apparent without ever having to challenge the prime minister directly. His position remained one of never striking out at his quarry. He would merely wait for her to fall and hope to claim the leadership when the opportunity arose. With this objective in mind, Heseltine worked tirelessly for the party, visiting constituencies, making speeches supporting local MPs and offering any form of assistance he could provide. This prodigious activity protected his flanks from accusations of party disloyalty. At the same time, it allowed Heseltine the opportunity to cultivate support in the party's grass roots. Heseltine worked for the party assiduously and was a tireless publicist for its election campaigns. After nearly five years in exile, Heseltine now struck to reclaim what he regarded as his rightful patrimony.

Michael Heseltine's decision to challenge the prime minister was seen in many quarters as an act of courage. He had openly departed from his previous strategy of refraining from a direct challenge to Margaret Thatcher. He was now placing himself in a very precarious political position by this shift of position. One immediate benefit of this sudden challenge was that Heseltine had wrested the initiative from both the leader and the rest of her cabinet. In being so spectacularly outside the cabinet for four years, Michael Heseltine was not tainted with its recent failures and miscalculations. His departure from government now looked more prescient and principled with each passing day. He could now convincingly assert that only an 'outsider' could recognise the need for new leadership and provide that refreshment at the top. Heseltine gave the appearance of an individual whose convictions and integrity had led him into the wilderness. That vantage point had given him the perspective and authority from outside government to see the need for a new leader with 'a new style and new personality, different phrases and a different way of presenting arguments'.[21] The challenger was highly skilled in the arts of making no direct criticism of the party leader and in shrouding his leadership challenge in the propriety of seeking a revival of cabinet government.

Notwithstanding Heseltine's sober emphasis upon the self-effacing virtues of collective decision-making, his challenge electrified the party and the media with the prospect of a titanic personal struggle between the prime minister and a contender who was comparable in self-belief and self-promotion. In the febrile atmosphere of Westminster, Heseltine suddenly became not merely the focus of a rich diversity of Conservative anxiety and dissent, but the subject of intense national and international speculation over the implications of a leadership change. The challenger quickly achieved impressive levels over the prime minister in the polls.[22] Opinion surveys also revealed that the leadership contest itself was contributing to a renewed public interest in the Conservative party, which in turn was leading to increased voter support.[23]

Despite this immediate surge, Michael Heseltine was pursuing a high-risk strategy. Apart from suffering defeat by the prime minister, it was possible that his campaign could be used as a stalking horse operation for other senior and more conventional Conservative figures to enter the race once the indignity of Mrs Thatcher's departure had been completed. Heseltine knew that his challenge would unleash a profusion of scenarios and permutations that might lead to the prize going elsewhere. The optimum outcome to those loyal to Heseltine believed that if the challenger failed to win the first ballot, he would prevail in the second ballot against a prime minister damaged and weakened by the insurgency of the first round.

In his campaign, Heseltine had the advantage of surprise and momentum. He was assisted by the cabinet ethos of collective responsibility. Margaret Thatcher expected to win the battle and assumed that her cabinet would support the prime minister. This was a wholly legitimate but not an altogether secure assumption. She underlined these expectations by insisting that her two leading ministers – Douglas Hurd and John Major – sign her nomination papers. With the cabinet heavyweights locked morally and politically into an enforced closure of ranks, the contest proceeded as a straight fight between the prime minister and a candidate who was rising in prominence, popularity and leverage on a daily basis. Michael Heseltine hoped that he could develop enough of an ecumenical movement of protest either to win on the first ballot, or else to achieve the kind of momentum to secure the leadership on the second ballot as Margaret Thatcher herself had done in the 1975 leadership contest.

In the event, the challenger was to be disappointed on both counts. The result of the first ballot revealed that the prime minister had won more votes than her challenger but not enough to secure victory.

Margaret Thatcher	204
Michael Heseltine	152

However, Heseltine had acquired the support of over 40 per cent of the parliamentary party. In doing so, the challenger had in effect destroyed the prestige and hold of Margaret Thatcher's personal leadership. For such leadership to be effective, it had to be seen as being never less than predominant. Mrs Thatcher initially considered remaining in the contest and competing in the second ballot. She was advised against this on the grounds that she would in all probability lose, thereby allowing her arch rival, Michael Heseltine, to secure the leadership of both the party and the Conservative administration. By withdrawing her name she in effect reconfigured the whole shape of the leadership contest. It allowed senior members of the cabinet to compete openly for her position. Heseltine recognised that his chances of the leadership immediately began to diminish. To have 'defeat[ed] her in open combat was one thing; to be held accountable for making her quit the field was quite another'.[24] In Heseltine's view, 'my hope of being Mrs Thatcher's successor vanished when she resolved to give up the contest'.[25] He continues:

> [I]f I made an error, it lay in thinking that her Cabinet colleagues would not be able to get her to change her mind. I knew, of course, of the pressure on her to stand down, but ... there remained, it appeared to me, a real chance that she would indeed fight on ... I never had the slightest doubt that in a head-to-head second ballot contest with Margaret Thatcher I would win ... But now other candidates would come in and I, as the notional front-runner, would inevitably become their target.[26]

Heseltine was now confronted by two new contenders – namely the Foreign Secretary Douglas Hurd and the Chancellor of the Exchequer John Major. Both had the advantage of not having been associated with the 'assassination'. This was a credential of growing value in the aftershock of Margaret Thatcher's humiliating withdrawal and resignation. Despite their own ambitions, both ministers had remained loyal to the prime minister. Hurd and Major had only put themselves forward for elevation after she had stood down (i.e. exactly what Heseltine had always planned to do during his wilderness years). They also had a far superior claim to building party unity at a time of potentially chronic disunity. Furthermore, they had powerful backing from different sectors of the cabinet. Heseltine by contrast had virtually no support from the cabinet. He was now stained with the responsibility both for having eliminated Mrs Thatcher – even though she had beaten him in the first ballot – and for having brought a leadership crisis upon the party. The discomfort and embarrassment even on the part of those who had opposed her, but who had perhaps willed the end rather more than the means, led to something of a backlash against Michael Heseltine.

Of the two new contenders, it was John Major who acquired greater gravitational force. At first sight, it might have been thought that the experienced Douglas Hurd would have become the chief rival to Michael Heseltine. John Major was young (forty-seven years) to the point where his inexperience was thought by many to be a bar to the premiership this time round. He had been in the House of Commons for only eleven years. Although he had held two prestigious posts (i.e. Foreign Secretary and Chancellor of the Exchequer), he had done so for only short periods of time. Moreover, he had been Chancellor during a deepening recession and, as a consequence, had been the government's chief spokesman for an economy in decline. Finally, Major had to contend with a personal image that was grey and technocratic in nature, and implied a lack of guiding principles and with it an opaque personal identity.

On the other hand, Major was well known and well liked in Parliament. He had assiduously built up a profusion of contacts and friendships in the party. He had a reputation for being disarmingly honest, and courteous to his colleagues and opponents alike. At Westminster, Major was universally liked as a person. He was known to work immensely hard and to have an ability to mix high ambition with emollient good humour and private charm. Although he had a sufficient following in parliament to constitute a power base, his was not a provocative or polarising presence. Major's courtesy together with his capacity to listen and to conciliate now became much valued properties at a time of turmoil for the party. By the same token, he was enough of a politician to know how to cultivate and to deploy such personal resources to the maximum effect. Major's style was built on caution, persuasion and accommodation. While this led some to question his ability to resist pressure, it appealed to many in the party looking for a leader who could assimilate the party's vociferous factions into a common purpose. Major was highly adept at providing suggestive signs and hints to different groups. He stressed continuity and the defence of the Thatcherite legacy, while implying that adjustments in areas like local government finance and European integration were necessary. He could claim with conviction that he was of Mrs Thatcher's persuasion but was not the lady herself. This was in itself a very effective form of balanced appeal.

Between the first and second ballots Michael Heseltine's momentum was arrested. His populist appeal was confronted by the sudden surge in public support for John Major. On the weekend before the second ballot, a profusion of polls showed that Major's support was not only comparable to that of Heseltine but in some instances now exceeded it. On the day of the ballot, Tuesday, 27 November 1990, a NOP/*Independent* poll reported that a greater proportion of the electorate would be more likely to vote Conservative with John Major as leader than with Heseltine as leader.[27] A Gallup poll in the *Daily Telegraph* confirmed that Major had 'substantially improved his standing with the general public during the Conservatives' short leadership election campaign and now rivals Mr Michael Heseltine as the candidate most likely to win the next general election for the Conservatives'.[28] The poll showed that Major, after being behind by five points two days earlier, now had a one-point lead over his rival in Conservative voting intentions. It also revealed that Major was more appealing than Heseltine to Conservative defectors; that Major had overtaken Heseltine in being seen to be better at handling the NHS and education; and that he was regarded by the public as equal to Heseltine in being 'prime ministerial material'.[29] Major had effectively taken up Heseltine's challenge that a leadership change could make all the difference to the party's public appeal and electoral prospects. The Chancellor promoted himself as the individual who, in his own words, had 'a very clear instinct for what the people in this country feel'.[30] His implied intimacy with the drives and anxieties of the ordinary person now appeared to pay dividends. It allowed Major to claim that his leadership could make just as much difference as Heseltine's leadership. As a consequence, Heseltine's position began to falter while Major's candidacy appeared to be on a rising curve. Once Major was seriously in contention, Heseltine's public image suffered from comparison with the Chancellor. Major appealed to the public as warmer and friendlier than Heseltine. The Chancellor was seen as being more trustworthy, caring and sincere. While Heseltine was regarded as being more experienced and forceful than Major, he was also seen as being palpably more ambitious for himself and more willing to take risks as a politician.[31]

In the intense conditions of this leadership contest, the more cautious and statesmanlike campaign of Douglas Hurd visibly withered. Hurd's discreet qualities of authoritative experience, sober diplomacy and self-effacing collegiality would have been formidable attributes in a more traditional conservative leadership contest. In this context, where the emphasis lay either on securing the leadership for Heseltine or on preventing such an eventuality, Hurd was squeezed into the position of a third party distraction. As the contest sharpened into a head-to-head competition for maximum party appeal and public outreach, Hurd's private virtues and Old Etonian gravitas were overwhelmed by Heseltine's parading flair and Major's avowed"classlessness". Although Hurd objected to being effectively sidelined into a declining establishment by the deployment of John Major's colourful family history, he could do little to resist the movement towards his junior cabinet colleague.

In the second ballot for the Conservative Party leadership, John Major topped the poll:

John Major	185
Michael Heseltine	131
Douglas Hurd	56

The Chancellor had not achieved the required margin of victory to secure the leadership. Nevertheless, the process was ended when both Hurd and Heseltine immediately withdrew their candidacies and pledged their support to the new leader. Heseltine had been stopped. Margaret Thatcher's supporters had switched to the candidate whom she had endorsed and for whom she had actively campaigned. Within a matter of days and with the support of fewer Conservative MPs than those who had backed Margaret Thatcher, the Chancellor had become party leader and prime minister. He had been suddenly propelled into the same position as his formidable predecessor and patron. For over ten years, Margaret Thatcher's leadership had been an impregnable fortress. Unexpectedly, it had now fallen. John Major had negotiated himself into a position of contention without challenge. He had not only replaced his patron, but had succeeded in attracting her support and blessing as the chosen successor. 'Whether by accident or design … he had navigated between the Scylla of being dragged down with her and the Charybdis of alienating her through disloyalty, and achieved his ideal result.'[32]

John Major had benefited from Margaret Thatcher's imprimatur. But he had also gained from the party's need and desire to curtail the process of leadership change to the barest minimum. The publicity generated by a leadership contest can be two-edged, especially if the competition becomes sufficiently prolonged and acrimonious to raise doubts over a party's unity of purpose, or its competence to govern. The Conservative party has traditionally been very inhibited, not just in relation to the public exposure of its internal processes, but in connection to the establishment of structures of consultation and participation within the party. The party's hierarchical ethos and internal discipline are widely seen as being the necessary concomitants to electoral success. For a cautious but always ambitious organisation, a party leadership contest can be a high-risk event and one not to be undertaken lightly. The resistance to them and even fear of them is considerable, especially when it involves a challenge to an incumbent leader. In November 1990, enough Conservative MPs believed that there was no alternative other than to displace Margaret Thatcher. However, the act of forcing her out set in motion a related impulse to acquire a replacement as soon and as decisively as possible. By electing Hurd, the party would have risked appointing a caretaker leader who would not have been able to subdue other competitors for the leadership for very long. Michael Heseltine was popular but threatened further instability and even turmoil. By opting for the distinctive youth of John Major, the party signalled its drive to produce a conclusive result that would effectively end the leadership ambitions of all those more senior to him in age, experience and government service.

Themes, style and authority

John Major had acquired the premiership through good fortune and a sustained application of a consensus building approach to political management. He was a self-confessed 'politics addict'[33] and retained the whip's outlook of identifying potential problems, in order to pre-empt them by manouevre and practical accommodation. Major may have come to the premiership prematurely but, within the party, he had already achieved the status of a possible future leader by 1988. Major's conscientious attitude to ministerial work and his close attention both to detail and to the predicament of others, combined with his professional integrity, personal warmth and social skills made him a formidable parliamentary politician. In entering Number 10 Downing Street, the new prime minister saw no reason to change his modus operandi. On the contrary, it appeared evident that the turmoil within the party and the country as a whole made it imperative that John Major play to his strengths – that John Major be allowed to be John Major.

The times appeared to require precisely what the new prime minister had structured his political career upon – namely conciliation. Major's presence in the leadership had infused an immediate tranquility in his own party. He now hoped to transpose that calmness to the country as a whole. Major believed that his background and experience would allow him to reach across various social divisions and to find common ground to the mutual benefit of all the participants. He expressly linked this kind of brokerage politics with a commitment to social mobility and the erosion of class distinction. To John Major, social privilege was an attitude that had been 'engraved for a 100 years in the British instinct'.[34] It was now time for it to be 'disengraved [sic]'.[35] In the leadership campaign, Major had made it clear that he was committed to 'a genuinely classless society in which people can rise to whatever level that their own abilities and good fortune may take them, from whatever their starting point'.[36] His intention was to make this kind of fluid society and pliable politics the centrepiece of his premiership. Initially, it appeared possible that such a programme might make some headway. However, several conditions militated against his preferred option of consensus politics.

Even though the new prime minister had reversed the Conservative party's deficit on the polls, Major was aware that the recovery in the government's public approval could be construed as having more to do with the absence of Margaret Thatcher and the crisis over Iraq's invasion of Kuwait than any deep groundswell of support for the new administration. The new government was faced with the divisiveness of the poll tax and the European question. It was confronted by a deepening recession, high interest rates and rising unemployment. Moreover, it was challenged by a rejuvenated Labour party that was now confident of finally breaking the Conservative run of successive general election victories. In spite of the appearances of stability, therefore, Major was conscious that the new administration and his premiership were in a tenuous position. Apart from the question of immediate policy decisions, the new prime minister could see the potential for serious problems in three key areas.

First, was the division in the party between the neo-liberal, free market right and the socially compassionate instincts of 'one nation' Toryism. This tension was compounded by splits over the utilitarian cost-benefit analyses of European integration and over the fundamental principles of British identity within an increasingly European context. In these circumstances, Major's government would be closely monitored for signs of overall policy direction. The second source of concern was the nature of the leadership election aftermath and in particular the repercussions following Margaret Thatcher's resignation. Prior to her departure, Major had been 'masterful at managing her, at relating to her personally in the way she liked, while also being confident enough to stand up to her without causing offence'.[37] The subtleties of this balance had been the key to Major's elevation to the premiership. But as Anthony Seldon points out, the need for balance remained even after the change of administration. Moreover just as any balance would be more difficult to achieve, so any failure to accommodate Thatcher and her supporters would be commensurately damaging to the new government: 'the Major team did not know exactly how to handle the deposed leader. This uncertainty, rather than Major's successful management of her in 1989–90, was to be the motif of his premiership.'[38]

The third source of conditioning anxiety for Major was derived from the circumstances of his promotion to the party leadership and the premiership. It is true that he had the support of a majority of the parliamentary party in the election and that he received a form of public endorsement from opinion poll ratings. Nevertheless, he had no popular mandate or clear basis of personal authority. Margaret Thatcher had not been defeated at the polls. Major's legitimacy was sustained by a cabinet that had been pivotal in the removal of his predecessor. As a consequence, the new prime minister could not be sure what expectations were attached to his leadership, or what opportunities and limits there would be in establishing a new identity for the party and administration.

Just as these three problem areas were connected to one another, so the responses of John Major to them were related to a broadly unified outlook upon his position and responsibilities. That he wanted a change in the style and method of leadership, there can be little doubt. An integral part of his original appeal had been that he was *not* Margaret Thatcher. Major understood this and appreciated his own value in the role of an antidote. However, his reaction reached much further than the recognition of a political resource. As a matter of deep conviction, Major was determined to draw a line under the overbearing, abrasive and lacerating leadership methods of his benefactor. She maximised her personal authority to intimidate adversaries, to dominate colleagues and to sweep objections aside in a relentless campaign to control the political agenda and to drive her programme through government. Major saw these characteristics not as devices of effective government but as the characteristics of an increasingly irascible and isolated premier. They were disruptive, counterproductive and, ultimately, destructive.

Even if Major had had the temperament, he had no wish to try and emulate Thatcher's forceful leadership. The conviction of the new prime minister was that his own style of consultative consensus building was more effective both in achieving objectives and in retaining the organisational integrity of the government and the party. In addition, this style of pragmatic brokerage politics was firmly in the mainstream traditions of Conservative leadership. In Major's view, he had been selected leader in order to restore this form of parliamentary leadership to the party. It was consistent with the indictment of Margaret Thatcher and the sectarian acrimony surrounding her resignation, that John Major should believe that he had been chosen to be not merely a different leader but a different kind of leader. His personal philosophy of effective and legitimate political conduct seemed to converge with the immediate demands of a party and government in recuperation. The new prime minister's considered view was that '[b]y and large events are the greatest single determinant of policy over any measurable run of years'.[39] As a consequence, he was content with the widespread perception that the country would now be 'governed by a Conservative party in which ideology, vision, conviction are no longer to be the principal driving forces'.[40]

Integral both to his personal outlook and to his self-defined role of prime minister as healer was John Major's suspicion of ideas. He distrusted their usage in politics and particularly their contribution to grand visions, sweeping programmes and fragmented power bases. This distaste had a variety of roots and outlets. For example, Major's limited education generated an unease with those colleagues whose intellectualism gave them an analytical and social edge in the competition for position and leverage. However, in Major's view the inclination towards intellectualising politics was both a cause and a symptom of an elitism, whose macro but one-dimensional view of politics overlooked the effects of doctrine upon individual lives. Major's depiction of William Waldegrave, for example, is redolent with this suspicion of the best and brightest: 'William Waldegrave had a brilliant academic mind, and was often talked of as a future prime minister. He had a phenomenal breadth of know-ledge, but his intellect was not invariably an asset: it did not always equip him to understand the hope and fears of lesser minds.'[41] In this particular realm, Major's social vulnerability was intense. He had been well aware that he had been compared unfavourably with Nigel Lawson when he replaced him as Chancellor of the Exchequer. Major could not hope to compete with his pre-decessor's strategic vision of economic management. Therefore, he did not attempt to do so. He played to his political strengths, which were more in the mould of a skilled craftsman than that of a designer. Similarly, Major's dis-comfort with Margaret Thatcher was born out of her doctrinal preoccu-pations and her sudden excursions into dogma, which would be at the expense of carefully constructed political arrangements.

This led to another element in Major's wariness of political ideas – they disrupted the natural channels of communication, negotiation and compro-mise. For a gifted political broker like John Major, intellectual intransigence contributed neither to party integration nor to governmental coherence. On the contrary, it represented a danger to both. Group attachments to particular ideological projects could become ingrown and self-centred forms of anti-social behaviour. These could devalue and threaten the medium of political exchange. To a political leader like Major, there was a danger in anything which subverted the basis of persuasion and accommodation. The new prime minister was explicitly attached to the traditional conservative antipathy towards rationalism in politics. This was because he was inclined to an incre-mental and evolutionary conception of adaptive change. It was also because he had just experienced an era when the strident assertion of new philosophical orthodoxies had produced an insensitivity to the social and personal costs of an ideologically driven crusade of reform. The net effect of the Conservative party's prolonged engagement with the battle of political ideas had produced a marked power differential within the government that had led to an increasingly inflated and isolated leadership and to a polarisation of opinions and attitudes within the party and society as a whole.

Given these perspectives, Major was intent upon ensuring that his administration would be as free as possible from doctrinal conflict and that his premiership would not become an ideological lodestar. He resisted being questioned on his relative position in the left-right continuum: 'I have always studiously avoided labels on the grounds that they are grotesquely misleading.'[42] He strenuously objected to being unilaterally assigned to an ideological location. In his view, all such assignments were deceptive and ultimately false: 'There has never been a politician who can be truly docketed as right, left or centre. If people come to you bearing a package labelled in that way, treat it carefully.'[43] That insistent independence, which had marred his period at Rutlish Grammar, remained an integral part of his of outlook as party leader.

Even if it might be to his advantage, he refused absolutely to be pigeon-holed. 'I don't have a great deal of affection or indeed admiration', he said, 'for the kind of political thought which claps itself on the back and says I'm a right-winger, I'm a left-winger, I'm a liberal. The truth is that people are much more complex than that. I don't think you ought to put people in boxes.'[44] When he succeeded Margaret Thatcher, profile-writers searched for clues to Major's animating beliefs. Political analysis and commentary had become accustomed to defining political leadership through the context of a personal credo. But with Major, they were confounded: '[T]his man has held no unnecessary opinions or at any rate has not expressed them.'[45] In the end, the tendency was to use one particular quotation from a speech that Major had made in June 1988 to the Adam Smith Institute. On that occasion, he wished to make clear that he was not disposed to the world of ideas: 'Unlike Adam Smith, I am not a moral philosopher. Nor an economist. Nor an intellectual. I am a practical politician.'[46] Major made no apologies for the protean nature of his ideas and even sought to make a virtue of the pragmatic utility of his own freedom from dogma during his rapid rise to prominence: 'I was moving through government faster than a counter moves around a Monopoly board. So there wasn't a great deal of time to back and make philosophic speeches. I was too busy dealing with the practicalities of the day.'[47]

At the beginning of his premiership, members of Major's staff were keen to experiment with the notion of trying to use his name to provide the administration with an identity that would be distinct from that of Margaret Thatcher. The attempt to formulate a position that could be characterised as 'Majorism', however, was quickly abandoned partly because of the ambiguity of any projected content, but mostly because of the uncooperativeness of the principal party. The prime minister later recollected that there were calls for his policy views to be given a single theme. 'This prompted some talk of "Majorism". I discouraged it. The Conservative party does not belong to any one individual. The "ism" I wished to promote was a traditional Conservatism tempered with an understanding of and sympathy for life at many levels.'[48] As Dennis Kavanagh notes, the new prime minister wished to be strongly distinguished from his predecessor but not on the grounds of discernible ideological posture. 'John

Major rejected the comparison with his predecessor, in the sense of not wishing to be identified with an "ism". Being a Conservative was sufficient for him, and, after all, by 1990 nearly half of the Conservative MPs had wanted Mrs Thatcher to go. At one stage, he expressly forbade his Downing Street staff to use the term Majorism.'[49] Sarah Hogg and Jonathan Hill confirm that from the beginning, the prime minister 'resisted any talk of "Majorism". His team knew that they could expect a Prime Ministerial talking-to if he saw it creeping into the newspapers.'[50] To John Major, traditional conservatism required a more pragmatic, fluid and open-textured approach to political management.

Nowhere was this perspective more evident than in Major's revival of the cabinet as a collaborative and discursive device. From the outset of his administration, the prime minister made it clear that he was resolved to make the cabinet into a facility for defining problems, widening participation, sharing responsibility and unifying the party and government.[51] The impetus behind this objective had a number of sources. For example, because his was a new administration whose legitimacy was ambiguous, Major was aware that his personal authority might be limited and, therefore, in need of a more explicit support structure. The party and government had also undergone a period of sudden and unexpected change. This made cabinet continuity a necessary form of reassurance. It also underlined the importance of the cabinet in facilitating the transition to a post-Thatcher regime.

Another reason for Major giving prominence to the cabinet lay in its ability to limit criticism and ambition to manageable proportions. Major had had first-hand experience of the pathology of his predecessor's leadership. He had witnessed both the organisational damage and the personal benefits of indiscipline, disaffection and internecine rivalry at the highest levels of government. He knew the symptoms and was intent upon preventing any recurrence of the chronic condition that had undermined Margaret Thatcher's premiership. A further contributory factor in Major's attachment to cabinet inclusiveness was the simple imperative of an imminent general election. After such an intense period of high exposure when its divisions had been plainly apparent, the party needed to close ranks in preparation for its severest test in over fifteen years. Major had the advantage of such a stimulus to unity, but he also had to ensure that he maximised the opportunity of a disciplined and unified front. Developing the cabinet into a mutually supportive team was deemed the most effective way of achieving governmental and party coherence and, with it, a sense of corporate responsibility for individual decisions.

But by far the most significant factor in John Major's attachment to enhanced cabinet deliberation was that of personal temperament. He had a strong personal preference to decision-making by prior discussion. Major believed that it improved both the quality of choices and the strength of subsequent support behind them. This outlook lay at the heart of Major's adopted form of leadership. He advocated it as a more democratic and, therefore, more productive style of leadership than that of his predecessor. Major was determined to extend this strategy to the premiership and, in doing so, to provide a corrective contrast to the dysfunctional elements of the Thatcher era.

> Margaret had often introduced subjects in Cabinet by setting out her own favoured solution: shameless but effective. I, by contrast, preferred to let my views be known in private, see potential dissenters ahead of the meeting, encourage discussion, and sum up after it. A different approach, but, I believe, one that is equally effective. Margaret had been at her happiest confronting political dragons; I chose consensus in policy-making, if not always in policy.[52]

These intentions were successfully translated into action. As a consequence, the cabinet came to have 'a more prominent role in policy-making and ministers had more significance'.[53] A greater volume of 'matters were dealt with in Cabinet committees' and there were 'fewer bilateral meetings and 'ad hoc groups', which reflected the 'differences in style and approach'.[54] The literature on the Major government is accordingly replete with references to the sharp change in prime ministerial styles and the consequences that flowed from it. Sir Charles Powell, for example, sensed an immediate difference between the mood and operation of the cabinet under Major compared with the tenor of discussion that prevailed in the cabinets under Thatcher. 'John Major was more disposed to listen to his Cabinet colleagues than Mrs Thatcher was.'[55] Thatcher was an 'instinctive leader' who used to declare what the conclusions of a cabinet should be at the outset and then 'challenge anyone to fight her'.[56] Powell thought John Major was quite different: '[H]e's a natural chairman. He likes to hear points of view and then he will draw his conclusions. That's why, on the whole, officials love him because he chairs an orderly meeting and you can write minutes quite simply. I used to have to invent the minutes of Mrs Thatcher's meetings because otherwise government couldn't have got on.'[57]

In his recent study of the prime ministerial office, Peter Hennessy refers to the views of 'a very senior Cabinet minister'[58] who in 1991 analysed the changed context in the following way:

> The Prime Minister sums up but he doesn't prejudge the question. So that changes the discussion. It has a rather odd effect on ministers. In the old days, a Secretary of State would discuss a proposal with the Prime Minister [Mrs Thatcher]. If after one meeting or two he had persuaded her that it was right, she would say: 'we'd better put it to Cabinet'. Then he wouldn't have to worry about it *because he had gone through the difficult part*. Now he has to persuade the prime minister *and* he has to persuade a lot of other people in the Cabinet as well.[59]

Michael Heseltine had more reason than most to discern the nature of the transition. He recollected that in Margaret Thatcher's cabinets, 'it was all too easy to find one's arguments by prime ministerial interruption, to have the case one wished to deploy highjacked by premature conclusions and often hectoring interventions'.[60] Heseltine discovered that if he wished to make a contribution he needed to persevere to the point of stubborn persistence.

> Hard experience taught me to wait until Mrs Thatcher paused for breath and then I began again – and again – and again – until I was satisfied that what I had to say had been clearly heard. It was wearying, but those who shrank form it soon found themselves marginalised in the endless power struggle of Cabinet life. Those who were around in the late 1980s told me it became a great deal worse after the middle of the decade, when some of the older and more formidable members of the Cabinet had left or been sacked and Mrs Thatcher came to dominate her colleagues in a way that was simply unhealthy.[61]

When Michael Heseltine returned to the cabinet in John Major's government, he was struck by the 'improved atmosphere', which he attributed largely to the new prime minister: 'In contrast to the Thatcher years, everyone was allowed their say. Arguments were countered by reason and not interrupted or shouted down. Personal abuse and raised voices were never part of the currency'.[62]

By the end of his first administration, the new prime minister had reason to think that his leadership style had been vindicated. Major had successfully defused the divisive issue of the poll tax by negotiating a scheme to replace it as the basis of local government finance. In doing so, Major had 'achieved his goal of removing one of the most serious political disasters inherited from the Thatcher years by playing a long-drawn-out political game, by careful compromise and by an emollient style'.[63] He also managed to keep the cabinet united on the issue of Europe. Major felt it necessary to improve relations with the European Community after the convulsive period of Thatcherite Euroscepticism. His posture was controversial but he managed to secure the acquiescence of Margaret Thatcher's sympathisers in government. 'Mr Major's wish to see Britain "at the very heart of Europe" was balanced by his dismissal of federalism.'[64]

This emphasis upon compromise and equilibrium was a discernible pattern in other key areas. Although public expenditure needed to be sustained in the period prior to a general election, the economy was in a downturn and the Public Sector Borrowing Requirement was increasing. The room for tax reduction, therefore, was very limited. The Major administration balanced the political need for spending with the Thatcherite impulse to reduce the sphere of the state by targeting tax cuts to the lowest paid. In another field, Major sought to broaden the party's appeal by a commitment to raise government support for health and education, and to show a greater awareness of minorities and the socially disadvantaged. At the same time, he remained firmly in favour of privatisation and reasserted a tough attitude towards law and order. The Citizen's Charter provided another example of this balanced approach. The Charter was a showpiece initiative designed not only to demonstrate a populist concern for the standards of public services, but also to protect established public bureaucracies from the threat of further privatisation measures. His immediate successes may have been deceptive in that they were achieved during extraordinary circumstances. Even Major himself may have overestimated his capacity to finesse the divisions within the party by compromise and party management'.[65] But at least during his first administration, the new prime minister had few doubts that deep consultation, quiet negotiation and practical goodwill could be made to square any circle.

Leadership contingencies and constraints

John Major's preferred posture was that of a facilitator. He believed that such a role was consistent not only with his own personal temperament but with the traditions of the Conservative party. A facilitating prime minister also seemed appropriate to the conditions that prevailed in the immediate aftermath of Margaret Thatcher's departure from the premiership, when the emphasis lay upon recovery, consolidation and party unity. Major was the beneficiary of several factors in favour of his adopted role as an agency of integration. He was credited with preventing the party's decline into long-term civil strife as a consequence of Thatcher's fall. His passage to the premiership reversed the party's slump in public estimation and placed the Conservatives it into electoral contention once again. The party's deficit in the polls that had stretched to over 20 points in the spring of 1990 had now been reduced to a level where the government could reasonably aspire to a fourth general election victory. In essence, 'the country behaved as if last November [1990] there had been a change of government, and the new government had been given a remarkable honeymoon'.[66]

The prime beneficiary of these trends was John Major himself. He sought to cultivate this appearance of revival and unity into a political resource. Fortunately for the prime minister, he was immediately placed in a position of embodying his ideal of 'one nation' leadership. He successfully symbolised the country's war effort in the allied attack upon Iraqi forces in Kuwait. Thereafter, he sought to re-enact the unifying properties of the Gulf War's coalitional engagement. His attempt to transpose such leadership to the sphere of normal politics seemed a plausible proposition. In many respects, the new prime minister's style appeared congruent with the need to construct new relationships with Europe, to engage in the subtle processes of readjustment incurred by the end of the cold war, and to defuse domestic issues that were divisive in nature. By being youthful, accommodating, courteous and constructively ambiguous, Major was the recipient of substantial public goodwill. He had been a leading figure in Mrs Thatcher's first administration. He had also been a conspicuous supporter of Thatcher and the chief beneficiary of her patronage. Nevertheless, he had apparently broken free from her and had done so without incurring the dishonour of open disloyalty. The shift from the confrontational style of his predecessor was facilitated not only by the disappearance of Thatcher from the cabinet along with many of her senior ministerial supporters, but also by the successful reinstatement and rehabilitation of Michael Heseltine as a cabinet minister.

The image of party unity that resonated from the Major administration, combined with the resurgence in public support for the party, the government and the leadership, supplemented the political leverage available to a prime minister. Major had calmed the turmoil of a regime change and had instituted a tone and a culture of conciliation. Just as his leadership style appeared to be correlated to the political position in which he had to operate, so Major's immediate success in acting as a negotiating broker to the various segments of the party seemed to vindicate his own view that this kind of leadership was more constructive, more functional and more in the grain of British political experience.

But Major's conception of leadership – its requirements, supports and effects – were not unproblematic. Far from being the mere extension of political conditions and customary practices, both the leader and his style were confronted with a series of potential and actual difficulties that constituted a set of conditioning constraints. First, Major did not have a well-developed base within the party. He had been acknowledged as a long-term prospect for the leadership but he had not had the time to build up a deeply rooted and durable personal following. As a consequence, he was dependent upon the status of several senior ministers like Douglas Hurd, Kenneth Clarke, Kenneth Baker, Tom King and Michael Heseltine. Major was aware that his record was that of a largely unproven minister who had not served the appropriate apprenticeship for a party leader within government. The new prime minister's deficiency in cabinet experience was further compounded by the evidently limited nature of his electoral legitimacy as premier. His leadership style therefore, reflected not merely a personal preference, or a recuperative need for the party, but a political accommodation in its own right. Major had little incentive or leverage to be anything other than a collegiate figure. Second, while Major's victory in the leadership election resolved the immediate issue of a succession to Thatcher, it did not mark a point of finality for the ambitions of those figures with more experience or more talent than the prime minister. Major's accession to the premiership may have coincided with a moratorium on competitive manœuvrings and mutual hostilities, but it could never have satisfactorily resolved them. Those with frustrated ambitions were now quiet because it was politically prudent to be so. The prime minister's more consensual approach may have served his immediate interests, but it was also a sign of the leader's need to cater for the varied segments of the party and to maintain some equilibrium between them.

A third constraint was that of time. During the leadership election and at the outset of his administration, Major was able to broaden his appeal and to reassure doubters by spreading himself across many of the party's divisions. Major generated hope by offering varied intimations of his guiding convictions and future policy directions. The strategic imprecision of his position succeeded in generating a host of speculations over the nature and intensity of his likely policy choices. But this ambiguity over the potential direction of his premiership was difficult to sustain over a prolonged period. Following the primary colours of his predecessor, John Major's early caution and his grey image of opaque neutrality in effect raised expectations in a variety of directions that could not all be fulfilled.

This problem was further exacerbated by a fourth limitation. Major began to be unfavourably compared with Margaret Thatcher. Increasingly, the antidote came to be seen as the anticlimax especially to those who had become accustomed to leadership in the form of personal vision, strategic drive and purposive direction. Major may have been Thatcher's preferred successor, but his presence in Number 10 inevitably represented the 'dissipation of the energy, the radicalism and the conviction that suffused the Thatcher decade'.[67] As early as March 1991, Thatcher herself was turning against her successor for being insufficiently Thatcherite in substance or style. Moreover, some of her most dedicated lieutenants (e.g. Norman Tebbit, Cecil Parkinson, Nicholas Ridley) had left the cabinet and were now in a position to subject the new administration to continued review on the issue of its guardianship of the 'Thatcherite inheritance'. Thatcherism and Thatcherite leadership became a point of critical reference for John Major, whose own leadership by contrast was beginning to be equated with political and personal weakness. Just as in the past a range of issues could be calibrated into the central issue of Margaret Thatcher's position in government, so now Major's mode of leadership was increasingly used as an instrument of general political critique upon the government and the Conservative party.

This dynamic was deepened by a fifth factor. This was the government's decline in reputation and popularity after June 1991. As the Labour party recovered its opinion poll lead and the economy headed for deep recession, Major's position became more problematic. As the election approached, he would receive the vociferous support of the party but it would be qualified by internal doubts over Major's competence as prime minister. Amongst many sectors of the party, there was an expectation that the Conservatives would lose office at which point the real process of a post-Thatcherite adjustment would finally commence.

Many of these contexts and contingencies of John Major's leadership remained implicit and undeveloped during his first administration. The forthcoming general election acted as both a suppressant and a disguise to many of the problems inherent in the new prime minister's position. After the election, the tensions within Major's own leadership style, together with the problems involved in juxtaposing such a leadership with that of Margaret Thatcher, would become increasingly evident. But before these developments became explicit, one other dynamic was added to the matrix. This was derived from the immediate context of the election itself and related to the urgent need of the Conservative party to project John Major as a public personality and as an electoral commodity in his own right.

Notes

1 Quoted in Peter Norman, 'Tory leader who rose without trace', *Financial Times*, 28 November 1990.

2 Quoted in John Major, 'Who I am and whence I came', interview with Nicholas Wapshott, *The Observer*, 2 December 1990.

3 Anthony Seldon, *Major: A Political Life* (London: Phoenix, 1997), p. 68.

4 Nigel Lawson, *The View From No. 11: Memoirs of a Tory Radical* (London: Corgi, 1993), p. 711.

5 Lawson, *The View From No. 11*, p. 711.

6 Edward Pearce, *The Quiet Rise of John Major* (London: Weidenfeld and Nicolson, 1991), p. 114.

7 Joe Rogaly, 'Will the real Mr Major stand up', *Financial Times*, 28 November 1990.

8 Margaret Thatcher, *The Downing Street Years* (London: HarperCollins, 1993), pp. 757–8.

9 John Major, *The Autobiography* (London: HarperCollins, 1999), p. 112.

10 Major, *The Autobiography*, p. 112.

11 Major, *The Autobiography*, p. 116.

12 Seldon, *Major: A Political Life*, p. 85.

13 Pearce, *The Quiet Rise of John Major*, p. 126.

14 The deterioration in the government's position had reached the point where a quarter of the party's parliamentary seats risked becoming marginal at the next general election.

15 John Major, *The Autobiography*, p. 167.

16 Michael Foley, *The Rise of the British Presidency* (Manchester: Manchester University Press, 1993), p. 178.

17 Major, *The Autobiography*, p. 176.

18 Hansard, House of Commons, 13 October 1990, col. 464.

19 Hansard, House of Commons, 13 October 1990, col. 465.

20 Hansard, House of Commons, 13 October 1990, col. 465.

21 Quoted in an interview with Christopher Huhne, *Independent on Sunday*, 25 November 1990.

22 For example, see the Harris poll in *The Observer*, 18 November 1990; the Gallup poll in the *Sunday Telegraph*, 18 November 1990.

23 Ivor Crewe, 'Leadership Fight Revives Tory Vote', *Independent on Sunday*, 18 November 1990.

24 Michael Heseltine, *Life in the Jungle: My Autobiography* (London: Hodder and Stoughton, 2000), p. 369.

25 Heseltine, *Life in the Jungle*, p. 370.

26 Heseltine, *Life in the Jungle*, p. 369.

27 *The Independent*, 27 November 1990.

28 Anthony King, 'Major rivals Heseltine as candidate most likely to lead Tories to victory', *Daily Telegraph*, 27 November 1990.

29 King, 'Major rivals Heseltine as candidate most likely to lead Tories to victory'.

30 Quoted in an interview with Charles Moore, *Daily Telegraph*, 26 November 1990.

31 Gallup poll, *Daily Telegraph*, 27 November 1990.

32 Seldon, *Major: A Political Life*, p. 128.

33 Major, *The Autobiography*, p. 89.

34 Quoted in an interview with David Wastell, *Sunday Telegraph*, 24 November 1990.

35 Quoted in an interview with David Wastell, *Sunday Telegraph*, 24 November 1990.

36 Quoted in Jon Hibbs, 'Major vision of classless new Britain', *Daily Telegraph*, 24 November 1990.

37 Seldon, *Major: A Political Life*, p. 129.

38 Seldon, *Major: A Political Life*, p. 128.

39 Quoted in Joe Rogaly, 'Now events, not vision, will be driving policy', *Financial Times*, 30 November 1990.

40 Rogaly, 'Now events, not vision, will be driving policy'.

41 Major, *The Autobiography*, p. 116.

42 John Major quoted in Major, *The Autobiography*, p. 193.

43 Quoted in an interview with Robin Oakley, *The Times*, 24 November 1990.

44 Quoted in John Major, 'Who I am and whence I came'.

45 Pearce, *The Quiet Rise of John Major*, p. 167. See also Frank Johnson, 'Is there a spark in the machine?' *Sunday Telegraph*, 9 December 1990.

46 For example, see 'Unlike Adam Smith, I am not a moral philosopher. Nor an economist … I am a practical politician', *Financial Times*, 28 November 19990; and Adam Raphael and Victor Smart, 'Tears, fears, plots … and toothache', *The Observer*, 2 December 1990.

47 Quoted in BBC1, *The Major Years*, broadcast 11 October 1999.

48 Major, *The Autobiography*, p. 204.

49 Dennis Kavanagh, *The Reordering of British Politics: Politics after Thatcher* (Oxford: Oxford University Press, 1997), pp. 200–1.

50 Susan Hogg and Jonathan Hill, *Too Close to Call: Power and Politics – John Major in No. 10* (London: Warner, 1996), p. 86.

51 See Colin Brown, 'Happy days are here again …', *The Independent*, 17 December 1990.

52 Major, *The Autobiography*, p. 209.

53 Graham P. Thomas, *Prime Minister and Cabinet Today* (Manchester: Manchester University Press, 1998), p. 44.

54 Thomas, *Prime Minister and Cabinet Today*, p. 44.

55 Sir Charles Powell, quoted in Penny Junor, *John Major: From Brixton to Downing Street* (London: Penguin, 1996), p. 209.

56 Powell, quoted in Junor, *Major: From Brixton to Downing Street*, p. 209.

57 Powell, quoted in Junor, *Major: From Brixton to Downing Street*, p. 209.
58 Peter Hennessy, *The Prime Minister: The Office and its Holders since 1945* (London: Allen Lane, 2000), p. 439.
59 Hennessy, *The Prime Minister: The Office and its Holders since 1945*, p. 439.
60 Heseltine, *Life in the Jungle*, p. 232.
61 Heseltine, *Life in the Jungle*, p. 232.
62 Heseltine, *Life in the Jungle*, p. 488.
63 Brendan Evans, *Thatcherism and British Politics 1975–1999* (Stroud: Sutton, 1999), p. 156.
64 David Butler and Dennis Kavanagh, *The British General Election 1992* (Basingstoke: Macmillan, 1992), p. 39.
65 Evans, *Thatcherism and British Politics 1975–1999*, pp. 146–7.
66 Peter Jenkins, 'A vital U-turn for Mr Major', *The Independent*, 7 March 1991.
67 Andrew Gamble, 'Following the leader', *Marxism Today*, January 1991.

3 The imploding premiership

The 1992 general election and the personalisation of leadership

An integral element in the evolution of John Major's premiership, and in the development of leadership politics in Britain, was provided by the 1992 general election. This election would determine whether or not the period of Conservative ascendancy would be ended. Equally significant, it would reveal the extent to which Major's leadership marked either an interim period between Margaret Thatcher's fall and the emergence of a Labour government, or a genuine reconstitution of the Conservative party's identity and, with it, an opportunity to secure a fourth term of office. The prospect of an election had been a conditioning factor in the closure of Conservative ranks in November 1990. Now John Major would have to fulfil the hopes and expectations engendered by his premiership and take charge of the government's battle for survival. To this end, he would need to retain the virtue of his merits but at the same time to combine this theme with a different set of acquired skills.

From the outset of his administration, John Major's personal approval rating had outstripped the support for the Conservative government. Whether or not this differential was caused by a negative disposition towards Margaret Thatcher, or a positive attitude to her successor was difficult to determine with any accuracy. But even if it were more the former than the latter, Major's style and behaviour had successfully accommodated the anti-Thatcher impulse. He had not deterred the movement of support from one Conservative leader to another, or from a particularly robust type of leadership to his studiously restrained vision of a post-Thatcher premiership. And yet, Major had been unable to bring the party up to his levels of public support. In fact, this was less a failure and more a concerted strength. It was certainly recognised as such by party strategists.

> John Major was pulling the party up above the level of support that might have been expected given the state of the economy. But he could only pull it so far. During his 'honeymoon', the percentage saying they would vote Conservative had, according to Gallup, risen way ahead of what might have been predicted from the figures for consumer confidence. Since then, the gap

between two measures had narrowed, but seem to have stabilised at about 4 per cent. That was reckoned to be a measure of the boost John Major had given to his party's chances in the polls.[1]

The key question was how to exploit Major's electoral potential for the party. Prior to November 1990, Conservative Central Office had proceeded on the basis that the next general election would feature the familiar scenario of a triumphant prime minister battling against the scourge of Labour's closet socialism and endemic incompetence. This role had been exactly matched to Margaret Thatcher's naturally aggressive stance. John Major, however, was a quite different politician. He would require a new approach and altered style of party projection. Compared to Thatcher, he was a 'very different personality and, in terms of party management and electoral appeal, it paid dividends to emphasise the difference'.[2] Major himself was adjudged to be the party's central electoral asset. As early as spring 1991, the Conservatives' advertising agency Saatchi and Saatchi concluded that the campaign should focus upon John Major pressing for his first full term of office rather than for the continuity of Conservative government. This view was based not just upon a differentiation at the top but upon Major's capacity to suggest differentiation from the Conservative party itself: 'Surveys suggested that while Mrs Thatcher dominated the image of the Conservative party, with her strengths and weaknesses defining those of the party, voters drew a distinction between Mr Major and the Conservative party.'[3] The prime minister, therefore, represented an opportunity for the Conservatives. They could retreat into victory by allowing the leader to eclipse the party and, in doing so, to generate an altered conception of his own party.

Actualising John Major's potential as a campaign spearhead was not without its problems. First, even though much of his appeal would be based upon not being Margaret Thatcher, the distinction would have to be implicit. Major could not afford to antagonise the party by any critical references to his predecessor. Second, John Major was inexperienced as a national campaigner. He would be confronted by the oratorical skills and predatory aggression of Neil Kinnock. Apart from the danger of being simply overwhelmed by his main opponent, Major's well-known sensitivity to criticism could be a severe handicap. In the abrasive atmosphere of a general election, Major might inflict damage upon his own reputation as a calming influence and a builder of consensus. This danger would become particularly acute when the Labour campaign intensified its assault upon Major as the 'son of Thatcher' and, therefore, as a leader who was not his own man – a leader who would forever be in her debt and in her guiding shadow.

The third problem relating to the prime minister's electoral potential was the familiar question over Major's message to the public. It could be said that

Thatcherism had won the battle of ideas and that Major had no need of a 'big idea' to inform his discrete proposals for reform. Nevertheless, it would be difficult to run a campaign centred upon an individual without a unifying theme. And finally, Major was ill disposed and temperamentally unsuited to the personalisation of politics. He detested the pretension and the hauteur of ideological solutions. He was a self-confessed pragmatist who valued practical politics, social cohesion and national traditions. He was conceived as caring, compassionate, honest and sincere. His merits had a private interior character to them that might not translate well to public presentation. It was possible that Major was perhaps simply 'too unheroic and uncommanding a figure to be able to bank for long on public favour'.[4] Major was popular for being ordinary. The question was whether ordinariness could be marketed as a political resource that would motivate voters to opt for the Conservative party in preference to the programmes of more flamboyant leaders.

These problems generated a grand solution. Early in Major's premiership, Conservative strategists decided to take active steps to project the prime minister into a public persona. In order to allow his private merits and intrinsic character strengths to resonate amongst the electorate, it was necessary to turn John Major from an image of introversion into one of self-conscious personal exposure. This would allow him not only to capitalise upon his distance from the party's overall image, but to develop an individual base within the party and government. Conservative strategists determined that the best chance for the party lay in running a presidential-style election campaign over an extended period of time. Major would be marketed as a highly personalised package to a public, which during the Thatcher era had become increasingly conditioned to the strategies and styles of leadership politics. Such a decision would have been contrary to the prime minister's natural preferences and inclinations. Major would have to overcome his diffidence as well as his customary defensiveness over his background and formative experiences. The change was gradual and at times reluctant, yet during the 1991–92 period Major acquired the appearance of a far more assertive and outwardly autonomous figure.

As both Major and his leadership became more visible, the party and government became increasingly identified with the accelerated personal status of the prime minister. With their complicity, Major assumed the personal licence and responsibility of public leadership. Any inhibitions he may have had at the beginning of his administration were dismissed as he went to considerable and conspicuous lengths both to impress himself visibly upon government and to deploy his office as an immediate point of contact between government and the public. The prime minister took to making conspicuous prime ministerial interventions into governmental machinery (e.g. compensation settlement for HIV haemophiliacs, a relaxation of the eligibility rules for cold weather payments), in order to demonstrate a sensitivity to public concerns and a leader's responsibility to redress grievances. His interventions were usually well publicised and designed to give the impression of an attentive prime minister breaking free from collective restraints and personally turning on some aspect of government policy or government machinery on behalf of the public. The Citizen's Charter was promoted as a device that patented prime ministerial intervention on a mass basis within the complaint-ridden public services. The prime minister also sought to take himself directly to the people by inaugurating informal question and answer sessions with members of the public. The change of outlook was underlined in his agreement to take the nation through his childhood and inner thoughts on the fiftieth anniversary edition of the radio programme *Desert Island Discs* in January 1991.[5]

The scale and consequences of the transformation were evident in the prime minister's speech to the Conservative Party Conference in October 1991. This was his first address to the conference as leader and prime minister. It was also the final conference before a general election that threatened to end the Conservatives' period in government. In addition, it marked the first occasion that the party had assembled following the enforced resignation of Margaret Thatcher. In these conditions, it was vital that Major stamp his mark on the party and establish its theme for the forthcoming electoral struggle. It was in this arena that Major uncovered not only his guiding theme, but the lengths to which both he and the party would go in order to promote it. The party's post-Thatcherite identity and appeal for the 1990s would be based not so much on policy as on John Major himself and what he and his career symbolised. Major's problem with personalised politics was that he had always equated it with the explanation of concepts and the propagation of ideology. In a remarkable transformation, he and his party's solution to this problem was to subsume the realm of ideas under the narrative and meaning of Major's own experience in rising through society to achieve the premiership.

His story acted as the living embodiment of his own conservatism. It was the affirmation and vindication of a culture of individual opportunity. His credo was synonymous with his passage to power. His experience constituted the personal guarantee to maintain and improve the individual opportunity and social provision which he had enjoyed. Major's background gave him insights and instincts into the aspirations and anxieties of the lower middle classes and other struggling sectors. His vision was the vision of his past. Through him, his past could become an inspiration to others to follow the Major models, and to trust Major's leadership. 'He invited people to identify in his personal mythology and to follow in his footsteps from Coldharbour Lane, Brixton to Number 10, Downing Street.'[6] He explicitly linked his present principles and programme to his own underprivileged background and his rise to prominence as an outsider. Because of *his* experience, the party – *his* party – was not indifferent to the plight of the unemployed: 'I know how they feel – I know what it's like for a family when a business collapses. What it's like when you're unemployed and when you have to search for the next job. I haven't forgotten – and I never will.'[7] Because of these hard knocks, he would 'never play fast and loose with the economy'.[8] His private difficulties in the past were now not only publicly aired by Major himself, but openly deployed to justify his occupancy of Number 10 and to vindicate the values of his party – 'the power to choose and the right to own … Ordinary values perhaps, but over which ordinary people have, in our time, fought an extraordinary fight'.[9]

Major made it perfectly clear that he had used the office, and would continue to exert his incumbency, in the furtherance of his values. He played due deference to the constitutional virtues of cabinet government and collective leadership, but at the same time he underlined the public value of his private leverage. He sought to reassure the public by reference to the benign nature of prime ministerial power. Major's message was that he could be trusted with the exercise of power because of who he was and what he had been through. He claimed the right to be believed especially where the NHS was involved. It was 'unthinkable that I, of all people, would try to take that security away'.[10] As a consequence, there would be 'no charges for hospital treatment, no charges for visits to the doctor, no privatisation of health care, neither piecemeal, nor in part, nor in whole. Not today. Not tomorrow. Not after the next election. Not ever while I'm Prime Minister.'[11]

It was precisely his background and character that would prevent his incumbency from becoming one of detachment and insensitivity. His memory of being just one of a crowd would always ensure a genuine, and electorally attractive, identity with the average person. 'Here was an authentic product of the post-war meritocracy'[12] intent upon developing a 'skill in relating policy to his own life'.[13] For a modest man, Major's exploitation of his personality had been extraordinary. In Hugo Young's view, the speech 'made clear that the Conservatives' visionary appeal [was] built, to a startling extent, around one model: himself'.[14] Young concluded that in this respect Major had surpassed his mentor: 'This was the unexpected coda to the Thatcher era. Mrs Thatcher was often charged with hubristic domination, and her conference speech was delivered and received as an annual consummation of one-woman government. But she was never so shameless in representing her own life as the proof of all she had to say.'[15] Major's transformation as an exponent of leadership politics was now complete.

This form of self-promotion was not merely different in scale to that of Margaret Thatcher. It represented a more premeditated and concerted effort to produce a highly symbolic construction of leadership that was designed to produce a personal engagement with the public and a displacement of popular interest away from the party and its immediate past. Margaret Thatcher's self-promotion had been secondary and incidental to the task-driven crusades of her policy leadership. John Major's self-promotion was more an end in its own right in terms of serving party management and pursuing populist credentials. Margaret Thatcher's highly conspicuous leadership had the properties of an elemental force. By contrast, the attempts to project John Major's leadership were intended to demonstrate that he remained integrally related and unusually connected to the public. Margaret Thatcher's advocacy of personal empowerment had never reached the level of accepting that anyone could act as prime minister. John Major's personal story on the other hand was an epic expression of neoliberal values. As an exemplar of social mobility, his very presence in the premiership suggested that individual opportunity could reach as far as the Conservative party leadership and Number 10 Downing Street.

When the 1992 general election was finally called, the strategy of the Conservative party campaign had already been long established. It would be a long and heavily personalised campaign to allow John Major both the time and the platform to steer public perceptions away from the party's collective parts and towards its individualised sense of the future. The objective was to create as great a disjunction between Thatcher administrations and a new Major government. Major himself had come to realise that in order both to establish a break with Margaret Thatcher and to wear down the Labour party's lead and the leadership credentials of Neil Kinnock, it was necessary to alter radically his previous style and mode of operation. Prior to the election, Major had had to transform himself into a skilled exponent of the personalised and publicised requirements of leadership politics. Now the election had been called the process of self-promotion geared up to their point of culmination.

The Conservative campaign was unreservedly and unashamedly leader-centric in design and application. Its manifesto launch reaffirmed the adopted strategy. Even though Major was surrounded by his cabinet, he answered nearly all the questions. He went on to assure the audience that the manifesto embodied his principles and his objectives: 'It's all me, every last word of it is me.'[16] The occasion prompted one celebrated Thatcher-watcher to draw parallels between the two prime ministers. In his view, the comparison revealed the extent to which John Major had not merely emulated, but superseded his predecessor in the personalisation of the campaign.

> The Tories' projection of John Major as the prime issue in this campaign has a startling intensity … It is to be seen on the cover of the manifesto, the first the Conservatives have published where the image of the leader entirely dominates the words. Mrs Thatcher, for all her presidentialism, declined, out of prudence or fastidiousness, to wallow in such excess. Her face never appeared on the cover. Hers were years of austerity by comparison.[17]

John Major had been 'predictably uncomfortable about the picture, worrying that it smacked of a personality cult … [b]ut the campaign needed all the help it could get'.[18] The launch was also coordinated with the first prime ministerial mailshot in British political history with over a million letters sent out to voters in sixty-seven marginal seats.

Another keynote feature that characterised the campaign was the party election broadcast that concentrated wholly upon Major's life and formative experiences. Once again the prime minister had been very reluctant in agreeing to the production of such a film. It took the party chairman, Chris Patten, over six months to persuade hum to use his past in this way for political gain. The film was shot by John Schlesinger and used Major's background to underline his achievements and to convey his reflections and feelings as an individual. *The Journey* was an evocation of Major's odyssey from Brixton to Downing Street and gave visible expression to the sentiments conveyed in his conference speech. Employing the same formula that he used before, he sought to translate his own personal experiences into qualifications for leadership and public office. In it, Major affirmed that his background was 'an asset not a disadvantage'. It was only when you had 'done something, or seen it, or been it or felt it' that you could understand what it meant and how it affected 'other people in their individual lives'.[19] To devote a quarter of million pounds of the Conservative campaign budget to making *The Journey* and then to select it to fill the party's only prime PEB slot[20] provided further evidence of the campaign's dependence upon not merely the prime minister but more especially his personality and individual qualities. It was thoroughly consistent with Conservative strategy that the film's narrative was provided exclusively by John Major speaking in the first person and that no mention was made throughout the film of the Conservative party. The fact that John Major never watched the film was similarly consistent with his own outlook of a parliamentary politician reluctantly coming to terms with the demands of modern leadership politics.

The campaign included a variety of other forms of leadership projection. The prime minister was deployed in small informal 'Meet John Major' sessions where party members could engage with the prime minister in unscripted question and answer sessions. On other occasions, Major was placed in the centre of a custom-built circular video theatre which allowed the prime minister to engage closely with the audience while video clips of John Major as leader circled the auditorium. The most celebrated instance of public promotion came with Major's sudden decision to revert to old-style street campaigning through the use of a soapbox and megaphone. Major had been prompted into such a course of action by reports that the campaign was lacklustre, by accusations that the prime minister was not connecting with the public and by John Major's own personal irritation with staged events constructed for television. After the first of these encounters in Luton, the format was repeated on other visits to the hustings. On each occasion it drew large crowds, generated demonstrations and ensured extensive coverage. The prime minister was shown being jostled and heckled. Abuse and eggs were hurled at him. These events would allow Major to appear as the non-conformist politician, breaking campaign norms, defying security, dropping his guard and risking everything by trusting the people. Of all the devices used to personalise the campaign this was the one with which Major felt most at ease: 'This aspect of electioneering suited me well. I felt at ease hemmed in by a noisy mass of jostling humanity. The people were there because they chose to be. So was I. I like the unpredictability and the dialogue with the crowds. I was invigorated when things went well.'[21]

Apart from being leader centred, this form of campaigning was motivated by a reaction against the more cultivated, stylish and controlled devices of leadership projection being used by the Labour party. Although it was ostensibly against the pretensions of leadership, Major's actions were designed both to devalue Kinnock's campaign and to enhance his own. The same fusion of self-effacement, self-interest and leadership presumption was evident in Major's flamboyant eleventh-hour appeal for the electorate to consider the fate of the United Kingdom. On this occasion, Major assumed the mantle of a visionary as he beseeched a large rally in Scotland to heed his warnings on devolution.

> The message I would give you, to the British nation, we have 72 hours to save the union, 72 hours to make sure that the nature of our government is not changed irrevocably for the worse, with power draining away from Westminster. There are 72 hours in which to save the Union, 72 hours to make sure that the system of Government that has prevailed in this country for a very long time is protected and enshrined, and … not broken up and divided in one direction towards the EU and the other to a devolved Parliament across the United Kingdom.[22]

A tale of caution and prime ministerial obligation was married effectively to party benefit and enhanced national leadership.

The 1992 general election was dominated by leaders and pervaded by the issue of leadership. The conduct of the campaigns, the selection of themes, the organisation of events and travel schedules, and the media coverage of the election were all geared to the presentation and promotion of the leaders. The Labour party had been expected to use Neil Kinnock as the centrepiece of a presidential campaign, but in the event the strategy was surpassed by the Conservatives' deployment of John Major. Together with Paddy Ashdown, all three leaders ensured that their individual campaigns would collectively intensify the trend towards a leadership-centred general election. Each leader was not only regarded as being responsible for his party's campaign, he was seen as personifying its principles, its programme and its general fitness to govern. All three dominated both their parties' media strategies and the news-gathering priorities of the major news organisations. The coverage generated a profusion of observations, analyses and speculations on the subject of leader-ship and, in particular, on the relationship between leaders, and their parties' campaigns and electoral prospects. The controlling premise of such intense coverage was that leaders mattered; that they had an indeterminate, but material influence upon electoral choice.

John Major's campaign had been a high-exposure and high-risk venture. He and his team were continually confronted with polls that showed the Labour lead to be intact. They also revealed that the public believed the Con-servative campaign to be the worst of the three main parties, and that John Major's own lead over Neil Kinnock, which in January 1992 had been 26 points, had been eroded to 11 points by the final week of the campaign.[23] Nevertheless, the Major team remained defiantly committed to its selected strategy and even finished the campaign with full-page advertisements in the national press. They featured the prime minister enumerating fifteen objec-tives for 'The Britain I am fighting for'. Once again, the name of John Major was considered a sufficient branding device. Suggestively, the term Conserva-tive party was missing from the advertisement. The subtext, however, was clear. In order to secure the continued services of the prime minister and to support his personal vision of Britain's future, it was necessary to vote Conservative. The party was by implication the instrument, while Major's leadership was couched as the objective.

On 9 April 1992, the Conservative party won an unexpected victory. A succession of opinion polls had pointed to a Labour win. John Major's efforts throughout the campaign had been repeatedly dismissed as having had no effect upon a durable Labour advantage. And yet, the election result yielded a fourth succession Conservative victory. Polling organisations and survey analysts variously asserted that there had been a late swing to the Conserva-tives and that while Labour had underperformed in the volume of votes it had exceeded expectations in its target seats based upon the swing achieved against the Conservatives. It was even asserted that Labour may never have had a lead either prior to, or during, the election. Irrespective of these technical explan-ations, the party and much of the infrastructure of opinion perceived it to be a peculiarly personal and dramatic reversal of political fortune. The tone and the folklore were established immediately after election day with a profusion of reviews and post-mortems. It was simply assumed that the campaigns had made a difference and that John Major had been the critical factor in securing Conservative victory. The prevailing response was that the prime minister had turned the tide with a highly individualised and even idiosyncratic campaign. It was Major who 'against the odds of historical precedent' had allegedly 'won

a remarkable victory'.[24] The Conservative party was reported as having benefited from the 'personal success of John Major in wooing substantial numbers
of Labour's traditional supporters'.[25] The prime minister proved to be 'a
national leader' who had 'risen to the challenge of combat'.[26] The conclusion
that was widely drawn was that in essence 'it was Mr Major's victory'.[27]

In the euphoria of such an electoral upset, these claims were simply
accepted as self-evident axioms. John Major did nothing to discourage such
equations. He had taken the political risk of running a campaign centred upon
himself. If it had failed, it would have broken both his premiership and his
leadership. Now that it had succeeded, Major rushed to draw the appropriate
conclusions. Even though 'Major's personal boost to the Conservative vote
was probably very small,'[28] the result was immediately claimed to be a vindication of his judgement, his competence and his leadership credentials. It also
signified a democratic mandate and a constitutional legitimacy. John Major
was wholly uninhibited in his interpretation of the achievement. He conspicuously summed up the Conservative victory in the first person: 'I now have a
clear majority ... I am prime minister of all this country, for everyone,
whether they voted for me or not.'[29]

Prior to the 1992 general election, John Major felt that many of the difficulties he had encountered upon succeeding Margaret Thatcher had been
attributable to his limited authority as a leader and prime minister. The British
parliamentary system permits parties to change leaders without recourse to
the electorate. The internal coup that forced Margaret Thatcher to resign,
therefore, was entirely within the rules of parliamentary politics. Nevertheless,
Major was acutely aware that this action was still seen in some quarters as
outside the spirit of representative democracy and also against the grain of
contemporary leadership politics. As a consequence, Major always felt in his
first administration that he was missing the direct infusion of democratic
authority that a modern prime minister requires. The deficiency was further
underlined by having to follow on from a premier who had won three general
elections and had engaged in a sustained and highly conspicuous form of
populist leadership. During his first administration, Major had been discomforted by this dimension of his premiership: 'The interval between assuming
that office and seeking my democratic mandate to keep it was not without a
certain ambiguity ... Throughout that year and a half, I had the sneaking
feeling that I was living in sin and the electorate.'[30] Major's relief in winning
the 1992 general election therefore was tangible. At last it appeared that he
would no longer be a provisional prime minister who was in Downing Street
on approval. Major was now entitled to regard himself as a prime minister
firmly in his own right and one who could at last emerge from the shadows of
Margaret Thatcher.

Leading to descent

The second most outstanding aspect of John Major's electoral triumph in 1992 was how short lived his success proved to be. In fact the key significance of his victory was the extent to which it failed to resolve the problems of his leadership. In many respects the election campaign had merely concealed the problematic properties of his position and style. After the election, the initial doubts and restrained disquiet over John Major's premiership generated a debilitating process of corrosive complaint. The early reservations of the first administration were merely the precursors of a second administration that came to be characterised by an almost continuous crisis of leadership. In retrospect, it became apparent that the problems that John Major confronted in the immediate post-Thatcher period represented a largely untapped potential for discord. The extent of the potential and the repercussions following from it not only dominated the development of Major's second administration but also profoundly influenced the character of leadership politics within the British system.

The full pathology of the 1992–97 government is a matter of historical record and does not need to be elaborated upon in detail for the purposes of this analysis. What is noteworthy is that the government was adversely affected by a succession of policy disasters, political reversals, personal scandals and investigative inquiries, which progressively depleted its reputation for integrity and competence. The 'Major years' became synonymous with an apparently unbreakable spiral of declining public confidence and intensifying divisions within the governing party. The administration was damaged by a series of assertive initiatives that were made under pressure and were then followed either by retreats, or by public perceptions of retrenchment (e.g. the pit closure plan in 1992; the 'Back to Basics' crusade in 1993; the issue of an amended scheme of EU Qualified Majority Voting in 1994). The most extreme example of the government's reputation for losing control of events came with the decision to suspend Britain's membership of the Exchange Rate Mechanism. Coming in the wake of a tidal flow of currency movements that culminated in Black Wednesday (16 September 1992), when interest rates were repeatedly raised and the Bank of England's reserves were squandered in a vain attempt to support sterling, the government had little choice but to accept that the market had devalued the pound. The ERM had been the centrepiece of John Major's economic policy and the symbol of the government's claim that counter-inflation was its highest priority. The ignominious defeat was compounded by the subsequent need for the government to raise taxes and in doing so to break the central campaign commitment of the 1992 general election. The ERM fiasco destroyed the Conservatives' reputation for economic management, which had already been undermined by the deepest recession since

World War II. The episode was also instrumental in defining a pattern of 'compromise, muddle and error'[31] which rapidly came to characterise the Major administration.

If the collapse of Britain's membership of the ERM was initially responsible for undermining the reputation of the government, it was followed by a series of events and developments that served to diminish the administration's authority even further. Whether it was the prolonged war of attrition within the Conservative party over the ratification of the Maastricht Treaty, or the damaging revelations that emanated from both the Nolan Committee[32] and the Scott Inquiry,[33] the Major administration appeared to be locked into a dynamic of enduring crisis. The condition was further exacerbated by the continuing acrimony of the party's public strife over the future of the European Union, by a succession of dramatic Conservative defeats in by-elections, local elections and European elections, and by the BSE crisis which 'inflict[ed] lasting damage to the government's credibility at home and abroad'.[34] Against this background, it became commonplace for commentators simply to be lost for comparisons and points of reference. Apart from numerous references to 'never [having] seen this country worse governed than it is today',[35] the Major administration continually plumbed the depths of opinion poll ratings. Within six months of receiving a renewed electoral mandate, the support for the government slumped in the wake of the debacles over the ERM, the pit closure programme and increases in taxation.

As early as June 1993, the government was experiencing a huge 24-point deficit (i.e. 25 per cent to 49 per cent) in relation to the Labour party. This represented the second biggest lead recorded since Gallup began polling in 1937. Only one other government since the war had been more unpopular. This was the administration of Harold Wilson following the devaluation of the pound in 1967. The 1992–93 period represented the 'worst first year for any government in recent times'.[36] It only took another month for the administration to achieve the distinction of being the most unpopular government ever recorded in British polling history. Support for the government had slipped to 24.5 per cent. Moreover, the Conservative party had sunk to third place behind the Liberal Democrats. By October 1993, the position had worsened still further. According to Gallup, 88 per cent thought the government did not inspire confidence, 85 per cent believed it was divided and 78 per cent did not think it was in touch with the country. Three-quarters of voters thought the government was ineffective and two-thirds were of the opinion that it was weak and dishonest. Anthony King concluded that it would be 'hard to imagine a more damning indictment of a freely-elected administration by the people of any country'.[37]

The Major government's standing in 1993 set a basic pattern that lasted throughout the tenure of the administration. Despite the trend lines of an

Figure 3.1 Conservative party image in decline (1992–93)

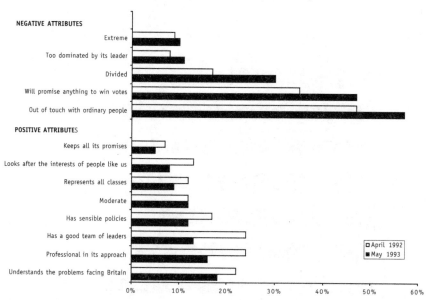

Source: MORI/*Times* (3 May 1993)

improving economy, low inflation and falling unemployment, the government became rooted in the basement of public support and political esteem.
The government's decline was not only deep but broad in scope. The Conservatives lost ground in virtually all the component categories of political
evaluation. The perceived ineptitude, weakness and incoherence of the government led to a decline in political support and public trust and to a corresponding increase in scepticism over its interests and motives. In May 1993,
MORI reported that Labour now outranked the Conservatives in thirteen out
of the fourteen benchmarks of party image (Figure 3.1). This represented a
dramatic reversal of the configuration that characterised the Thatcher years
when the Conservatives remained ahead of Labour on most of the benchmarks. Within a year of the general election, the Conservatives' positive
attributes had all contracted while its negatives had grown slightly larger.
Gallup's survey of attitudes using a split choice of statements conformed the
multidimensional nature of the government's unpopularity (Figure 3.2).

Initially, the government could claim that it was suffering from the
complex and prolonged effects of the recession and that, given the exceptional
nature of the Conservatives' fourth successive general election victory, the
customary mid-term reversals for any governing party would inevitably be
early and severe. As the levels of public scepticism and antipathy showed no
signs of abating in any substantive way, the Major administration swiftly

Figure 3.2 Positive and negative perceptions of the Major government (May 1993)

Q. Which word or phrase more applies to the Government?

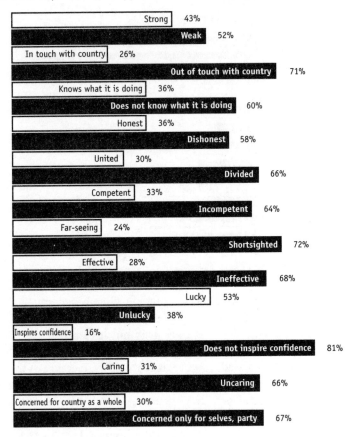

Source: Gallup/*Daily Telegraph* (7 May 1993)

acquired a reputation for defiant endurance in the face of chronic adversity. The chief attribute of the government became that of pioneering survival in a context that featured the continuous erosion of the government's power base. As Major's parliamentary majority progressively diminished and as the Conservative party remained rooted behind Labour in public support and voting intentions by at least 10 points during 1993, diagnosis and prognosis converged at the point of impending electoral disaster.

The collective disarray in the Conservative party and in the government found several expressions but the most conspicuous, and arguably the most damaging, was the concerted criticism of John Major himself. Disquiet over the content of decisions became increasingly extended not only to the perceived nature of the decision-making process at the highest levels, but also to the presentation, coherence and support of policy. These multiple concerns tended to devolve upon the single dimension of prime ministerial leadership as the primary location of governmental image, competence and accountability. In the same way that John Major had sought to personalise the electoral appeal of party and government of 1992, so the process was reversed in the long, fractious aftermath of the election. Major became increasingly synonymous with the general deficiencies and failures of the Conservatives, the administration and the state of the British economy. From being a talisman of positives, Major's reputation rapidly degenerated into a defining symbol, drift, vacillation and loss of purpose. Ivor Crewe observed the way that John Major's premiership became the visible expression of a government in retreat: 'Previous governments presided over recessions, sterling crises or other national traumas and suffered mid-term electoral reverses as a result. Yet none have sunk so low in public esteem ... No previous government has undergone a post-election reverse so early in its life and of such severity and duration.'[38]

The critical assault on Major came in various guises. All of them had appeared in a preliminary and muted form during his first administration. In 1991, the prolonged period of consultation over how to replace the poll tax generated a number of reservations over the merits of revived cabinet government. The hiatus that this issue entailed had prevented the calling of a general election in 1991. It had also prompted concerns over the extent to which Major's style of policy-making owed more to the virtues of participation or more to the vices of indecisiveness. Nigel Lawson had detected this lack of apparent direction at an early stage. In March 1991, the former Chancellor complained that extended negotiations over the reform of local government finance carried the risk of losing the initiative: 'Consultation is an aid to government, but we are in danger of seeing consultation as a substitute for government.' Lawson concluded that '[t]o appear to be unable to choose is to appear to be unable to govern'.[39]

Lawson had drawn public attention to the possible demerits of providing an antidote to Margaret Thatcher. In Major's first administration, the new prime minister had emphasised the need to restore cabinet government by devolving greater responsibilities upon senior ministers and by creating consensus-based agreements upon strategy within government. Soon after his accession to the premiership it was widely asserted that he had indeed achieved this laudable objective. The question then raised was whether this development amounted to confirmation that he was not his own man and that the revival of the cabinet was synonymous with a lack of personal authority and leadership. In some respects, Major did appear to be a captive of his own desire to move forward by collective accommodation. According to this perspective, Major opened himself up to the charge of dithering by the lengths he would go to in order to reach satisfactory settlements. Significantly, he was accused by those who had once been critical of Margaret Thatcher's style for being too accommodating and inclusive in the process of decision-making. Rather than making tough decisions, the new prime minister was thought of having succeeded merely in evading them: 'Almost everything has been a balancing act – the whip as prime minister.'[40]

Prior to the election, Major was in a position of having inherited both the premiership and a divided and demoralised party that required recuperation and consolidation. Major's adoption of a flatter and more collegial type of organisation appeared wholly appropriate to the immediate post-Thatcher context. The position became far less clear after Major had secured electoral victory for himself. The questions over his assimilative style and his use of the cabinet and senior colleagues became more persistent and acquired a greater significance than they had done in the interim period of 1991–92. Although the consultative style of Major's cabinet chairmanship had initially been welcomed as an attractive counterpoint to the methods of Margaret Thatcher, it generated a succession of problems. It inevitably produced what were seen to be delays in decision-making. In comparison to Margaret Thatcher's period in office, important decisions appeared to emerge more slowly than before. Connected to this change was the perception that decisions lacked conviction because they were seen as representing the outcome of prolonged accommodation. They had the appearance of segmented and portmanteau devices oriented more to balancing internal cabinet coalitions than to clear-cut choices. Another problem arose with the emphasis given to the cabinet as a conspicuous element of John Major's highly publicised style of leadership. When the system operated effectively then Major could claim to be personally vindicated; when it did not, then Major was politically exposed in a context that compounded a systemic failure with a self-evident personal failure. Moreover, to raise the cabinet to such a high-profile position of political management set expectations at an unrealistically high level. Many issues simply could not flow through such a structure.

In the ERM crisis, for example, not only had events moved too quickly to engage in cabinet-style decision-making, the issue was one that required urgent executive action. Even then Major had insisted that Douglas Hurd the Foreign Secretary, Kenneth Clarke the Home Secretary, and Michael Heseltine the Secretary of State for the Environment should all become involved in the decision to withdraw from the ERM. This infuriated the Chancellor of the Exchequer, Norman Lamont, who was appalled by what he saw as the needless delays incurred by the prime minister's need to share the decision and by extension, the responsibility for it with senior colleagues. Lamont thought the events of 'Black Wednesday' typified the prime minister's evasive style of decision-making. The Chancellor declared himself to be 'completely flabber-gasted'[41] by the choice to involve Hurd, Clarke and Heseltine in the decision to withdraw from the ERM:

> They had nothing to do with the Treasury and frankly they did not under-stand the issues at all. I rather came to the conclusion that he [Major] just couldn't face it. He could not bring himself to make a decision, and more and more people had to be involved; we had to spend more time and the results were disastrous ... We were losing reserves rapidly. We needed a decision. He was able to concentrate on the details but he did not seem able to concentrate on the big decision that had to be made.[42]

The pit closure plan provided another example of the administration publicly subscribing to one process while operating one at variance behind the scenes. The plan was hugely controversial and entailed serious political risks. Nevertheless, it was not seen to be sufficiently significant to either John Major or to Michael Heseltine, the Secretary of State for the Department of Trade and Industry, for the plan to be taken to the full cabinet. When the furore over the plan subsequently arose, the rest of the cabinet were expected to support and defend the policy. As a consequence, Major's public embarrassment was compounded by the private irritation of senior colleagues. They were expected to share responsibility for a decision that had not been taken collectively but which had nonetheless emerged from a system that was publicly associated with collective deliberation and accountability.

But probably the greatest difficulty that Major encountered with his conception of cabinet government was that the very reason for its adoption ultimately subverted its operational effectiveness. Major's striving for a post-Thatcher consensus was in effect predicated upon the existence of internal tensions and divisions. By adopting a more open-textured and conciliatory posture, Major not only acknowledged those strains but also contributed towards their legitimation. For a prime minister so explicitly dedicated to accommodation and stability, it was important not to reveal his position too early for fear of disrupting the process of collective choice or of sending opposition underground. Nevertheless, the net effect of this discretion was to give greater rein to dissent, and to provide further licence to splits, to leaks and to a lack of finality in decisions. In the process, the prime minister's stature was diminished within government. During the Thatcher era, the system had long grown accustomed to a strong steer from the prime minister's known position on issues. John Major's more cautious and opaque style now pro-duced a disorientating absence of individual location within the topography of government. To Norman Lamont, it seemed as if we had 'swung to the other extreme'[43] to that of Margaret Thatcher: 'I confessed my frustrations to Douglas Hurd, who agreed that he too was finding it difficult to get decisions from the PM.'[44] Lamont observed the difficulties of a prime minister seeking agreement in conditions of deepening disagreement.

> At one cabinet meeting during the pit closure crisis, the prime minister opened a discussion without offering a view. There was then a 'tour de table' where a number of views were expressed one by one. When everyone had spoken John ended the discussion abruptly by saying without conclusion, 'We don't seem to be agreed then', and then moved on to the next item … On other occasions of differences between cabinet ministers, the prime minister's usual tactic was to refer these to a cabinet sub-committee to be chaired by Lord Wakeham, who was now Leader of the House of Lords and always a subtle operator. But it was unfair to expect him to solve every problem of government, and inevitably he couldn't.[45]

As Major's working methods further signalled a tolerance of dispute and a freedom of expression, the load placed upon him for conciliation increased proportionately. This in turn fostered a supply of divisions that exceeded the capacity for resolution: 'Increasingly, if there was a disagreement between colleagues, the prime minister seemed to expect them to settle it themselves without leadership from him.'[46] Ultimately, this dynamic deterred ministers from revealing their positions in cabinet for fear of compromising their political resources in a context that increasingly lacked privacy and a seriousness of intent to reach a common position. 'Eventually, the Cabinet became as leaky as a sieve and no minister wished to raise any serious business there. The Cabinet Secretary [Butler] became concerned that ministers would not bring their business to Cabinet.'[47] Serious issues now became 'too sensitive to discuss in Cabinet'[48] as its clearing house function declined in the face of often uninhibited strife operating at deeper levels. Far from being the facilitating agency for quelling disputes and maximising unity, the cabinet instead came to embody the limits of Major's recuperative objectives for party and government.

Another element of Major's first administration that became more evident in the second administration was the challenge of party management. The context of a small and progressively declining majority combined with a chronic and apparently irreversible deficit in the polls placed huge demands on the prime minister to maintain party unity. Massive swings against the government in successive by-elections were compounded by episodes such as the elections to the European parliament in 1994. These marked the Conservatives poorest ever performance in a national election with only 29 per cent of the mainland vote. As private and corporate contributions to the Conservatives declined in response to their electoral prospects, the party's conspicuous reliance upon an ageing and eroded core of activists was thrown into high relief.[49] Increasing numbers of Conservative MPs were fearful of losing their seats and became progressively more agitated over the urgent need for the tidal loss of public support to the stemmed. To an increasing extent, '[v]oters decided that Major was not decent and dependable but weak and useless'.[50] As a result, his problems in managing the party grew commensurately.

Squaring the circles of Europe and Thatcher

The chronic position of the party was exemplified by the issue of Europe, which had been intensified by the ramifications of the Maastricht Treaty. More issues now had a European dimension. Furthermore, the polarising effect of Europe injected controversy into a range of political themes that ostensibly had little or no relationship to the immediate phenomenon of European integration. Eurosceptic concerns were directed towards the perceived pro-European orientation of key Whitehall departments, the presence of declared Europhiles within the senior ranks of the government (e.g. Michael Heseltine, Kenneth Clarke, David Hunt) and the prime minister's well-known ambiguity on the issue. Those who were opposed to, or who were suspicious of, the government's position developed a defiance of party discipline that was based upon the higher-cause justification of defending the integrity of the nation state.

Although the dissenters' arguments were highly principled in tone, John Major's background as a whip led him to regard such rebels as mischievous grandstanders who courted publicity at the expense of their own party's reputation for governing competence. Those who were openly defiant and who threatened abstention or worse in key votes represented a direct threat to the government's majority and, therefore, to its ability to manage parliamentary business. To a leader like Major who placed enormous emphasis upon carefully constructed and balanced arguments to maximise party coherence, these public demonstrations of opposition were an anathema. They undermined policy accommodations and threatened to subvert arrangements that had involved the expenditure of limited political resources. In November 1994, for example, the prime minister felt he had no alternative but withdrew the whip from eight Eurosceptic rebels. They had abstained on a Finance Bill even though it had been classified as the equivalent of a vote of confidence. In doing so, however, Major further undermined his own already weakened support base in parliament, thereby, making the task of party management even more problematic.

But a greater threat to his position came from those who kept their Euroscepticism private but who manoeuvred behind the scenes to pursue an ideological and political agenda at variance from that of the government. Although there were many variants of Euroscepticism, they collectively constituted a network of dissent and in many respects an alternative power base within the party. These discreet and often highly placed figures were part of a wider infrastructure of scepticism that extended to think tanks, foundations, much of the Conservative press, to Lady Thatcher and even to the cabinet. In the bitter debate on the Maastricht Treaty in 1993, rebels had humiliated the government but then had stopped short of bringing it down. Following this bruising encounter, Major mused on the question of whether he could replace three ministers who were suspected to be active Eurosceptic plotters (i.e. Michael Portillo, John Redwood, Peter Lilley): 'I could bring in other people. But where do you think most of this poison is coming from? From the dispossessed and the never-possessed. You can think of ex-Ministers who are going around causing all sorts of trouble. We don't want another three more of the bastards out there.'[51] High-level leaks, private briefings and leadership plots became a characteristic feature of the Major government and fed into the disarray of the parliamentary party which by November 1996 had lost its majority. The prime minister himself described the febrile atmosphere in the following terms: 'The drama-a-day mentality of parts of the parliamentary party had colleagues huddling together to exchange gossip. Whenever a cabinet member was spied talking to sceptics, opinion was divided as to whether he was urging dissent or conformity. It was a madhouse.'[52]

The repercussions of this sectarian atmosphere continually resonated through government. In June 1996, for example, Major tried to negotiate a complex and delicate deal with the European Union that would resolve the issue of the EU's ban on British beef exports. But as in no many other instances of subtly shaded arrangements in Europe, Major's plans were disrupted by what he took to be the gestured simplicities of the Eurosceptics' jihad against the EU. A year earlier, he was reported as having had a 'bellyful'[53] of the Conservatives' divisions over Europe. The development of the EU persisted in being the issue upon which Major was tested, monitored and evaluated. It had become a litmus test that divided the party and fuelled both explicit and clandestine disloyalty. It was also the issue that dramatised Major's failures in party management and which fostered continuous speculation over whether, and by whom, the prime minister would be challenged for the leadership of the party.

A further feature of Major's first administration that intensified in the period following the 1992 general election was the issue of his individual leadership. After his personal appeal had been vindicated in the election, it might have been thought that the criticisms of his style would have subsided in accordance with his new status as an elected prime minister. Unfortunately for Major, this did not occur. On the contrary, the critiques became more intense and widespread as the numerous afflictions of the party and the government tended to become associated with the personal failings of the prime minister. Only a year after his general election triumph, Major had become more unpopular than Margaret Thatcher had been at the height of the poll tax crisis. A NOP/*Independent on Sunday* poll showed not only that Major's approval rating had 'plumbed new depths', but that he was no longer regarded as being the best prime minister that the Conservative Party could offer to the voters. Asked who would be the most effective Conservative prime minister, Major was registered in only fourth place behind Lady Thatcher, Kenneth Clarke and Michael Heseltine. Amongst Conservative voters, only 22 per cent thought he was the best leader compared to 28 per cent who still hankered for the Thatcher effect.

A Gallup poll in the same period confirmed that the government's poor record was compounded by the prime minister, whose level of public approval (21 per cent) was the lowest recorded for any prime minister in Gallup's history. This configuration of public opinion in June 1993 quickly settled into a durable pattern that persisted for the remainder of the parliament. Major continued to be regarded as a person of integrity who was seen to be sincere, honest, patient and moderate. However, the value assigned to such character-istics was not sufficient to outweigh the prime minister's perceived deficiencies in a highly charged political environment. Within two years of his accession to the premiership, the political context had changed dramatically. The indivi-dual qualities of the prime minister that were praised as offering all the advantages of Thatcherism without the disadvantages of Thatcher had been re-evaluated to the detriment of John Major. Now asked who would make the best prime minister amongst the party leaders, Major was always ranked well behind John Smith or Tony Blair and often below Paddy Ashdown. Even more demoralising for the prime minister was the fact even four years after suc-ceeding Margaret Thatcher, he was still seen as less of a leader than his predecessor by Conservative voters and by the general public.

The figure of Margaret Thatcher highlighted the extraordinary difficulties that plagued John Major's premiership. Just as Major had attempted to steer the party and the country back to what he defined as the normality of measured and consensus-based government, it increasingly became evident that Margaret Thatcher had redefined the evaluative and performance-related categories of British political leadership. While Major sought to present a pragmatic and assimilative style of government in the traditional grain of the Conservative party and the British constitution, he found himself increasingly entangled in a critical web of asserted requirements of strong leadership, radical vision and personal power. He was repeatedly admonished for not developing the same aura of leadership authority that Margaret Thatcher had exerted in her premiership.

This was not simply a question of nostalgia for a lost leader. Lady Thatcher had an active and material effect upon Major's position in his party and in his government. He suffered from a sustained and concerted comparison with his patron. She remained a permanent conditioning agent to John Major's own premiership. 'It would have difficult for any leader to follow one who had been in office for over eleven years but the position was made even more problematic by Major's stated intention to depart from Mrs Thatcher's style of government. The situation was further exacerbated by the active presence of his predecessor in the febrile atmosphere of a party and government riven by the polarities that had initially been induced by Thatcher herself.[54] When she was prime minister, Margaret Thatcher had been concerned over the 'lack of a successor whom I could trust both to keep my legacy secure and to build on it'.[55] Thatcher's legacy became a frame of reference that only she could define with any authority. It became a device by which the deposed prime minister could retain some sense of controlling influence. Margaret Thatcher herself made this quite clear following John Major's general election victory in 1992: 'I don't accept the idea that all of a sudden Major is his own man. He has been prime minister for 17 months, and he inherited all these great achievements of the past eleven and half years which have fundamentally changed Britain … There is no such thing as Majorism.'[56]

Major bridled over the implication of a displaced but superior leader. He objected to the impression that he 'was a prime minister "on trial", that he was somehow temporary'.[57] He also resented the way that his predecessor and her allies were 'still harking back to a golden age that never was, and is now invented'.[58] Moreover, he was aggravated by the presumption of Thatcher and her supporters to subject his leadership to critical review. As Margaret Thatcher began to muse on when she first 'became conscious that there was a certain ambiguity in his stance',[59] Major took issue with her public criticism of the Maastricht Treaty, which he had negotiated and which had now become a litmus test of Thatcherite allegiance. Major felt increasingly targeted as a heretic.

> [S]he felt dispossessed and betrayed by those who she had led. Cut loose from the Downing Street support mechanism, lesser men than those who had once advised her now poured poison in her ear – perhaps with the intention of cheering her up. The target was, inevitably – who else could it be? – her successor.[60]

In the view of Michael Heseltine, the prime minister was 'under remorseless pressure to move the party, one stage after another, into ever more determined Euroscepticism'.[61] Margaret Thatcher was instrumental in maintaining such pressure.

> Mrs Thatcher more than fulfilled her threat – when John Major became Prime Minister – to be a backseat driver, with incessant leaks of her bizarre contradictions of much that she herself had done in government. A strange collection of never-promoted, never-would-be promoted and once-promoted-and-now demoted backbenchers spent every waking moment on College Green outside the Palace of Westminster, feeding the airwaves of the national media with their views.[62]

The activities of these dissident backbenchers were complemented by cabinet ministers like Michael Howard, Peter Lilley, Michael Forsyth, John Redwood, Michael Portillo and William Hague who in their different ways all claimed an association with the mission of Margaret Thatcher. The combination of the polarising effects of Europe, the division between 'consolidators' and 'radicals' in the party, and the problems of the prime minister's adopted role as a conciliator all generated intense frustration with John Major as an individual who seemed to distance himself not only from opposing factions but also from Margaret Thatcher's model of strong leadership.

Even though Major had disavowed Margaret Thatcher's style of leadership and even though he had been selected to be a different kind of leader, he was Increasingly being appraised in precisely the terms that Thatcher had established during her premiership. In the same way that Mrs Thatcher had stamped her authority on government, so strong leadership had become equated with her personal qualities. This dynamic had generated a profusion of premises, associations and equations concerning the relationship between governing competence, political leadership and individual character. Discussions of power were invariably centred upon the personal qualities she brought to the role of premier. It was precisely this nexus of power and personality that stimulated such a habitual interest in the formative influences and social impact of Mrs Thatcher's character.

Initially, John Major's rise to the premiership diminished public interest in the relationship between position and personality. After less than a year into his second administration, Major was besieged by a series of political problems that tended to become indistinguishable from individual failings. Increasingly, critical discussion moved from the political choices of the prime minister to the personal and psychological constituents of his character. Some of this process was linked to the need to assign responsibility and accountability to governmental decisions. Anthony King's comment on one of the Major administration's many poor polling performances is both representative and instructive: 'His problem seems to be that both he and his Government are seen to be indecisive and ineffective; and because the Government is his Government he inevitably takes much of the blame.'[63] Another dimension of this process related more to attributed explanation than to the location of answerability. The chronic array of setbacks, failures and crises became conjoined to John Major as an individual.

> It was not simply that Major had become identified as an abstracted centre of accountability for an unpopular government. It was that he was being continually subjected to the proposition that there was something about him and his personal make-up that was undermining the government. As a consequence, he did not merely characterise decline, he was made to embody it through personal flaws and deficiencies.[64]

This fusion of government and leader was expressed in different ways. For example, the disturbed and incoherent nature of the government was routinely regarded as being synonymous with the state of the prime minister's mind. Major was often quoted as being depressed and occasionally disturbed by the unfolding of events. An occasion in point was the ERM episode of 1992. During this period, Major was widely reported as having been under severe strain. This generated a form of speculation that arose intermittently throughout the rest of his tenure. It centred upon the sate of the prime minister's mind and the extent to which he could withstand the stress of the premiership.[65]

A different element of this personalisation of government and politics was expressed by an alleged association between Major's temperament and the lack of leadership. In effect, weak leadership was equated with personal weaknesses. The prime minister was criticised for being ill equipped even for the performance of his own adopted role of conciliator and consensus builder. He was seen as being too sensitive to criticism and too insecure to discount it. More significantly, Major was continually subjected to critical review in respect to the question: 'Is he up to the job?'[66] The problem for Major was that 'the job' was almost invariably defined according to the specifications of Margaret Thatcher.

On some occasions the comparison was implicit in nature. Roy Jenkins, for example, thought that John Major lacked Margaret Thatcher's basis of a set of clear, motivating ideas. This had resulted in the 'unfortunate effect of making him disengage from her only hesitantly and apologetically'. The contrast between the two prime ministers contributed to the 'steadily mounting impression that neither in breadth of personality, nor in depth of knowledge and experience, [was] the prime minister up to the job'.[67] William Rees-Mogg took Winston Churchill and Margaret Thatcher as examples of effective leaders and prime ministers. Anthony Eden and Alec Douglas-Hume by contrast were representative cases of ineffective leadership. In the view of Rees-Mogg, Major belonged to the latter category and, therefore, could be 'regarded as a failure as a prime minister'.[68]

On other occasions, the presence of a guiding standard and the prime minister's inability to meet it were wholly explicit. Philip Stephens, for example, observed that the political mood, which had initially favoured Major's style of leadership, had shifted to a more critical disposition. Time-consuming exercises in conflict resolution now looked more like forms of simple appeasement: 'So enthusiasm for the consensualism with which he replaced the blinding conviction of his predecessor has given way to doubts about whether he can set his policies within a long-term strategy.'[69] In May 1993, Paul Johnson pointed out to his readers that Margaret Thatcher remained in 'sparkling form', and therefore should still be considered a model of leadership, and even a leader in waiting: '[H]er performance, contrasting with the government's obvious disarray, reminded us all that strong national leadership is still available if the Conservative Party, or the nation as a whole, calls for it.'[70]

These complaints and many others like them could partially be attributed to class snobbery and intellectual prejudice. But many of the critiques were driven more by a genuine concern that the Conservative party was disintegrating because of an organisational weakness that emanated from the top. On numerous occasions, the prime minister was called upon to 'get a grip', to impress his leadership upon the party and, in doing so, to reinstate discipline upon the party. These exhortations were often unrealistic and unfair, but they were also self-nullifying in effect. Prescriptions for strong leadership tend not only to be made in conditions that are highly unfavourable to its exercise but undermine any subsequent leadership action as being necessarily delayed, reactive and 'other directed'. John Major experienced this paradox to the full. He was criticised when he did not act and criticised when he did respond in accordance with widely expressed calls for action. For example, he was condemned for keeping ministers like Norman Lamont and David Mellor in the cabinet when there was public pressure for their removal. When the prime minister finally asked for their resignations, his actions were greeted with disdain and dismissed as belated U-turns that reflected nothing more than the prime minister's weakness.

John Major felt that his leadership was mostly misunderstood. According to his perspective, its chief virtues had been preventative in nature. His achievements were that the party had not split over Europe, that the cabinet had been held together, and that the Conservatives had not demonstrably declined as an electoral force. He had secured a general election victory in the midst of a deep recession and remained convinced that, notwithstanding the worst polling slump on record for a government in mid-term, he could preside over both an economic and political recovery. Major's leadership, however, continued to present serious problems to the party and to the government. His alleged achievements were largely invisible and depended upon the persuasiveness of speculative counter-factual assertions related to what would have occurred if Major had not been prime minister. By contrast, his failures seemed only too evident. It is arguable that the palpable nature of his setbacks was in inverse proportion to the implicit properties of his alleged successes.

The party was well aware of the duality implicit in Major's premiership. The prime minister was poorly versed in the arts of oratory and public speaking. He had disavowed big ideas, refuted any identifying themes, and had a personal distaste for the language of populist agitation. Major's open-textured and consensual style of leadership had widened the licence for dissent and division. Nonetheless, he was far from being dispensable as a leader. In fact, Major was the only senior Tory capable of brokering a form of peaceful co-existence between the different wings of the party, and yet his authority was continually undermined by precisely this role. He was dogged not only by the model and the continual presence of his predecessor but also by a proliferation of surreptitious contenders for the leadership. Ironically, what was seen to be one of the chief problems for the Conservatives was also regarded as representing the party's best chance of overcoming its difficulties and achieving re-election. John Major believed by conviction, while the party reluctantly conceded through resignation, that the much-maligned prime minister represented the Conservatives' best chance of re-election and therefore of power retention.

Notes

1 Susan Hogg and Jonathan Hill, *Too Close to Call: Power and Politics – John Major in No. 10* (London: Warner, 1996), p. 122.

2 David Butler and Dennis Kavanagh, *The British General Election of 1992* (Houndmills: Macmillan, 1992), p. 29.

3 Butler and Kavanagh, *The British General Election of 1992*, p. 30.

4 David Selbourne, 'One of us?' *Sunday Times*, 8 March 1992.

5 BBC Radio 4, *Desert Island Discs*, broadcast on 26 January 1991.

6 Peter Jenkins, 'Just a Brixton boy made man of the people', *The Independent*, 12 October 1991.

7 Leader's speech to the Conservative Party Conference 1991, *The Independent*, 12 October 1991.

8 Leader's speech to the Conservative Party Conference 1991, *The Guardian*, 12 October 1991.

9 Leader's speech to the Conservative Party Conference 1991, *The Independent*, 12 October 1991.

10 Leader's speech to the Conservative Party Conference 1991, *The Independent*, 12 October 1991.

11 Leader's speech to the Conservative Party Conference 1991, *The Guardian*, 12 October 1991.

12 'John Major', *The Times*, 12 October 1991.

13 'Mr Major provides a strong finish', *The Independent*, 12 October 1991.

14 Hugo Young, 'Surprising egotist proves he is more equal than others', *The Guardian*, 12 October 1991.

15 Young, 'Surprising egotist proves he is more equal than others'.

16 Quoted in Michael White, 'Modest plans fail to fire campaign', *The Guardian*, 19 March 1991.

17 Hugo Young, 'Mr Major and his albatross', *The Guardian*, 19 March 1992.

18 Hogg and Hill, *Too Close to Call*, p. 218.

19 Party Election Broadcast, *The Journey*, 18 March 1992.

20 Each of the main parties was given one broadcasting slot that was twice as long in duration as the normal four-minute PEB.

21 John Major, *The Autobiography* (London: HarperCollins, 1999), p. 290.

22 Quoted in Philip Webster, Jane Landale and Arthur Leatley, '72 hours left to save UK, says Major', *The Times*, 29 April 1997.

23 See Kenneth Newton, 'Caring and Competence: The Long, Long Campaign', in Anthony King, Ivor Crewe, David Denver, Kenneth Newton, Philip Norton, David Sanders and Patrick Seyd, *Britain At The Polls* (Chatham NJ: Chatham House, 1993), pp. 150–1.

24 'Mr Major's "100 days"', *The Times*, 11 April 1992.

25 Nicholas Wapshott, 'John Major's discreet charm to the British bourgeoisie', *The Observer*, 12 April 1992.

26 'Mr Major's "100 days"', *The Times*, 11 April 1992.

27 'A Mandate for Major', *Sunday Telegraph*, 12 April 1992.

28 Ivor Crewe, 'Electoral Behaviour', in Dennis Kavanagh and Anthony Seldon (eds), *The Major Effect* (London: Macmillan, 1994), p. 104.

29 Quoted in *The Times*, 11 April 1992.

30 Major, *The Autobiography*, p. 291.

31 Noel Malcolm, 'What verdict on Major', *Daily Telegraph*, 23 June 1997.

32 The Committee on Standards in Public Life.

33 The Inquiry into the Export of Defence Equipment and Dual-Use Goods to Iraq and Related Prosecutions.

34 Anthony Seldon, *Major: A Political Life* (London: Phoenix, 1997), p. 641.

35 Roy Jenkins, 'Major is not up to the job', *The Observer*, 18 October 1992.

36 Anthony King, 'Major's team tops unpopularity stakes', *Daily Telegraph*, 4 June 1993.

37 Anthony King, 'Outlook bleak for Tories as they plumb new depths', *Daily Telegraph*, 4 October 1999.

38 Crewe, 'Electoral Behaviour', in Kavanagh and Seldon (eds), *The Major Effect*, pp. 116, 119.

39 Quoted in Robert Morgan, 'Stop consulting, start deciding, Lawson advises government', *The Times*, 26 March 1990.

40 Robin Oakley, 'Major's balancing acts break with Thatcher style', *The Times*, 29 November 1991.

41 Quoted in BBC1, *The Major Years*, broadcast 18 October 1999.

42 Quoted in BBC1, *The Major Years*, broadcast 18 October 1999.

43 Norman Lamont, *In Office* (London: Warner, 2000), p. 318.

44 Lamont, *In Office*, p. 318.

45 Lamont, *In Office*, pp. 318, 319.

46 Lamont, *In Office*, p. 319.

47 Kenneth Clarke, quoted in Peter Hennessy, *The Prime Minister: The Office and its Holders* (London: Allen Lane, 2000), p. 445.

48 Sir Robin Butler, quoted in Hennessy, *The Prime Minister*, p. 445.

49 For example, see Patrick Seyd, Paul Whiteley, Jeremy Richardson, *True Blues* (Oxford: Oxford University Press, 1994).

50 Crewe, 'Electoral Behaviour', in Kavanagh and Seldon (eds), *The Major Effect*, p. 99.

51 Seldon, *Major: A Political Life*, p. 390.

52 Major, *The Autobiography*, pp. 601–2.

53 Seldon, *Major: A Political Life* , p. 652.

54 Michael Foley, *The British Presidency: Tony Blair and the Politics of Public Leadership* (Manchester: Manchester University Press, 2000), p. 250.

55 Margaret Thatcher, *The Downing Street Years* (London: HarperCollins, 1993), p. 831.

56 Margaret Thatcher, 'Don't undo what I have done', *The Guardian*, 22 April 1992.

57 Graham P. Thomas, *Prime Minister and Cabinet Today* (Manchester: Manchester University Press, 1998), p. 45.

58 Quoted in Seldon, *Major: A Political Life*, p. 390.
59 Thatcher, *The Downing Street Years*, p. 861.
60 Major, *The Autobiography*, p. 215.
61 Michael Heseltine, *Life in the Jungle: My Autobiography* (London: Hodder and Stoughton, 2000), p. 519.
62 Heseltine, *Life in the Jungle*, p. 518.
63 Anthony King, 'Major's team top unpopularity stakes', *Daily Telegraph*, 4 June 1993.
64 Foley, *The British Presidency*, p. 251.
65 For example, Graham Paterson and Andrew Pierce, 'Can Major take the strain?', *The Times*, 21 October 1993.
66 For example, see 'Is John Major up to the job?' *Sunday Telegraph*, 28 February 1993; 'Is he up to the job?' *Independent on Sunday*, 4 April 1993.
67 Jenkins, 'Major is not up to the job'.
68 William Rees-Mogg, 'Major fails the leadership test', *The Times*, 10 May 1993.
69 Philip Stephens, 'Blurred vision of a split personality', *Financial Times*, 10/11 April 1993.
70 Paul Johnson, 'Major must consult the people, or go', *Sunday Telegraph*, 4 May 1993.

4 The Labour party in a context of leadership

Tony Blair was a winner at a time of Labour's most ignominious defeat. He entered parliament in 1983 when Labour had just been defeated for the second time by Margaret Thatcher. The scale of this electoral failure was a scarring experience for Labour and one that was to have deep and prolonged implications for the party and not least for the new member representing Sedgefield. The period of Blair's parliamentary apprenticeship coincided with a profound self-examination on the part of the Labour party. This period of critical and turbulent introspection led to a process of transformation coinciding not only with the election of a Blair government but with the emergence of a party possessing an altered view of its own identity and demonstrating an adaptive response to contemporary requirements of organisation and leadership. In acquiring the premiership, Blair had had to confront his party's past and to challenge its philosophy of leadership. Confronting the Conservative hegemony ultimately involved the need of coming to terms with its attributed political strengths and its own measures of coherence and drive.

Labour party leadership: logic and tradition

The Labour party has always had an ambiguous relationship to parliamentary democracy. In many respects, the party is closely associated with the widening of the franchise and the progressive democratisation of parliamentary representation to the point of reflecting working-class organisations and interests, and of facilitating the inclusion of working-class MPs. In other respects, the Labour party retains an organisational logic that is not centred upon Parliament. The party developed as a movement outside parliament. Its structures, traditions and procedures remain based in its origins as an amalgam of trade unions, cooperative societies and socialist organisations. As a consequence, the party's sovereign institution is still the party conference and its National Executive Committee (NEC). Apart from its segmented and federated structure incorporating a plurality of different priorities for sectional and social reform, the Labour party has been characterised by an unresolved tension between its extra-parliamentary origins and impulses on the one hand, and the demands and disciplines of parliamentary representation on the other.

These tensions have not been diminished by Labour's rise to the status of a party of alternative government and subsequently as a governing party. On the contrary, the strains have often been deepened by charges that Labour's parliamentary representatives have historically superseded their authority derived from the party. Labour's organisation has had to authorise the need for some discretionary freedom of action on the part of its parliamentary party, in order for that body to compete effectively for the privilege of forming a government and retaining its governing status. In effect, the Labour party outside parliament has had to give some recognition to the demands of the 'responsible party' model. Under this rubric, a party aspiring to government must have collective discipline, programmatic coherence and a competence to govern in the interests of the nation rather than a sector.

The problem for any political party in a system offering such a large prize of unified governmental responsibility is that the input in terms of prior intentions and planning can have a poor correspondence to the output of policy achievement. Even though governments are ultimately dependent upon their party organisations, they often have to distance themselves from their extra-parliamentary bodies and to depart from agreed priorities. It is only through this discretion that they can act as responsible governments and adapt to the changing conditions of governance. This problem of govern-mental and elite prerogative has been particularly difficult for Labour because it is both a member-based organisation and one that is intrinsically committed to large-scale social reconstruction requiring high political commitment within the limited time frames of four- to five-year parliaments.

Given the prevalence of Conservative-based government in the twentieth century, Labour's opportunities to form administrations have been few and far between. The paucity of openings and the magnitude of the historic agenda have traditionally aggravated the tension between the principles of Labour representation and the executive prerogatives of Labour government. This strain is exemplified in the relationship between Labour's leadership and the wider movement associated with the party. In formal terms, the Labour leadership is closely confined by structures and processes to ensure that it does not exceed its authority and that it remains subordinate to the Parliamentary Labour Party (PLP) and to the mass party outside Parliament. The leader is obligated to implement the programme upon which its representatives have been elected to pass into law.

In accordance with both Labour's dedication to intra-party democracy and its social philosophy of egalitarianism, the leader is in theory a derivative of the collective movement and, therefore, an extension of its choices. Such a leader is intended to act as a spokesperson of, and a facilitator for, the policy objectives determined in accordance with the socialist theory of represen-tation. This gives normative priority to the interests and needs of a particular sector within society rather than to an accumulation of individual preferences. In effect, the Labour party is designed to embody the economic interests of the working class, which is in every other respect politically deprived. The strong correspondence between the working class and the mass of electors allows the Labour party to claim that in representing the interests of a particular class, it gives democratic expression to that class which best represents the electorate as a whole. The scale of representation is matched by the magnitude of the prescribed programme of social transformation. This would require a massive expansion of the positive state to engage in economic planning, public ownership and social provision. It was envisaged that the party would operate in a context of tectonic social movement and transformed industrial infra-structures. In theory, the party leadership would effectively be swept along by the collective forces of Labour's mass movement and class-based representa-tion, and by the animating belief in a historical process of social development.

In spite of these formal, organisational and philosophical limitations on the leadership, the position of the Labour leader has been far more ambiguous than the party constitution would at first suggest. Given the rich potential for power that Britain's parliamentary system affords to victorious parties, and given the acknowledged need of a leadership to exploit political contingencies for the benefit of the movement, Labour leaders developed a discretionary licence to take policy initiatives and to shape party priorities. In his classic analysis of British political parties, Robert McKenzie observes how easy it is to mistake Labour's formalism for the reality of the leader's position. It is true that Labour's background as an outsider party, with roots laying in dissent and oppositionist politics, renders it more susceptible to dispute and disorder. Nevertheless, as McKenzie notes, the position of Labour leaders was ultimately not dissimilar to their Conservative counterparts in Parliament.

> It cannot be stressed too strongly that the leader of each of the great parties is either prime minister or a potential prime minister. And it is this fact, not the internal mechanisms of the party, which is the governing influence in deter-mining the role the leader plays in the affairs of his party ... [T]he wholly different 'style' of Labour politics, and the recurrent and bitter public quarrels over policy questions, tends to suggest that the party is perpetually on the verge of anarchy. But by accepting the conventions of cabinet and parliamen-tary government the party has ensured that in practice its leader acquires influence and authority nowhere laid down in the party constitution.[1]

This is not to say that the existence of leadership authority in the Labour party has been clarified and resolved. The opaque nature of the tension remains in evidence.

The forces of *realpolitik* and political discretion continue to confront the logic of the party's organisational and constitutional traditions of representation. Samuel Beer alludes to the recognised requirements of the leadership even in such an ostensibly highly regulated structure. Leaders have to attend to the timing, details and methods of achieving the party programme but according to Beer the 'decisive will and the main thrust of ideas must come from the rank and file'.[2] Beer reiterates the nature of the recurrent tension: 'In actual practice, leaders may at times – perhaps even most of the time – have exercised far greater power over program-making than this theory would allow. It cannot be seriously denied, however, that the persuasive belief of the party has been that the ultimate control over program belongs to the members acting through the democratic structures of the party constitution.'[3] The clear expression of a functional theory of representation was not extended to a precise or explicit acceptance of the functional attributes of leadership. As a consequence Labour leaders have traditionally operated on a fine line between on the one hand embodying the collective force of the movement and programme, whilst on the other, using the formidable solidarity and discipline of the party to pursue individual strategies of power acquisition and retention on the basis of a claim to promote the long-term interests of the party and the nation.

The leadership position has been further compounded by the difficulties attendant upon any one individual giving a precise representational expression to the aspirations and expectations of a mass movement. Leaders and potential leaders have often differed between each other, and between themselves and the party, over the role of the Labour movement in the pursuit of socialism; over the interpretation of socialist philosophy; over the methods and timetable of socialist reform; and over the scope for socialism in a liberal-democratic society. The party's leadership elites have had to give particular consideration to the need for Labour to prove it can act as a representative party of government, which can mean subordinating its members' immediate agendas to the long-term objective of acquiring a reputation for governing competence: '[L]eadership sponsored programmatic change is often a response to electoral difficulties, a determination to prioritise successful office seeking over policy seeking.'[4]

The net effect of Labour's structures and traditions has been to ensure that the 'Labour party's policy and its leader are chosen by two separate and only marginally overlapping bodies with different power bases'.[5] Because the scheme 'institutionalizes opposition between the party and its own leadership',[6] it often means that the 'official policy is one thing while what the party's leader and MPs actually do is something else'.[7] The strains in this relationship have usually been exemplified by conflict between the leadership and those who most closely associate themselves with the movement and its conference decisions. As a consequence, Labour history has been marked by a succession of disputes over ideology and policy, which have invariably involved the leadership in conflict with groupings usually located in the hard and soft left sectors of the party. On occasions, these conflicts would become long-standing and personalised around senior figures who would act as collection points for backbench dissent against the leadership. Stafford Cripps, for example, was a centre of left-wing opposition to Clement Attlee in the 1930s. Aneurin Bevan fulfilled a similar role in relation to Hugh Gaitskell during the 1950s. While Michael Foot could be a thorn in the side of Harold Wilson in the 1960s, so Tony Benn was a rallying point for those on the left disaffected with the leadership of Harold Wilson and James Callaghan in the 1970s and Neil Kinnock in the 1980s.

In one respect, the Labour party accords substantial authority to its leaders. In relation to its constitution, its animating ideas on equality, and its style of protest, assertion and critical analysis, the level of influence afforded to its leadership can appear to be wholly anomalous. The security of tenure, for example, has historically been superior to that offered by the Conservative party to its leaders. Apart from the unusual circumstances surrounding the departure of George Lansbury from the leadership in 1935, no Labour leader has had to face a concerted movement by the PLP to remove him from office. The extraordinary and even disproportionate tolerance shown towards the leadership, however, has often been balanced by a conspicuous assault upon leaders after they have left office or resigned from the leadership. The disaffection that had previously been suppressed by the claims of collective identity and consequently restricted to subterranean frustration can suddenly burst open when a change of leadership is required.

A past leader can quickly be reduced to a vilified figure of contempt as the disappointments and resentments of recent history turn into critical post-mortems on what might have been and what should have been. Critical retrospection more often than not leads to charges of failure and betrayal. These in turn generate proposals to revive the party's formal position of an attachment to a leader that is subservient to the Labour movement. Just as Labour leaders accrue enormous leverage over the party, they also become highly visible lightening rods of accountability. In doing so, they serve as catalysts for fundamentalist critiques and insurgency movements designed to interpret the past in terms not just of a failed leadership, but of a failure on the part of the party to control the leadership.

Leadership under strain: Harold Wilson, James Callaghan and Michael Foot

The formative years of Tony Blair's political education were permeated with indictments of Labour leaders. The administrations of Harold Wilson in 1964–70 and 1974–75 had become synonymous with drift, stagnation, inflation, sterling crises, industrial strife, unemployment and a corrosive imprecision at the centre of government. The high hopes and idealistic expectations of the incoming Labour government in 1964 were gradually eroded away by an administration beset with difficulties. Not the least of these problems was the strain between a disillusioned Labour party and a prime minister whose over-riding objective was to keep the party in equilibrium and establish Labour as the natural party of government. In David Walker's words, 'the "real thing" for Wilson was to make a Labour government – *his* Labour government – acceptable in British electoral circumstances. That meant, for policy, a social-democratic style and, for the Labour party at large, subordination to the national figurehead who could appeal beyond the party's core supporters.'[8] In the pursuit of these objectives, Harold Wilson acquired a reputation for prag-matism and flexibility that too often appeared to be synonymous with evasion, prevarication, delay and short-term accommodation.[9] Wilson's preoccupation with party management revealed a leadership without a sense of authenticat-ing vision. He was, 'constantly seeking to win the immediate game'[10] rather than working towards a long-term destination: 'Wilson was an empiricist and a meliorist. As such he did, and does, annoy utopians and visionaries, left, right and centre.'[11]

The consequence of Wilson's style of stopgap improvisations and tactical manœuvres was a political party that appeared to be dictated by events and which continually operated within an ambiguity of its own making. As the Wilson government suffered a number of policy setbacks (e.g. industrial rela-tions, sterling devaluation, economic planning, trade union reform), and as the Prime Minister became an isolated figure consumed by suspicions of plots and leadership challenges, the party became more disabled by claims of betrayal and allegations of the misuse of power. The left in particular became increasingly insistent upon the need to rein in future leaders. By the time he returned to power with an unexpected electoral victory in February 1974, Wilson was confronted with chronic economic conditions and with a resur-gence of left-wing insurgency within the party. In the 1960s, his improvisa-tions were designed to conceal and defuse intra-party conflict. In the 1970s, Wilson could no longer conceal the enmity. Instead he wearily resisted the exertions of the NEC and its allies to assume control of the government's agenda. If he found it difficult 'to articulate the party's vision of an alternative future', it was in Philip Whitehead's view 'because he did not share it. And just as he did not wish to be educated by his party, so he gave up trying to educate it.'[12] This time, Wilson openly sought to outmanœuvre his opponents. This was tantamount to an admission of a diminishing leadership.

The ingrown and febrile atmosphere of the Wilson years bequeathed a profusion of problems upon his successors. James Callaghan, who succeeded Wilson when he resigned from the premiership in March 1976, was in many respects a more secure leader than his predecessor. Callaghan's avuncular manner and his long-established links with the trade unions gave him a style and a power base, which led to a more open and less neurotic premiership. Callaghan's strength was that his personal identity merged with the traditional roots and contemporary impulses of the Labour movement: 'While other, more glamorous, politicians were blown away in the whirlwind of Labour politics in the troubled years of Gaitskell and Wilson, Callaghan remained durable and impregnable, probably more consistently attuned to the instincts of the average Labour voter than anyone else in politics.'[13]

And yet, despite these advantages and his personal toughness, James Callaghan became as beleaguered in government as Harold Wilson. He was confronted by mounting economic and industrial problems, which were aggravated by a small, and declining parliamentary majority. He had to defer to large cuts in public expenditure as part of an IMF package to defend sterling in the crisis of 1976. He had to persuade the party to recognise that there were limits to Keynesian economic management, which involved recognising the significance of the money supply and the need to control government spending. Even though the Callaghan government refused to consider statutory controls on incomes and on trade union actions, the pressure for wage inflation was too great to be contained by voluntary restraint. The succession of public service strikes in 1978–79 that were collectively termed the 'winter of discontent' underlined the government's fragility in economic management. They also showed that Callaghan no longer retained the sureness of touch which had once been his hallmark.[14]

The Callaghan leadership had for long periods been one of survival under difficult conditions. The Liberal–Labour pact had given some security of tenure for a minority government but at the price of further antagonising the left. In the end, the Callaghan administration fell on a vote of confidence precipitated by the issue of devolution for Scotland and Wales, support for which had been a condition of Liberal support. Callaghan himself did not blame devolution for his government's defeat or for Labour's defeat in the subsequent general election. He believed that the tide in public opinion had finally turned against Labour. It brought Margaret Thatcher into government with a prospectus of a disciplined and robust response to the ailments of public expenditure, taxation, the economy and industrial relations. The general election defeat in 1979 was widely attributed to Labour's perceived failures in government stretching back to 1966. The analysis and explanation of these failures coincided with the end of Callaghan's tenure as a leader and subsequently dominated the experience of his successor in the leadership.[15]

Unlike Callaghan, Michael Foot had had a comfortable background as a member of a patrician family dedicated to public service. He had strong left-wing credentials drawn from an elite association with Aneurin Bevan in the 1950s. While Callaghan's attachment to socialism was rooted in personal experience and in a visceral connection to the trade union movement, Foot's dedication to the cause was more of an intellectual enterprise drawing upon historical strands of the English dissenting tradition. Although Foot had established his reputation as a polemicist and rhetorician, he demonstrated an ability to subordinate his natural talents for non-conformity to the higher objectives of party loyalty, cabinet unity and collective responsibility. His experience, prominence and party record made him the natural successor to Callaghan.[16] In 1980 the PLP elected him its leader. Many in the party hoped that others would emulate his example of restrained radicalism in the strained period following Labour's defeat.

These hopes were largely misplaced. The tensions generated within the party by the experience of government were severe. The social democratic wing of the party had been discomforted by the myriad failures of its revisionist alternatives, by the increased militancy of the trade unions and by the party's refusal to embrace the EEC as an agency of progressive politics. The trade unions for their part had been aggravated by the pay restraint incurred by the 'social contract'. The left was frustrated by its own inability to hold the leadership to its constitutional and policy obligations towards a radical programme of public ownership and investment. Chris Mullin's indictment typified the jaundiced attitude on the left to Labour's leadership elite: 'Most of our leaders once in power treat the Labour Party as though it were one of number of rather irritating pressure groups.'[17]

While the Conservative leadership indicated an intention to move to the right, the internal balance of forces in the Labour party revealed a growing polarisation that began to erode its conventions of mutual tolerance and to expose its organisational ambiguities.[18] The radicalism of the 'new left' and the injection of socialist activism into many of the Constituency Labour Parties (CLPs) found their expression in the leadership figure of Tony Benn. This accumulation of pressures, which pivoted upon the disjunction between the high expectations and low achievement of recent Labour governments, opened up a deep rift within the movement. Kenneth O. Morgan described the resultant dynamics in the following terms:

> As the party in cabinet moved away from socialism, neutralizing the doctrinaire demands of Benn, and towards monetarism, cash limits, and a total accommodation with capitalism, the Labour party as entrenched in local

government as in the new metropolitan council and in Greater London, became associated with far-left postures, open resistance to demands for expenditure cuts, and association with Marxist and other groups not at all attracted to the pragmatic Labour tradition of Atlee, Gaitskell, and Wilson.[19]

Benn pursued the logic of representative and party democracy to what he saw as their necessary consequences; namely in the long term a device to secure a genuine working-class democracy, and in the short term the creation of a material nexus connecting a Labour government to the party conference and, through it, to the decisions of the constituency organisations and the interests of the rank and file.

The release from government allowed the party to engage in an uninhibited process of recrimination and in a renewed battle for the soul of the Labour movement. This catharsis reached its culmination in two related developments. First, was the emergence within the party of an insurgency movement dedicated to ensuring that Labour would become a more openly democratic organisation. This was the period when Tony Benn and his supporters were determined to press home their advantage. They not only sought changes in policy but also the introduction of constitutional devices to ensure that there should be no reversion to previous practices of the leadership either revising or suspending policy commitments. In restoring the bottom-up rationale of the party, the reforms would prevent the abuse of power by Labour prime ministers who invariably adopted the presumptions of the 'establishment' upon taking office. As a result of pressure exerted by Benn's supporters, the 1979 Party Conference approved the introduction of a mandatory process of reselection for Labour MPs. This measure was designed to monitor the record of adherence to party policy and to create a deterrent against party disloyalty. In an effort to limit the leadership's discretion in developing the party manifesto, conference also voted in favour of a measure assigning responsibility for the final draft of the manifesto solely to the NEC. The proposal that an electoral college of the party instead of the PLP should select the leader was defeated in 1979. However, it was passed in the 1980 Party Conference.

This period of party turmoil coincided with the change of leadership. The leadership passed from James Callaghan to Michael Foot[20] between the 1980 Party Conference and the special party conference at Wembley in January 1981, which had been convened to decide upon the exact configuration of the electoral college. Foot was widely seen to have been outmanoeuvred at Wembley when moves from the PLP to retain at least a 50 per cent holding in the selection process were defeated in favour of a college weighted accordingly: the unions with a 40 per cent weighting; the PLP with a 30 per cent weighting; and the CLPs with a 30 per cent weighting. Peter Jenkins acknowledged the leadership role of Tony Benn and the extreme radicalism of the reform programme with which he had been closely associated.

> What makes Mr Benn lethal, unappeasable and unlike … any previous left-wing rebel is that his quarrel with the parliamentary party is not about the substance of policy, and therefore is not susceptible to compromise; rather he is challenging the legitimacy of the parliamentary party itself by putting forward a novel constitutional doctrine which would make it the complete servant of the party in the country.[21]

According to Roy Hattersley, the constitutional reforms were the result of a 'reckless pursuit of a narrow sectarian view of socialism' held by a small yet influential group whose members showed 'neither respect nor regard for alternative views within the party'.[22] Adam Raphael agreed that the left's victories on constitutional change had effectively 'smashed the party's existing power structure'.[23]

The second main outcome of this turmoil was the formation of a right of centre dissident organisation (Council for Social Democracy) which led quickly to the formation of a new breakaway Social Democratic Party (SDP). Its leaders cited the factional irresponsibility and militant extremism of a declining Labour party as the primary reason for seeking to radicalise the centre of British politics. They wished to establish a progressive party free not only from trade union block votes but also from Labour's allegedly naive impulses against nuclear weapons, the EEC and leadership discretion.[24] Within a matter of months the SDP–Liberal Alliance had peeled away twenty-two Labour MPs to its ranks[25] and overtaken Labour in the opinion polls. The Alliance also won two dramatic by-election victories[26] and threatened to consolidate its position as the leading party in the public's voting intentions.[27]

As the parliamentary power base of the party's right of centre was being successively weakened by SDP defections, the 'new left' attempted to capitalise upon its constitutional victories by mobilising a challenge for the Labour's deputy leadership in 1981. Although Tony Benn only just failed to dislodge Denis Healey as deputy leader, the episode underlined the perilous state of a party engaged in a very public civil war at a time when intense voter volatility threatened Labour's position in the British two-party system. The groundswell against the myriad disappointments of the previous Labour governments focused upon the leadership behaviour of their prime ministers. In many respects, the insurgency against the party hierarchy amounted to a fundamental protest against the concept and practice of leadership *per se*. Leaders sought to rationalise their role in terms of representation, responsiveness and reaction to circumstances in the interests of party unity and general welfare. But dissidents saw only hierarchy, capriciousness, appeasement and the abuse of power. Conventional party leadership in these conditions of constitutional disruption and political dislocation became extraordinarily difficult. Leadership aspirants like Roy Jenkins, David Owen and Shirley Williams left the party to form a new vehicle of leadership possibilities. Meanwhile, Michael

Foot was marginalised into a conciliatory role within a crumbling coalition at precisely the time when Margaret Thatcher was acquiring an identity of formidable public and national leadership.[28]

The 1983 general election marked a watershed not only in Labour's contemporary political developments but also in its approach to party leadership. In normal circumstances Labour should have performed well. The Thatcher administration had presided over a severe recession, which left the economy in a worse condition than it had been in 1979. For example, manufacturing output had fallen by 19 per cent and investment by 35 per cent in the four years of Conservative government. As unemployment had breached the 3 million mark, Margaret Thatcher became the most unpopular prime minister since World War I. In addition, the Thatcher government was closely identified with a neo-liberal programme to dismantle much of the structural fabric of the post-war consensus. Thatcher's assault upon socialism included many features of British society that had strong Labour origins or associations – the positive state, welfare provision, nationalised industries, social and economic regulation, redistribution through direct taxation, trade union immunities, council housing, municipal socialism and high public expenditure. The Thatcher administration generated a groundswell of dissent and disaffection, which Labour should have been able to capitalise upon as an alternative government. But Labour was not seen in these terms. On the contrary, it was widely seen to be a party in barely suppressed turmoil.

The 1983 general election result revealed that far from improving its position after the turbulent period of Thatcher's first administration, Labour had actually lost ground on its 1979 performance. In that election Labour won 269 seats with 37.0 per cent of the popular vote. In 1983, Labour secured 209 seats with only 27.6 per cent of the popular vote. The party's number of seats and its level of electoral support represented its worst performance since 1935 and 1918 respectively. The SDP–Liberal Alliance with 25.4 per cent of the popular vote almost managed to squeeze Labour into third place. Although its traditional heartlands remained solid, the Labour party faired very badly in the south of England where apart from London it won only three seats.[29] In total, the Conservative party won 60.6 per cent of the combined Conservative and Labour vote – i.e. a far higher level than the other post-war peaks in the differential between the two main parties (54.8 per cent for Labour in 1945; 54.3 per cent for the Conservatives in 1979). Instead of establishing a base from which to compete effectively for the next general election, Labour had moved backwards and this in spite of the numerous provocations of the Thatcher government.

Labour strategists could point to the Falklands War, an improving economy, and the incursion of the SDP as contributory factors to the defeat. But it was also evident that Labour had comprehensively failed to mobilise the substantial level of anti-Tory sentiment that was present at the time. Nearly half of the non-Conservative vote had been drawn away to the Alliance. Moreover, many Alliance voters were supporting the third force in reaction to the perceived inadequacies of Labour. In addition, as many as 48 per cent of Conservative voters explained their choice in terms of fearing another Labour government.[30] In addition, 'surveys and politicians' doorstep encounters with voters, uncovered a "credibility gap" about the competence of the party and its ability to deliver on many of its promises'.[31] A capacity for governance had once again become an issue for Labour.

In many respects, the 1983 general election not only created the strong impression not so much that the Thatcher government had won the election, but that Labour had actively lost the encounter through gross incompetence. Michael Foot's dress sense and personal deportment evoked an earlier and less visual age when appearance was less significant than the integrity of ideas or the importance of reported speech. The manifesto was under-prepared and incoherent in design and content. It contained too many hostages to fortune in the form of bold statements and rash promises (e.g. the renationalisation of privatised industries, an end to racial and sexual discrimination, the termination of Britain's membership of the EEC, the introduction of industrial democracy, large increases in social provision and a commitment to unilateral nuclear disarmament). The Labour campaign itself was too often diverted away from attacking the Conservative government because of the need to explain, to refine and in some instances to revise the manifesto.

The contemporary centrality of the leader in election campaigns together with the leader's responsibility to manage the campaign were underlined by Michael Foot who failed to impress on either count. Foot not only presided over an inept and poorly organised campaign, he was portrayed as personally incompetent and ill equipped to be prime minister. At a time when Margaret Thatcher was deploying the latest American techniques in image projection, Foot was seen limping through crowds with a walking stick, addressing audiences with rambling speeches and making public appearances in ill-fitting clothes as his unkempt hair flew simultaneously in several directions. Foot's disabilities as a public leader were ruthlessly exposed during the campaign. He led his party to one of its worst defeats this century.[32] By not having adapted his leadership to the television age, Foot was accused of characterising the Labour party as ingrown, self-absorbed and insensitive to the need for adaptation.

In reality there was probably very little that the Labour campaign could have done to prevent a second Thatcher victory. A substantial case can be made in support of the proposition that political and economic conditions were always against a Labour victory. Nevertheless, Labour's myopia together with its presumption that it was the 'natural party of government' led to the conclusion that it had been responsible for its own defeat. In many respects, such a conclusion was welcome to the main factions in the party. The hard left could point to the fact that a quarter of those voting had chosen a party with an explicitly socialist message. Many more may have subscribed to this programme but for the 'betrayal' of Labour's leadership elite who during the campaign had softened various manifesto commitments, especially on defence. To the right, the election humiliation was proof positive that the party needed to move away as quickly as possible from those policies and that style of politics with which the party had become identified during the 1980-83 period. The consequences of the experiment were measured in terms of the party's collapse in election votes and in political stature. The urgent need for a response was made in the form of Michael Foot's immediate resignation and in the call for new leadership.

Labour leadership in the Thatcher era: (i) Neil Kinnock and the resuscitation of opposition

Even though Neil Kinnock had had no prior experience of working in government, he had for years assiduously cultivated the grass roots and key power centres of the Labour party. In 1983 those preparations came to fruition as Kinnock eased himself into the leadership. As the first Labour leader to be selected by the party's electoral college, Kinnock was able to overcome his failure to defeat Roy Hattersley in the vote of the PLP by overwhelming majorities in the trade union and CLP sections. Kinnock was a close friend and political protégé of Michael Foot. Like Foot, he secured the leadership by establishing himself on the left of the party. But in several other respects, Kinnock's selection was based upon his dissimilarity to Foot. In many respects, 'Foot's weaknesses served to accentuate Kinnock strengths.' The contrasts included the following: 'Foot was old; Kinnock projected an image of youthful vigour. Foot was ill at ease on television; Kinnock was a natural performer. Foot appeared weak, Kinnock strong. After two decades of leadership by a generation of politicians whose formative years had been in the immediate aftermath of the war, Kinnock held out the promise of a new and more exciting style.'[33]

Kinnock was chosen as leader almost by acclamation. Nevertheless his selection was greeted with only guarded enthusiasm by a party that remained deeply divided on policy agendas and principles. Some believed that the party needed to make only minor adjustments in order to claim the benefit from a radical and divisive Conservative government. Others believed that, if the party did not make large-scale changes, Labour would be in danger of being supplanted by the Alliance. Kinnock not only belonged to the latter category but was convinced that his leadership was the only agency capable of producing the required transformation of Labour's structure and culture. As a consequence, Kinnock established the 1983 general election defeat as the defining construction of the party's deficiencies and the motivating force behind the drive to correct them. Michael Foot had sought to accommodate the different sectors within the party through a process of mutual tolerance and traditional coexistence. Kinnock on the other hand was known to possess a confrontational personality, which operated on the need to prevail over opposition. Now he had been placed in an exposed position with a self-attributed mission to regain governmental power for the party. As a consequence, his robust character and visceral view of leadership were released in pursuit of a higher cause.[34]

To Kinnock the overriding need was to go out and win the next general election instead of depending upon the default position of the opposition in a traditional two-party system. It was necessary for the leadership to maximise the control of the party and to energise it into turning its attention away from internal controversies. In order to achieve this position, Kinnock engaged in a series of campaigns to change the views, the composition and the powers of the NEC; to make the conference more manageable and more amenable to leadership strategies; and to consolidate the leadership position over the PLP. Where he could, Kinnock attempted to marginalise the party structure in favour of alternative organisations that were directly responsible to the leadership. The Campaign Strategy Committee (CSC), for example, was answerable to the NEC and reported to it, but in every other respect it operated independently from the NEC and became in effect part of the leadership organisation. The Shadow Communications Agency (SCA) was set up by the leadership to provide expert advice and guidance in the field of political communications. The importance attached to media outreach, visual design, art direction, and campaign coordination succeeded in further enhancing the status of its chief sponsor and in increasing the leadership's leverage within the party structure. The net effect of these and other changes allowed Kinnock to consolidate his power base in the party and to establish a rolling programme of reform designed to widen Labour's appeal beyond its shrinking strongholds.

Kinnock's stated objective to make Labour electable prompted a reassessment of the party's policy position. This led to several revisions to soften some of those commitments which had made the 1983 manifesto so unpalatable to middle England. For example, the abolition of the House of Lords and the plan to close down US nuclear bases in Britain were dropped. The proposals to withdraw from the European Community and to take over private beds in NHS hospitals were also abandoned. Another key component of Kinnock's modernisation process was the introduction of a vigorous programme of political communications management. Under the leadership of Peter Mandelson and Patricia Hewitt, the party gradually reconciled itself to the need for a centrally planned and coherently co-ordinated campaign of public outreach that would maximise its access to the mass media to full effect. This plan involved the usage of advertising and marketing consultants, the need for media-centred campaigns and the direction of party activities in the light of news agendas and news cycles. It also embraced the need for cocoordinating party spokespersons around selected daily themes and the provision of visual material, photo opportunities and supportive news stories to match the party's priorities. Speeches, broadcasts, press conferences, backdrops and pictures all needed to be orchestrated by professionals in political communications, design, art direction, research and speechwriting. Political intelligence was also dramatically improved with a marked expansion of private polling and the introduction of focus groups. Labour's reputation for forward planning and public presentations was revolutionalised.[35]

The transformation was in many respects exemplified by the concentrated effort to change Labour's public image with a new corporate identity featuring a rose logo on a peach background, a new typeface and a dress code suggesting professional competence. Philip Gould who was a leading figure in the SCA described the scale of change in the following terms. When he had first started working on a communications strategy for Labour, Gould felt as if he had 'stepped into morass, entering a party at war with itself at every level'.[36] The party organisation was not easily susceptible to the proposition that it needed professional assistance.

> The left-dominated NEC, which had shown little interest in campaigns and communications in the past, saw us as a direct threat. Shadow cabinet members were at best suspicious, at worst openly hostile. Labour had become so distanced from the public that we were going to have to fight the party itself over every appeal to the voters.[37]

However, after two years, Gould felt that Labour had been 'dragged ... from a party which abhorred photo opportunities and still believed the way to address the public was to don a donkey jacket and harangue the party faithful at rallies into the glare of modern professional communications.'[38]

Despite the successes in repackaging the party, Kinnock's leadership faced a number of serious and debilitating problems. *First*, the Miners Strike (1984– 85) not only distracted the leadership from confronting the Conservative government on its overall record, but placed Kinnock in the invidious position of having to condemn the violence generated by the dispute, while at the same time giving guarded support to the miners and their families. Privately, Kinnock had opposed the calling of a strike without a ballot. He was also critical of the leadership of the National Union of Mineworkers in the strategy, timing and conduct of the industrial action. For over a year, the Labour leader looked indecisive and prevaricating as his attempts to modernise the party were continually undermined by Labour's sentimental attachments to an ageing industrial order, by the law and order dimensions of picket line violence and by the visible manifestations of trade union power.

The *second* problem centred upon the local activities of the hard left both in the CLPs and in those local authority councils controlled by the Labour party. The highly publicised insurgency by organisations like the Militant Tendency cut across the soberly restrained characteristics of Kinnock's reconfigured Labour party. The position was further exacerbated when new left organisations acquired policy-making influence in local government which they sought to use in order not only to further their agendas but also to challenge the power of central government policy head on. The robust and intransigent nature of their positions generated hostile media attention. This drew public attention away from the performance of the Thatcher government and focused it instead upon the alleged extremes and indulgences of 'loony left councils'. The reported extravagance, inefficiency and heavy handedness of these councils were used as a characterisation of Labour government in general and as a predictive model of a Kinnock administration in particular. The damaging publicity generated by Labour councils served to embarrass the Kinnock team in precisely the field of public presentation in which it was trying to excel. At the same time that Kinnock was trying to neutralise the negative effects of such perceived extremism within Labour councils, he also moved on the issue of Trotskyite 'entryism' within the party. Public denunciations and internal party tribunals were followed by a series of expulsions. Like the miners strike, the issue of extremist activities in the party threw Labour's own problems into high relief. It ensured that leadership activity often had to be publicly directed to the objective of damage limitation instead of establishing a convincing case of an alternative party of government.[39]

A *third* set of problems related to more generic disabilities. For example, Kinnock had to contend with the decline of manufacturing industry, the growth of home ownership, the expansion of the suburban middle classes, the progressive reduction of the manual working-class sector, the contraction of council tenancies, the rise of share ownership and the increase both in the numbers of skilled workers and in the volatility of their political allegiances. The repercussions of class de-alignment, combined with the continuing threat of the SDP displacing Labour as the chief opposition party, ensured that Kinnock would have considerable difficulties in mobilising Labour's core vote whilst attempting to broaden its appeal into untraditional constituencies. The leader's position was made even more difficult by the economic boom of the mid-1980s. This reduced inflation to below 5 per cent, increased average weekly earnings in real terms by 14 per cent and facilitated a regime of tax cuts.

Apart from being wrong footed by changing economic conditions, and social attitudes shifting away from collectivist solutions, Kinnock was also constrained by the organisational and political resistance of his own party. He had engaged in a modernisation process that had provided the party with a dramatic facelift and a more professional outlook upon marketing and positive projection. Nevertheless, the public image and policy content of Labour lagged behind the cultivated distractions of the leadership. Focus groups revealed a basic distrust of Labour, a discomfort with its trade union and special interest associations, and an anxiety over its reputation for division, extremism, pacifism and disorder. The attempts to make Labour policy commitments more palatable were only partially successful. The 1987 party manifesto was far more succinct and guarded than the now notorious 1983 manifesto. Even so, it still included grand schemes to reduce unemployment, large-scale increases in public expenditure, a reimposition of 'social ownership' upon privatised industries, a restoration of trade union rights (e.g. closed shop, secondary picketing), the removal of all nuclear weapons from Britain and an indeterminate method of costing and financing the whole programme.

Given these difficulties, Labour strategists feared that the party had no alternative other than to fight a leadership-centred election. They opted for such a campaign partly to focus attention on Margaret Thatcher as the Conservatives' main liability, partly to capitalise upon Labour's youthful and vigorous leader, and partly to divert attention away from Labour's more unattractive elements. The acceptance of the SCA's advice to run a presidential campaign was seen as a 'revolutionary'[40] departure from Labour's electoral traditions: 'Never before had Labour allowed the presentation of its party platform to be overridden by [the] purely personal projection of the party leader'.[41] The only problem with this strategy was that instead of the leader acting as the spearhead for a less popular party, Kinnock continually languished not only behind his party but behind Margaret Thatcher as well. In fact, Kinnock's leadership performance was persistently rated below that of all the other main party leaders. Notwithstanding his youth, his energetic espousal of social values and his folksy and sociable temperament, Kinnock found it difficult to compete with the personal authority of the prime minister.

In many respects, Kinnock personified a counterpoint to Margaret Thatcher, which was not always to his benefit. Within two years of his leadership, Kinnock found himself in the paradoxical situation of having to take a leadership role in confronting his party, whilst being criticised for insufficient leadership by forcing contentious internal issues further into the public eye. David Butler and Dennis Kavanagh captured the plight of the Labour leader.

> The halo effect of the leadership election in 1983 had worn off. Voters liked his personality; he outscored Mrs Thatcher on being in touch with ordinary people, personal warmth and uniting the country. But on questions relating more to leadership capability – strength of personality, decisiveness and gaining respect for Britain abroad – he lagged far behind. In some respects it was still the one-sided Foot v Thatcher contest. Rows, divisions, challenges to

> Mr Kinnock by Militant or black sections, and the 'extreme' image of some Labour-controlled London boroughs all contributed damagingly to a perception of weak leadership.[42]

Kinnock's inexperience of government, his limited administrative abilities, his parliamentary deficiencies and his lack of gravitas were not thought to be significant handicaps when he was elected party leader. By the mid-1980s, they were seen as areas of weakness both for him and the party. So much so that following Kinnock's poor handling of the Westland issue in 1986 when he was outperformed by John Smith, the shadow spokesman for Trade and Industry, rumours spread of moves to change the leadership. But no rival came forward to contest the position and the party settled down to implement its agreed plan for a presidential-style campaign.

The 1987 general election was the culmination of four years of preparations and planning by the Kinnock leadership team. Labour was widely credited with having devised the most professionally adept and media-conscious campaign.[43] And yet, despite its advanced, sophisticated usage of political communication techniques, the party made only marginal gains. Labour increased its vote by a mere 3.2 per cent on its 1983 performance. While the Conservative vote remained stable (42.3 per cent), it was the Alliance that lost ground leaving Labour firmly established as the main party of opposition. This had been the chief battleground for Labour. The party had retained its status as the alternative government, but at the same time it was very far from challenging for office. The election produced only 20 additional seats leaving Labour with a deficit of 229 to 376 Conservative seats. The Conservatives not only retained majority support of the skilled working class, but accounted for 58 per cent of the combined votes of the two main parties.

Labour had been unable to overcome continuing public perceptions that the party was extremist, divided and unreliable especially in respect to handling the economy. In spite of Labour's quantum leap in the modernisation of political communications, the Conservative party which, for nearly all of 1986 had been behind in the polls, had again imposed itself upon the electorate for a third successive general election majority.

Labour leadership in the Thatcher era: (ii) Neil Kinnock and the competition for power

To Neil Kinnock, electoral defeat further vindicated the leadership's strategy of modernisation. It re-emphasised the need for a more vigorous and convincing adjustment of public opinion and electoral attitudes. While Labour had been re-established as the primary counterforce to Thatcherite conservatism, Kinnock continued to use the SDP and the Liberals as leverage to exert even more pressure upon Labour's hard left. The most significant initiative undertaken by Kinnock was the introduction in 1987 of a two-year policy review designed not only to bury the public discussion of policy for an extended period but also to move the party more firmly towards the centre. The seven policy review groups duly reported their recommendations to the NEC and the party conference in 1989. The consensus-forming element of the exercise was highly successful. Policy was changed and used as the basis for the party to rally around the leadership.

Kinnock's policy review culminated in the publication of a 70,000-word report entitled 'Meet the Challenges, Make the Changes'. It implicitly acknow-ledged and accepted several key components of the Thatcherite agenda – e.g. the permanence of industrial relations legislation, the legitimacy of the market in allocating goods and services, the established fact of privatisation, the abandonment of Keynesian demand management, and the principle of tying public expenditure to a finite tax base.[44] As a result references to redistri-bution, egalitarianism, public ownership or social ownership were expunged from party policy statements. Contemporary socialism was largely redefined as a support structure of an enterprise economy and as a source of social purpose guiding the usage and value of capitalism's increasing surplus. Further embellishments upon the party's relocation were produced and accepted in 1990.[45] The net effect of this exercise in broad-scale consultation and central direction was to place the party in a position to challenge Margaret Thatcher in the next general election. The policy review succeeded in achieving its objective of establishing Labour's manifesto well in advance of the next election, and of removing most of those contentious and distracting proper-ties that had undermined previous campaigns.[46]

Under Kinnock's leadership, the ideology and policy repositioning of Labour was integrally connected to a parallel process of constitutional and organisational modification. The process of reforming the party machinery, which had, begun in the 1983–87 period, continued apace in Kinnock's second parliament as opposition leader. For example, an electoral college system weighted towards individual members over affiliated organisation was intro-duced for the local selection of parliamentary candidates. The mandatory element of the re-election procedure for sitting Labour MPs was abandoned, thereby giving incumbents greater security of tenure against the infiltration of left-wing activists in the CLPs. The two-year policy review was extended into a rolling programme of continual reassessment designed to reduce further the policy-making influence of the NEC and to diminish the role of the party conference in determining the party's agenda. Kinnock's campaign to con-solidate the party around the priorities and strategies of the leadership were assisted by a general shift towards the centre in the overall balance of the party. This was reflected both in the infusion of a new generation of moderate trade union leaders (e.g. Bill Jordan, Gavin Laird and John Edmonds) and in the rise to prominence of a set of new centrist Labour parliamentarians (e.g. Gordon Brown, Jack Cunningham, Robin Cook and Tony Blair). The ascendancy of Kinnock's coalitions of centre right and soft left was dramatically confirmed in 1988 when Tony Benn and Eric Heffer challenged Kinnock and Roy Hattersley for the leadership and deputy leadership of the party. The exemplars of the hard left won only 11.8 per cent and 9.5 per cent of the vote respectively.

Kinnock's strategy was to eliminate the negative public perceptions of Labour and to provide an impression of competence centred upon a leadership that could take advantage of any loss of popularity by the Thatcher government. In the 1989-90 period this strategy appeared to be highly effective. Labour increased in status when the Conservative party fell into disarray over the Exchange Rate Mechanism, the poll tax and the economy downturn. In February 1990, Labour's lead in the polls had soared to 24 points. Although the deficit was progressively reduced in subsequent months, Labour had established a persistent lead that threatened a swathe of Conservative marginals. Labour also profited from ill fortune elsewhere. The support for the SDP and the Liberals collapsed as a result of the internal turmoil generated by their disputed merger. Labour was suddenly placed in an unrivalled position not only as an alternative government, but as an administration in waiting. By April 1990, Kinnock and his senior advisors 'decided to tone down their personal attacks on Margaret Thatcher'.[47] They were concerned that Labour's lead might precipitate drastic action on the part of the Conservative party against its leader. As one Shadow Cabinet member later reflected: 'Most of us wanted her to stay. She was a running sore in the government, with people flaking off every time she intervened in anything, and every prospect that things would get worse before the next election.'[48] Labour strategists were anxious to keep Thatcher in the position where she would, in their opinion, do most harm to her party. Kinnock's advisors were 'anxious to prevent the Tories mounting a successful come-back by installing a new prime minister who could imply that the government's problems stemmed from Thatcher's leadership'.[49] Of the possible replacements, the figure of Michael Heseltine caused most consternation amidst Labour ranks.

The alarm within the Conservative party over the prospect of losing power not only propelled John Major into the premiership, but also disrupted Neil Kinnock's plan for acquiring office. Labour strategists had proceeded upon the premise that in her third term of office Mrs Thatcher and her style of government would become more of a force of controversy than ever before. Accordingly, the campaign strategy had been to use her as the defining feature of a failing Conservative government and a disintegrating Conservative hegemony. This largely negative but animating theme of dissent was quickly subverted by the sudden departure of Labour's talisman and by the equally sudden appearance of John Major as a *fait accompli* prime minister. In organising 'their own mini-General Election', the Conservatives had 'simul-taneously divested themselves of their biggest liability and cut much of the ground from beneath Labour's calls for change'.[50] In doing so, '[m]any of the most powerful weapons in the Labour armoury had been disabled overnight'.[51]

Labour found Major difficult both to define and to target as a political entity. His opaque yet genial manner combined with his political ambiguity was not the antidote to Margaret Thatcher that Labour had envisaged in the form of Neil Kinnock. Nevertheless, out of the Conservative party's catharsis, John Major emerged as a de facto post-Thatcher premier. In displacing Thatcher, the new premier altered the party's immediate identity and em-barked upon a process of implicit compensation for the personal excesses of his predecessor. In losing the leverage of the Thatcher issue, Labour's support was revealed to be alarmingly soft. In November 1990, Major overturned a 10-point deficit for the Conservatives and eased his party back into the lead for the first time in eighteen months. Given the strong possibility of a general election in 1991, Labour had little choice other than to adhere to the policy profile and campaign strategy that had been carefully crafted since 1987.

The chief problem that Labour faced was that it had expended enormous effort in reaching a position where the party could be seen as comparable to the Conservatives in terms of competence and electability. But in achieving this position, it had now lost its main source of differentiation in the form of Margaret Thatcher. In addition to losing the catalyst that they hoped would have driven voters into the Labour camp by default, labour strategists were conscious that Thatcher's departure had turned public attention back to the problems of Neil Kinnock's leadership. After only a few weeks of Major's premiership, Kinnock was being pressed to change his style away from the cultivated posture of a Thatcher alternative. In early December 1990, for example, Jon Hibbs reported that Kinnock was already being pressed to adapt to the new landscape of John Major's premiership: 'There are calls for Kinnock to shed the false image of a worthy but dull statesman, which he has been fostering in an effort to show he is a serious politician, and return to character with a burst of inspirational leadership.'[52] In the intense engagement for the centre ground, where marginal differences were thrown into high relief and attributed enormous critical significance, Kinnock's leadership became a focus of concern. While some in the party wanted him to alter the focus of his leadership, others returned to the theme that Kinnock was a liability to the party and should be replaced. He consistently trailed behind Major in leader-ship categories. In persistently languishing behind his own party, Kinnock was widely seen to be both Labour's champion and its most visible weakness. As an object of scorn, prejudice and ridicule, he remained the subject of successive tabloid campaigns against his leadership and by extension against the claims of Labour as a party of government.

When Kinnock was first elected leader in 1983, he was the youngest of the main party leaders. Now he was at a disadvantage. Kinnock was not only older than John Major, he had become the longest-serving leader of the opposition in the twentieth century. It was difficult to square Kinnock's message of new vision and innovation with the fact that he had been the Leader of the Opposition since 1983. Moreover, he was confronted both by John Major and Paddy Ashdown, who were facing their first election as leaders. Another problem was Kinnock's conspicuous shifts in policy position in areas such as unilateral disarmament, European integration and nationalism. In the past, Kinnock had made it clear that these were issues of personal and party principle. In abandoning them, Kinnock laid himself open to the claim that he had compromised his leadership and the party's moral standing for electoral advantage. These charges were added to the regular indictments of Kinnock's personal integrity, intelligence, temperament and judgement in the popular critiques of his leadership.

The significance of Kinnock's vulnerabilities was typified in September 1991 when Labour's case against the Major government was suddenly eclipsed by the issue of the party leader. The episode began with a flurry of headlines in early September. These related to Kinnock's abandonment of previous Labour party policies in areas such as nuclear defence and nationalisation. They were used to create public disquiet over his leadership qualities and over his personal credentials to run a government. Kinnock's own previous record in gaining public attention was now used against him with allegations of high-profile personal ineptitude. These claims provoked a set of polls revealing a sharp injection of public distrust in relation to Kinnock. They showed that voters' doubts over the Labour leader represented one of the main reasons for the party's decline in public support. In one poll, 25 per cent said they were more likely to vote Labour if there were a change of leadership. In another poll, 38 per cent reported that their dislike of Kinnock represented the main obstacle to voting Labour.[53] Such findings provoked a further series of front-page splashes, editorials and extended analyses, together with indications of disarray within the Shadow Cabinet over the leadership issue.[54]

In many respects, this assault represented a trial run of the Conservative campaign strategy to target the Labour leadership. To increase its value as a prototype ambush, it was especially timed to create a destructive prelude to the Labour party conference. If the aim was to subject Kinnock's leadership to further subversion without precipitating a change of leader, then it was successful. Given Labour's prolonged procedures for leadership selection, it was always probable that the party would not risk a leadership change during a period when a general election was likely to be called.

The ramifications of this sudden focus upon Kinnock in the news agendas of September 1991 were reflected by a Gallup/*Sunday Telegraph* poll. It disclosed that Kinnock was ahead of Major in only one category – strength of personality. On all the other categories (e.g. concern for country, trustworthiness, caring attitude, competence, decisiveness, listening to reason and appearance of a winner), Major was clearly ahead of Kinnock. Moreover, the belief that Kinnock would not make a good prime minister remained the number one complaint against Labour. It was cited by 30 per cent of voters including 21 per cent of Labour supporters. The poll also showed that of four possible contenders[55] to succeed Kinnock in the leadership, John Smith 'would seriously enhance the party's chances of winning the next general election'. Fifteen per locent of voters said that they would be more likely to support Labour with John Smith as leader. With the two main parties in close contention this margin of preference could be construed as critical.[56]

Such findings caused deep anxiety within the Labour party and generated muted contingency plans for a possible change of leadership.[57] Labour strategists knew, along with Conservative managers, that it would be politically very difficult to drop Kinnock so near to an election. Apart from the constitutional problems, such a course of action would utterly undermine the party's claims to unity, coherence, moderation and responsibility. Moreover, it was very much Kinnock's party in spirit and content. The programme on which Labour was committed to fight the election was one that had been devised and brought into existence by the leader. Given the extent to which personal leadership was now so central to party image, any doubts about the leader would be translated into doubts about the party as a whole. Labour had planned for a presidential-style election against Margaret Thatcher. It was now compelled to confront a new and popular prime minister with more gravitas than Kinnock and to challenge a governing party, which was determined to give maximum emphasis to John Major and the theme of personal leadership.

The public solution adopted by Labour to the problem of its leader was to close ranks and to emphasise the value of team leadership. Kinnock was increasingly located in a collective setting. The intention was to portray the leader as a facilitator who would allow others to excel in their respective positions. Normally the Shadow Cabinet provided the corporate context, but as the general election approached Kinnock relied mainly upon his 'Economic Team' (i.e. John Smith, Margaret Beckett, Gordon Brown and Tony Blair). This shift in emphasis was chiefly to allay fears over Labour's capacity for economic management. 'For all his strengths as a party manager, it was accepted – even by Kinnock himself – that he had to be seen as surrounded by solid, reassuring competence.'[58] Kinnock insisted that there had been no change of style, only a shift in emphasis: 'I have been and am, a very good captain of the team. You certainly don't drop winning captains.'[59] The next general election would be the litmus test of Kinnock's policy and organisational transformation. But as the election approached, it became evident that the chief architect of Labour's reconstruction remained the party's main electoral distraction.

In response to these concerns, Kinnock began to melt away from the role of party leader as the centre of attention. During the campaign, Kinnock kept the media at a distance both to prevent any distraction from the campaign's selected themes and also to conform to the adopted portrayal of a collective effort. Kinnock now openly equated leadership with the ability to construct and manage a team of able colleagues. After seeking for years to emulate Mrs Thatcher's leadership qualities, Kinnock now changed tack and sought to present himself as a consensus-building chairman of the board. Initially, the Conservatives were wrong-footed by this change of public projection. The Conservatives were relying upon the Labour leader to fall prey to his alleged vulgarity during the campaign. The party planners had organised the Conservative campaign around a choice between the proven leadership of 'honest John' against the doomsday scenario of Kinnock's unfitness to be prime minister.

The Labour leader's self-effacing caution threatened to deny the Conservatives the advantage of a Kinnock gaffe that could be exploited as typifying the incompetence and untrustworthiness of a Labour government. Nevertheless, the sober imperturbability of the Kinnock campaign came at a price. With the leader giving the appearance of concealing himself and with the party giving the appearance of complicity in keeping its leader from unscripted public contact, intense controversy was aroused over the Labour campaign and, in particular, over the role of the leadership within it. The public found it difficult to square Kinnock Mark I with Kinnock Mark II, or to reconcile either Kinnock with current Labour policies. The confusion of images suggested a hidden agenda, or worse, evidence of hidden incompetence.[60] These tensions remained unresolved at the end of the campaign when Labour lost the election and Kinnock immediately stated his intention to resign from the party leadership.[61]

In many respects, Labour's defeat in 1992 was worse than the result in 1983. It is true that Labour had achieved a 2.1 per cent swing against the Conservatives. This led to an increase of 42 seats, which, in parliamentary terms, placed Labour only 20 seats short of a hung parliament. Nevertheless, the near denial of a Conservative majority concealed the persistence of underlying weaknesses. The Conservative party had not only attracted more votes (14.9 million) than any party had ever won, but secured 55 per cent of the two-party vote. Labour needed to increase its number of seats by 97 on its 1987 performance. With a net gain of 42, Labour failed to achieve even half the required total. Labour had made inroads into the third-party vote but it had not dislodged the Conservative party from its previous level of 42 per cent of the popular vote. The last time that Labour had attracted that proportion of the vote was in the 1970 general election when it had been defeated by Edward Heath.

In 1970, Labour had lost even though it attracted 43.0 per cent of the popular vote. With a share of 34.4 per cent in 1992, the party remained well short of achieving its 1970 level of support. Labour had now lost four elections in a row with an average of 34.2 per cent of the vote. After all the policy and organisational preparations of the previous five years when the party was focused upon the need to achieve electability, the final result was a severe and painful public rejection. The Conservatives had won in conditions that were highly unfavourable to the governing party. Labour's latest reversal prompted concerns that the party was doomed to electoral decline. David Butler and Dennis Kavanagh concluded that 'if Labour could not win in 1992, it was hard, given the present electoral system and the Conservative base in a seemingly solid 42 per cent of the vote, to envisage it ever winning again.'[62] It was entirely appropriate, therefore, for Anthony King too ruminate upon whether the 1992 election offered final confirmation that the two-party pendulum had stopped swinging in favour of a steady state Conservative dominance. King arrived at the wholly logical and unavoidable conclusion that under such conditions 'British government [would] remain one-party government into the next millennium.'[63]

Labour leadership in question

After any defeat, a political party looks in on itself and to its recent past. This was a particularly painful form of introspection for Labour in 1992. A prolonged experiment in reorganising the party around a model of strong leadership had culminated in failure. Many contributory factors were considered in Labour's numerous post-mortems and recriminations. The difficulty of confronting John Major; the hostility of the tabloid press; the graduated nature of party reform; the fear of increased taxation; Labour's reputation for economic incompetence; and the internal disarray within the campaign between the leadership, party headquarters and the Shadow Communications Agency were all cited as factors in Labour's defeat. Nevertheless, the element that received most critical attention and, which more than any other came to characterise Labour's failure, was the 'Kinnock factor'. This was cited repeatedly as a generic explanation for overall inability on the part of Labour to make an electoral breakthrough.

Neil Kinnock's perceived lack of personal credentials to be prime minister had long been an issue for Labour. Even though Kinnock had excelled in the role of party manager, his public image remained that of an emotive orator espousing high causes, deep principles and moral outrage. Kinnock's excitability and occasional indiscipline only served to deepen the doubts concerning his appropriateness for high office. Kinnock himself was aware 'from the start that that public did not warm to him as a leader … He agonised about it, he felt the pain of it constantly. Before the election, he considered standing down on more than one occasion.'[64] Prior to the election, the

'Kinnock factor' had become a recognised feature of Labour and Conservative planning. Kinnock's high-profile position fulfilled several functions in party management, but in doing so it created a series of major diversions for Labour. In many respects, Kinnock came to be seen as a liability (i) for having raised questions over his own competence in the arena of public leadership; (ii) for diverting party resources in order to counter allegations of personal incompetence; (iii) for distracting the party's agenda away from topics that were sensitive to other parties; and (iv) for raising damaging doubts about Labour's leadership and, therefore, about the party's ability to provide effective governance.

After the election, there were numerous references to Kinnock's inability to break out of his own past. Robert Garner and Richard Kelly believed that 'he was probably the only senior Labour politician who could have persuaded the party to adopt the organisational and policy changes required to make it electable again'. And yet ironically, it was these very abilities, which 'made Kinnock a transitional figure, too rooted in Labour's traditions to appeal successfully to the wider electorate'.[65] In optimising the declining core vote, Stuart Hall thought that Kinnock 'embodied exactly those things that the constituency that Labour was trying to woo back – the new working class – [was] trying its damnest to escape from. The Welsh working class bonhomie and the "boyo" body language kept breaking through.' As a consequence, Kinnock revealed himself to be 'resolutely of his place' and therefore 'not for these times'.[66]

Kinnock was said to epitomise the party's absorption with itself. In the same manner, the party's electoral post-mortems tended to attribute the defeat to in-house problems and to autonomous choices. Just as much controversy surrounded what Kinnock had *not* done for example as that which circulated around the actual courses adopted. Philip Gould reports that there was 'much talk after the election about Neil was constrained by his advisers, that if he had been his natural self he would have done better ... We had a plan called Operation Liberation, in which Neil would cut loose, and become his real self. But it didn't work because his real self had changed, become older, wiser, different.'[67] Gould concluded that '[n]othing Neil could have done would have endeared him to the voters'.[68] According to this perspective, Kinnock had simply been the wrong choice. This implied that the right choice would have altered the outcome to the party's advantage.

The 1992 general election underlined the central difficulty that Labour faced in respect to leadership. This related on the one hand to the need to have both a capacity to work within the processes and traditions of the party's constitution, and an ability to mobilise the movement's core vote. On the other hand, a leader had to reach outward beyond the party. He or she had to build a broader electoral coalition by dramatically diminishing the public's fear and distrust of Labour as a party of government. These two components were in many respects mutually contradictory. Neil Kinnock appeared to have maximised the potential for achieving such a compound. That such a protracted experiment had failed seemed tantamount to a generic failure of Labour leadership. At the time, it appeared to provide conclusive proof that Labour was inherently unable to compete with the Conservatives at this level. Labour leaders may have aspired to the position of Conservative leaders. However, they could not match the Tories' aptitude for the public projection of leadership or their ability to confound polling evidence through effective leadership-centred appeals relating to public trust and governing competence. After three broken Labour leaderships and four general election defeats, it was difficult to conceive of a way for Labour to adapt itself sufficiently to challenge the Conservative hegemony. And yet, within two years of the disaster of Kinnock's defeat, the emergence of Tony Blair had wholly transformed Labour's position. Suddenly, Labour had a leader who could simultaneously appeal to party and public alike. He showed that Labour could not only challenge the Conservatives in the competition for increasingly de-aligned and volatile voters, but confront the Conservative ascendancy in national leadership.

Notes

1 Robert McKenzie, *British Political Parties: The Distribution of Power within the Conservative and Labour Parties,* 2nd edn (London: Heinemann, 1963), p. 300.

2 Samuel H. Beer, *Modern British Politics* (London: Faber and Faber, 1969), p. 88.

3 Beer, *Modern British Politics,* p. 90.

4 Richard Heffernan, 'Leaders and Followers: The Politics of the Parliamentary Labour Party', in Brian Brivati and Richard Heffernan (eds), *The Labour Party: A Centenary History* (Houndmills: Macmillan, 2000), p. 264.

5 Bryan Magee, 'A strange way to run a party, but it works', *The Times,* 4 December 1974.

6 Magee, 'A strange way to run a party, but it works'.

7 Magee, 'A strange way to run a party, but it works'.

8 David Walker, 'The First Wilson Governments, 1964–1970', in Peter Hennessy and Anthony Seldon (eds), *Ruling Performance: British Governments from Attlee to Thatcher* (Oxford: Basil Blackwell, 1989), p. 200.

9 See Paul Foot, *The Politics of Harold Wilson* (Harmondsworth: Penguin, 1968), ch. 11; Ben Pimlott, *Harold Wilson* (London: HarperCollins, 1992), pp. 560–7.

10 Walker, 'The First Wilson Governments, 1964–1970', p. 201.

11 Walker, 'The First Wilson Governments, 1964–1970', p. 201.

12 Philip Whitehead, 'The Labour Governments, 1974–1979', in Hennessy and Seldon (eds), *Ruling Performance,* p. 254.

13 Kenneth O. Morgan, *Labour People: Leaders and Lieutenants, Hardie to Kinnock* (Oxford: Oxford University Press, 1992), p. 267.

14 See Eric Shaw, *The Labour Party Since 1945* (Oxford: Blackwell, 1996), pp. 132–61; Kenneth O. Morgan, *Callaghan: A Life* (Oxford: Oxford University Press, 1997), chs 26–8.

15 See David Coates, *Labour in Power? A Study of the Labour Government 1974–1979* (London: Longman, 1980), chs 4–6; Martin Holmes, *The Labour Government 1974–79: Political Aims and Economic Reality* (London: Macmillan, 1984), chs 7–9.

16 Mervyn Jones, *Michael Foot* (London: Gollanz, 1994), pp. 448–56.

17 Quoted in Jones, *Michael Foot*, p. 436.

18 Jones, *Michael Foot*, pp. 498–502, 507–19.

19 Kenneth O. Morgan, *The People's Peace: British History 1945–1989* (Oxford: Oxford University Press, 1990), p. 389.

20 Michael Foot secured the leadership under the old system in which the competition was restricted to MPs.

21 Peter Jenkins, 'Fecklessness versus the wrecker', *Guardian Weekly*, 29 November 1981.

22 Roy Hattersley, 'Why I will stay on and fight', *The Observer*, 25 January 1981.

23 Adam Raphael, 'Benn's October Revolution', *The Observer*, 5 October 1980. See also Austin Mitchell, *Four Years in the Death of the Labour Party* (London: Methuen, 1983); David Kogan and Maurice Kogan, *The Battle for the Labour Party* (London: Kogan Page, 1983); Eric Shaw, *The Labour Party since 1979: Crisis and Transformation* (London: Routledge, 1994), pp. 162–8.

24 See Ian Bradley, *Breaking the Mould: The Birth and Prospects of the Social Democratic Party* (Oxford: Martin Robertson, 1981), chs 4–6.

25 Figures timed at November 1981.

26 Shirley Williams in Crosby (26 November 1981); Roy Jenkins in Glasgow, Hillhead (25 March 1982). In the by-elections, where the SDP fielded candidates during the 1979–83 parliament, the party secured an impressive average vote share of 33.81 per cent.

27 Ivor Crewe and Anthony King, *SDP: The Birth, Life and Death of the Social Democratic Party* (Oxford: Oxford University Press, 1995), ch. 8.

28 Mervyn Jones, *Michael Foot* (London: Gollanz, 1994), pp. 456–516.

29 The south of England in this context refers to an area lying below a line drawn from The Wash to the River Severn.

30 David Butler and Dennis Kavanagh, *The British General Election of 1983* (London: Macmillan, 1984), p. 293.

31 Butler and Kavanagh, *The British General Election of 1983*, p. 296.

32 The Conservative lead over the second party in the popular vote was 14.8 per cent. This made Labour's performance comparable to its record defeat in the 1935 general election. In terms of its overall share of the popular vote (27.6 per cent), it was Labour's poorest performance since 1918.

33 Robert Harris, *The Making of Neil Kinnock* (London: Faber and Faber, 1984), p. 224.

34 Eileen Jones, *Neil Kinnock* (London: Hale, 1994), ch. 3; Harris, *The Making of Neil Kinnock*, pp. 214–40.

35 See Martin Westlake, *Kinnock: The Biography* (London: Little, Brown, 2001), chs 12, 15; Colin Hughes and Patrick Wintour, *Labour Rebuilt: The New Model Party* (London: Fourth Estate, 1990), ch. 4.

36 Philip Gould, *The Unfinished Revolution: How the Modernisers Saved the Labour Party* (London: Little, Brown, 1998), p. 58.

37 Gould, *The Unfinished Revolution*, p. 58.

38 Gould, *The Unfinished Revolution*, p. 81.

39 See Michael Leapman, *Kinnock* (London: Unwin Hyman, 1987), chs 3–5.

40 Hughes and Wintour, *Labour Rebuilt*, p. 25.

41 Hughes and Wintour, *Labour Rebuilt*, p. 25.

42 David Butler and Dennis Kavanagh, *The British General Election of 1987* (Houndmills: Macmillan, 1988), pp. 68–9.

43 Philip Gould, Peter Herd and Chris Powell, 'The Labour Party's Campaign Communications', in Ivor Crewe and Martin Harrop (eds), *Political Communications: The General Election Campaign of 1987* (Cambridge: Cambridge University Press, 1989), pp. 72–86; Shaw, *The Labour Party since 1979*, pp. 63–80.

44 Shaw, *The Labour Party since 1979*, ch. 4.

45 For example, see *Looking to the Future: A Dynamic Economy, a Decent Society, Strong in Europe* (London: Labour Party, 1990).

46 See Westlake, *Kinnock: The Biography*, ch. 18.

47 Andrew Grice, 'Labour to tone down attacks on Thatcher', *Sunday Times,* 29 April 1990.

48 Quoted in Jon Hibbs, 'The dent she left in their dream', *Daily Telegraph,* 2 December 1990.

49 Grice, 'Labour to tone down attacks on Thatcher'.

50 Westlake, *Kinnock: The Biography*, p. 505.

51 Westlake, *Kinnock: The Biography*, p. 505.

52 Hibbs, 'The dent she left in their dream'.

53 See 'The Kinnock problem', *Daily Telegraph*, 16 September 1991.

54 'The Kinnock Problem'; Phil Hooley, 'Labour hit by Kinnock crisis', *Daily Express*, 16 September 1991; 'Labour captain to set sail for disaster', *Daily Express*, 17 September 1991; John Deans, 'Kinnock crisis of confidence', *Daily Mail*, 17 September 1991; Paul Wilenius, 'Wipeout', *Today*, 18 September 1991; Andrew Grice, 'Oh, when will I be loved?', *Sunday Times*, 22 September, 1991; Donald Macintyre, 'Kinnock: How the man became the issue', *Independent on Sunday*, 22 September 1991; Nicholas Wapshott, 'The Kinnock factor', *The Observer*, 22 September 1991.

55 John Smith, Roy Hattersley, Bryan Gould, Gordon Brown.

56 See David Wastell and Anthony King, 'Kinnock trails in popularity race', *Sunday Telegraph*, 22 September 1991.

57 See Nicholas Wapshott, 'Labour's top men twice tried to oust Kinnock', *The Observer*, 21 June 1992.

58 John Rentoul, *Tony Blair*, rev edn (London: Warner, 1996), p. 230.

59 Quoted in Wapshott, 'The Kinnock Factor'.

60 See Patrick Wintour, 'Labour sifts through the dust of defeat', *The Guardian*, 17 June 1992.

61 Richard Heffernan and Mike Marqusee, *Defeat from the Jaws of Victory: Inside Kinnock's Labour Party* (London: Verso, 1992).

62 David Butler and Dennis Kavanagh, *The General Election of 1992* (Houndmills: Macmillan, 1992), p. 275.

63 Anthony King, 'The Implications of One-Party Government', in Anthony King, Ivor Crewe, David Denver, Kenneth Newton, Philip Norton, David Sanders and Patrick Seyd, *Britain at the Polls 1992* (Chatham NJ: Chatham Houise, 1993), p. 246.

64 Gould, *The Unfinished Revolution*, p. 144.

65 Robert Garner and Richard Kelly, *British Political Parties Today*, 2nd edn (Manchester: Manchester University Press, 1998), pp. 150–1.

66 Stuart Hall, 'No new vision, no new votes', *New Statesman and Society*, 17 April 1992.

67 Gould, *The Unfinished Revolution*, p. 146.

68 Gould, *The Unfinished Revolution*, p. 146.

5 New Labour as a project of leadership confrontation

Personal foundations of leadership

In contrast to John Major, Tony Blair had had a privileged and sheltered background, which provided the basis for an apparently seamless advance into politics. Blair's father, Leo, was a highly ambitious law lecturer at Durham University. He was also chairman of the local Conservative Association and was intent upon becoming a Member of Parliament and, ultimately, Prime Minister. Leo was concerned that his family should consolidate upon the social position he had acquired from the very modest background of his own father who had been a shipyard worker. Accordingly, Tony was provided with a private education that took him first to the Chorister School in Durham and then to the elite public school of Fettes College in Edinburgh. Blair's biographers are agreed that he was a highly gifted student who was not only intellectually bright but also accomplished at sports – especially athletics, cricket and rugby. Another point of agreement was that Blair was rebellious. He was said to bend the rules rather than to break them. Unlike John Major's disaffection with school, which came from social insecurity, Blair's resistance to structures came more from a self-assured impulse to question the logic and consistency of rules from an analytical viewpoint. Although sometimes obstructive, Blair was neither abrasive, disrespectful nor openly defiant. He remained confident, affable and socially at ease as he secured passage to St John's College, Oxford.

The only substantial reversal of fortune expressed by Blair during his school career came when his father suffered a stroke. This effectively ended all hope of securing a nomination for a party constituency. It also led to the family having to move out of the centre of Durham to a more modest house on a suburban estate. The only compensation for Blair and his brother and sister was that their father now devoted himself to them. He did so with the same single-mindedness that used to take him away from the family home for extended periods when he pursued his academic and political career. When Blair reached Oxford, his father's influence guided his choice of degree subject. Blair applied himself to his legal studies but also ensured that he contributed to the social element of the Oxford experience. This included various 'blazers and boaters' activities. At the same time, he also became the lead singer of a rock band called Ugly Rumours. But impersonating Mick Jagger had its limitations for during this period Blair also developed an earnest interest in moral philosophy and the relationship between religion and politics.

In particular, Blair pursued the communitarian ideas of John Macmurray with particular interest and laid the foundations of a Christian socialist perspective of society. These concepts appealed to his impulse towards an anti-establishment stance and to his disposition for social engagement and critique. Blair's interest in religion was more associated with a rationale for ethical action rather than with an inward piety or an evangelical zeal. Accordingly, he did not make his Christianity into a conspicuous attachment. His commitment was not even known to most of his contemporaries. By the same token, Blair's interest in wider political issues was not translated into participating in student politics or the university Labour party. He came into contact with the staple radicalism of undergraduate political philosophy but it did not achieve any significant leverage within him: 'I went through all the bit about reading Trotsky and attempting a Marxist analysis. But it never went very deep … and there was the self-evident wrongness of what was happening in Eastern Europe.'[1] Cal McCrystal speculates that Blair had come to university at a particular period when Marxist nostrums had lost their earlier appeal. As he had arrived too late for the campus rebellions of the 1960s, 'his years at Oxford were stirred by no great ideological crises to make great claim on his loyalties, sear his conscience or dilute his ambitions'.[2] Certainly, upon leaving Oxford, Blair's aspirations were as high as his father's had been a generation earlier. After a short period of indecision, Blair decided in 1976 to continue in his father's footsteps and to opt for a legal career as a barrister.

Blair's interest in the law was not profound; '[H]e had gone into law for want of any other string pull in any other direction.'[3] Nevertheless, the choice served at least two purposes. First, it would provide him with a base to pursue other career options. Second, it appealed to his liking for public performance. From an early age, Blair had enjoyed appearing on stage and collecting the plaudits of an audience. At Fettes, he was heavily engaged in amateur dramatics and comedies. Blair and his St John's room-mate, Duncan Foster, produced and acted in satirical parodies of contemporary television programmes. The Bar now promised an outlet not just for Blair's intellectual competence but also for the attention-seeking element of his personality. Blair specialised in employment and trade union law at a time when industrial relations and the role of legal restraint upon union privileges and immunities were at the centre of political controversy. His interest in political participation developed at the same time. He had had joined the London party in 1975 after he had left university. Blair's head of chambers, Derry Irvine, now encouraged him to use his professional position to pursue a political career at the highest level.

Foregoing the route of local government, Blair began the search for a constituency that might adopt him as a party candidate.

This was not the most propitious period in Labour party history for a young public school and Oxford-educated barrister to find an opening. In 1982, he was selected to contest the safe Conservative seat in the Beaconsfield by-election. Blair was beaten into third place with just 10 per cent of the vote. In 1983, his fortunes changed when he was selected for the newly formed constituency of Sedgefield. Unlike John Major who had had to suffer many disappointments in the search for a parliamentary seat, Blair's question had been short-lived. He was a late entrant to the Sedgefield contest and had the benefit of a deadlock between the two leading contenders. Blair's intervention was decisive and he was made prospective parliamentary candidate. His chances of election were high. Sedgefield was solid Labour territory set in the mining communities of the old Durham coalfield. Consequently, Blair was elected to parliament in that year's general election with 47.6 per cent of the vote.[4]

Blair was quickly recognised as one of the new intake with political potential. His path was to some extent prepared by the linkages between Derry Irvine and John Smith who were professional colleagues. But Blair's patrons were not limited to the Bar. Roy Hattersley had also spotted Blair and recommended him to senior colleagues. It was Neil Kinnock, however, to whom Blair attached himself. The new member quickly became a vociferous disciple of Kinnock's crusade to transform the party and in 1984 was made an opposition spokesman on treasury and economic affairs. Although Blair was only an assistant on Labour's Treasury team, he had been placed in a policy area of central significance both to the issue agendas of the time (e.g. Exchange Rate Mechanism) and to the party's effort to build up its credentials of economic competence. His contribution had been solid if unspectacular during the years of the Lawson boom, but neither Blair nor Labour as a whole could dislodge the Conservatives' now entrenched reputation for economic management.

After the 1987 general election, Kinnock appointed Blair to the 'People at Work' policy review group, which would lead the party's policy review in the highly sensitive area of employment and trade union rights. At the same time, Blair was made deputy to Bryan Gould who had come top in elections to the shadow cabinet and who had been given the post of shadow trade and industry secretary. A year later, Blair himself won a place on the shadow cabinet and was made shadow energy secretary. After a year of applying himself to the parliamentary detail of opposing Cecil Parkinson's bill to privatise Britain's electricity provision, Blair moved from ninth to fourth in the shadow cabinet elections. As a result, in 1989 he was given the employment portfolio. Blair continued to impress his colleagues by his professionalism, commitment and, at times, his audacity. For example, he moved decisively to defuse and reconfigure Labour's position in such controversial areas as the closed shop,

Table 5.1 Responses to possible contenders to replace Neil Kinnock for the Labour leadership (%)

Q: If Neil Kinnock resigned, which of these Labour MPs would do the best job of leading the party?

	All	*Labour supporters*
John Smith	31	37
Roy Hattersley	18	22
Bryan Gould	6	4
John Prescott	5	6
Gerald Kaufman	4	5
Jack Cunningham	3	2
Robin Cook	3	4
Gordon Brown	3	4
Tony Blair	2	2
Margaret Beckett	2	1
Other	1	1
Don't know	23	12

Source: MORI/*Sunday Times* (22 September 1991)

secondary action, secondary picketing and employment law adjudication. By 1991, Blair had joined Gordon Brown, Margaret Beckett and John Smith to form Labour's high-profile economics team. This unit was very close to Neil Kinnock and in many ways provided the core of Kinnock's claim to team leadership and to Labour's new proficiency at economical management.

Between 1987 and 1991, Blair had succeeded in moving from the back-benches to become one of Kinnock's key lieutenants in the programme to change the posture and reputation of the party. He had proved himself as a party loyalist, parliamentary technician, a shadow cabinet trustee, a conference speaker and an appealing public figure. He had been instrumental in promoting a strong party association with new issues like environmental awareness and skills training. He had also begun to publicise a distinctive brand of radicalism based upon community ethics and mutual responsibilities. In the event of the party losing the 1992 general election and Neil Kinnock resigning the party leadership, Blair had become sufficiently established to move into the most senior ranks of the party alongside the next leader.

In September 1991, when Neil Kinnock had just faced the severest of the periodic crises that punctuated his leadership, MORI asked voters who they would prefer as leader if Kinnock were to resign (Table 5.1). The results showed a clear preponderance in favour of John Smith who was reaffirmed as

Labour's leader in waiting. But the responses also revealed an open field of other runners. They consisted of those who already had an established seniority, but also an array of rising figures who were achieving public prominence and becoming recognised as possible future candidates for the leadership.[5]

Tony Blair was listed but had only a nominal level of support. He had established himself as an individual with potential but was by no means seen as a likely leader. A year later, the landscape had markedly changed. Neil Kinnock and Roy Hattersley had resigned in the wake of the general election defeat in April 1992. John Smith was now leader with Margaret Beckett as deputy leader, Gordon Brown as shadow chancellor and Tony Blair in the second most important department assignment in the shadow cabinet – namely the shadow home affairs secretary. The transformation from one leader to another had been completed without rancour and the new blood appointments of Brown, Blair and Beckett had been successfully achieved. The party prepared itself for a further period of opposition, but this time without the constant undercurrent of controversy over the competence of the leadership.

Context of leadership acquisition

The moral integrity and measured professionalism of John Smith were greeted in many sectors of the party as a welcome relief from the bruising encounters of Kinnock's muscular leadership. Smith offered progress but also consolidation and a renewed appreciation of the value of organisational stability. Smith had been the *de facto* crown prince of the party for some years. Now he assumed the leadership with almost effortless ease by sweeping the challenge of Bryan Gould aside with 91 per cent of the Electoral College vote. The prospects for Smith's leadership looked highly favourable. He was solidly rooted in the Labour movement and in its traditions and understandings. He had made his reputation by applying his forensic skills as a Scottish advocate to a profusion of discomforted Conservative ministers. Smith was also well liked with very few political enemies. He had succeeded Kinnock as leader with remarkably little disturbance to the party and with a conspicuous level of goodwill.[6] Moreover, the period of accession coincided with the collapse of John Major's economic policy when the government was forced to leave the ERM. At the outset of the new parliament, Smith had looked in a good position to benefit from the prime minister's problems in managing a party with a small parliamentary majority. It was not long before Smith began to feel the positional advantage of being opposition leader at a time when the Conservative party had started to disintegrate over Europe, sleaze and charges relating to alleged abuses of power. As Labour's political lead began to grow, the more collegial and consensual style of John Smith looked as if it would pay dividends and allow Labour's popularity to be translated into electoral advantage.

Some elements in the party, however, had doubts over Smith's leadership. Anxiety was particularly acute with those who were most closely associated with the campaign to modernise the party. They could see the merits of a leader seeking to bring the isolated and disaffected component of the left back into the fold, but they were concerned over the costs of such a rapprochement. To reformers like Gordon Brown, Tony Blair and Peter Mandelson, modernisation was a process that had to be continued in order to maintain its effect. Temporary popularity built upon Tory misfortunes was regarded as being no substitute for structural change. The election campaigns of 1987 and 1992 had graphically illustrated not only the soft and volatile nature of opinion poll leads, but also the folly of opposition reliance upon a pendulum of alternating governments. Those most committed to the cause of modernisation were disturbed over the speed and intention of change under Smith. They felt less at the centre of leadership agendas and priorities than they had done under Kinnock. Smith was constructing a wider and more tolerant coalition with proportionally less room for the modernisers and less leverage to pursue cultural or constitutional innovations. Philip Gould, for example, felt the shift of emphasis to the extent where he was now only on 'the very fringes of the Smith leadership: out in the cold'.[7] Gould remained resolute about the need for structural and attitudinal change but under Smith he was forced to conclude that the priorities had changed: 'It was clear to me that Labour had to modernise completely or eventually it would die. We were going to have to wait, however. John Smith wanted to heal the party, not reform it.'[8]

Smith was prepared to allow cautious debates within the party. For example, he set up a committee to review Labour's links with the trade unions. A commission on social justice was also formed to examine the case for a reassessment of how social benefits were targeted. Another commission was established to assess the merits and implications of proportional representation. But as *The Economist* observed at the time, 'some of Labour's modernisers will grow impatient with the smoke-filled room approach to reform'.[9] They would prefer a more 'vigorous open argument to help move things along quicker' and to create the 'sort of spectacle that would show that Labour is really on the move'.[10] This was contrary to Smith's temperament and also to his instincts of party management, which had a Wilsonian quality to them. Like Howard Wilson, Smith felt that the role of leader was primarily one of holding the party together through a careful balancing of policies, plans and personnel. He was prepared to engage in reform but only through a considered process of progressive consultation and consensus formulation. For a party that needed to appeal to middle England, Smith's evident middle-class status and his capacity to portray personal probity and trust were valued as considerable assets. And yet Smith remained a Labour party insider. Like Neil Kinnock, he was deeply embedded in Labour party culture and in the labyrinthine complexities of its bureaucracy, language and rituals. As a consequence, Smith was seen as a figure, which moved continually on the issue of reform, believing that the party could only be politically effective when its explosive energies were kept in a quiescent condition. In the words of Kinnock's chief strategist, Charles Clarke, John Smith was 'essentially a fudge leader'.[11]

Traditionalists found Smith's style more congenial to their outlook. After the party's preoccupation with image building and public presentation, they believed it was now time to return to first principles and allow Labour's conventional strengths to take full advantage of the Conservative crisis. The most senior figures in the modernisation campaign, Gordon Brown and Tony Blair, were personally loyal and affectionate towards John Smith who had been their chief patron in parliament. Nevertheless, they harboured misgivings over the depth of Smith's convictions of the need for reconstruction and over his commitment to what they thought was necessary to achieve it. The leader's perceived authority over reform was highlighted in the struggle over the introduction of a 'one member one vote' (OMOV) procedure in the selection of party candidates. Although Smith had advocated the need to reduce the leverage of the trade union block vote in his leadership campaign, modernisers had to exert considerable pressure upon him to pursue the issue once he had become leader. Smith felt that OMOV would be disruptive because it would be seen as a challenge to trade unionists as well as an attack upon left-wing constituency activists. In the face of those misgivings, Smith campaigned through the trade union movement for the measure's adoption. It took an enormous expenditure of leadership resources and a threat of resignation to force the issue through a Labour conference that remained deeply divided on the issue.

Following this bruising and at times humiliating encounter, which had generated something of a crisis at the very outset of his leadership, Smith became far more cautious over the modernisers' agenda. He looked towards maintaining party equilibrium rather than to risking political capital and public goodwill, in order to engage in struggles for constitutional renewal or policy repositioning. Any substantive changes would have to wait until the party could assimilate them at its own pace. Eric Shaw observed the dynamic between Smith and the modernisers, and concluded that the party leader believed that accelerated changes would jeopardise the long-term campaign to reduce Labour's negative features: 'Though on most key items of policy which divided the modernisers from the left, Smith was more sympathetic to the former (especially on economic policy) he did not believe that any further dramatic alterations in policy were needed: the indispensable condition for victory at the polls had been met, he felt, when he had replaced Kinnock as leader'.[12] Others remained altogether less sanguine when on 12 May 1994, John Smith died suddenly from a massive heart attack.

The shocking demise of a leader, whose party and leadership had eclipsed an increasingly beleaguered government and prime minister, provoked a groundswell of public sympathy and loss. The sense of national tragedy provided an indication of the extent to which John Smith had been seen as a genuine alternative prime minister. By the same token, it also revealed that the extent to which the Labour party had been rehabilitated as a public good. It now provided a credible 'fall back' to a disintegrating government. The death of a leader in office is a very unusual event in British politics. Although the Labour party had well-defined procedures for leadership selection, these had been developed on the basis of a leader either being challenged through conventional means, or stepping down in an orderly manner. There was no detailed provision for an eventuality like this. It confounded the political calendar of party procedures and electoral events. In addition, a funeral and a period of mourning had to be factored into the arrangements. At the same time, Labour had to contest the elections to the European parliament as well as a set of by-elections in June. While the party needed a leader by the summer in order to prepare for the party conference in October, the party's large and complex Electoral College needed time to be organised. The solution chosen was to defer all announcements and activities relating to the leadership until after the elections on June 9.

This formal suspension of leadership politics led to an uncomfortable hiatus of clandestine canvassing and mutual jockeying for positions. The leading contenders were the shadow chancellor and shadow home secretary – Gordon Brown and Tony Blair. They were the party's two leading modernisers. In addition, they were both close political allies who had entered parliament together and shared an office with one another. For years, Gordon Brown was regarded as the senior partner. He was not only a Labour party thoroughbred with strong links to the party's Scottish heartlands but had been a long-established and widely respected politico prior to entering parliament. Brown had been highly active in student politics at Edinburgh University where he became Rector at the age of twenty-one. Before becoming an MP for John Smith's home constituency of South Edinburgh, Brown had been a university lecturer in politics, a writer of books on Scottish politics, a political journalist and chairman of the Scottish Labour party. This background helped to establish him as a significant figure in the party well before Blair had achieved comparable status. For example, Brown was elected to the shadow cabinet at his first attempt in 1987. He became shadow chief secretary and deputy to John Smith. When Blair was elected to the shadow cabinet at his second attempt in 1988, he had come ninth in the poll. His friend was registered in first place.

At that time, Blair's lack of political pedigree was regarded as significant. At university the new shadow home secretary had not been interested in student politics. He had had no background in trade union activities or local government, and had not even been a party member when Labour had last won a general election. As a consequence of his different apprenticeship and passage into the senior ranks of the party, Blair was altogether less reverential towards its conventions and traditions. While Brown was instinctively aware of the layered requirements of policy-making in the party, Blair still had the uninhibited directness of an outsider who was thought to have better connections with the media than the party.

Notwithstanding their differences, Brown and Blair constituted a formidable team that had become a recognised centre of modernisation within the party during the leaderships of Neil Kinnock and John Smith. Now they both had the opportunity to be leader and to promote the reconstruction of the party from a position of pivotal strength. Each also had the opportunity to deny the leadership to the other. They could run against each other and in doing so jeopardise the whole momentum towards modernisation. The key to the leadership succession and, through it, the future of the party, therefore would lie in the personal chemistry between these two elements of Blair–Brown partnership. For much of their relationship Gordon Brown was implicitly acknowledged to be the senior partner. Accordingly, it was generally understood that Tony Blair would not stand against his colleague in the event of a future leadership election. But in June 1994, it was Blair who declared his candidacy and Gordon Brown who deferred to the junior partner in deciding not to contest the leadership.

There were five factors involved in this painful decision. First, as shadow chancellor, Gordon Brown was more deeply implicated than Blair in Labour's unsuccessful financial strategy during the 1992 general election. The adoption of a shadow budget, including costings for child benefit and pension increases, together with plans to raise the ceiling on National Insurance contributions, allowed the Conservatives to invoke fears of a Labour 'tax bombshell'. Although John Smith had ably defended his budget design, it was widely cited as having been instrumental in losing the election. The second factor relates to Labour's continuing drive to establish a requisition for economic competence. In setting out to rethink the left's position on economic management, Brown had been instrumental in repositioning the party against devaluation, large-scale tax increases and demand-led economic expansion. Trade unionists and left-wing activists, however, bridled over the shadow chancellor's embrace of market economics and supply side growth and objected to its implications for public services, the welfare state and redistributive measures. They were also concerned over Brown's long-established advocacy of the ERM, which allegedly gave priority to the objective of currency stability over traditional commitments like full employment and social justice. In the crisis of 1992, the hardline defence of the ERM on the part of the shadow cabinet may have allowed the party to disassociate itself from the resultant devaluation but, in doing so, it left Brown with a conspicuous attachment to exchange rate stability and with a subsequent economic policy wedded to the unpopular option of the European single currency.

A third factor was connected to Gordon Brown's increased association with the demands of financial prudence and with the related perceptions of Labour's restricted aspirations. In contrast to the reactive and defensive nature of Labour's economic positioning, Blair had developed a fresh approach to social problems that tried to assimilate the contemporary emphasis upon individual freedom to a revivalist appreciation of social morality and mutual dependence. Since becoming shadow home secretary in 1992, Blair had used the position not only to subject his opposite number to close public scrutiny, but also to open up a debate upon the relationship between individual opportunity and the importance of social cohesion and collective security. In underlining the reciprocal nature of individual rights and responsibilities, Blair was able to inject a perspective into social problems that tapped into public concerns over a declining sense of community and civic obligation.

Blair believed that a new age had been entered where the 'limitations of narrow individualism' were acknowledged but where there is also 'no desire to return to … the collectivist excesses of the past'.[13] There was now a need to develop a new balance between the individual and collective in which liberty could coexist with community values and social order: 'a healthy society depends on a balance of mutuality and independence, where what we do together enhances what we do alone. Rights go with responsibilities, for individuals and organisations, and the two together are the foundations of an inclusive society.'[14] Opportunities, therefore, implied obligations. Rights had to be balanced with social responsibilities. Individual incidents of crime had to be punished, but zero tolerance was only legitimate if it was founded upon an enhanced framework of community consciousness. By stressing the force of collective norms and moral citizenship, Blair managed to outpoint the Conservatives on the law and order issue whilst managing to claim a genuine left alternative to Thatcherite orthodoxies of social dynamics. The notion of a possible new social vision for Labour that could complement its policy of emulating the Conservatives in economic competence was an appealing prospect for a party that had been seeking a normative rationale since the collapse of socialism in the 1980s.

Tony Blair also offered another type of appeal to voters fatigued by Conservative governments and especially resentful towards the Major administration. This constituted the fourth factor in Blair's rise to the leadership and in Gordon Brown's decision to defer to his nominal junior. In essence, Blair was more congenial to middle England voters whose support Labour required to secure a general election victory. In addition to his social background and professional training, Blair was manifestly English in appearance and accent.

He was also young, good-looking, personable, articulate, well dressed, cultured and dynamic. He not only talked of family values, he had a family based upon a model marriage of middle-class professionals. Just as these characteristics had already made him an effective media representative for the party, so they also ensured that the media gravitated towards Blair for comments, statements, interviews and pictures. Gordon Brown found it difficult to compete with Tony Blair's telegenic properties, or with the public attention and professional leverage that accompanied them.

Gordon Brown was manifestly Scottish in background and speech. Compared to Blair, he was a less engaging speaker who was given to making speeches laden with Treasury statistics and analyses of taxation regimes. Although he was only two years older than Blair, he looked older and often appeared dour and prickly. He was a private man with a bachelor's commitment to the details of politics. This intensity brought with it a reputation for creating deep enmities amongst colleagues. The reported tensions between him and both Robin Cook and John Prescott, for example, made Blair in effect 'the only leader with whom all corners of the top triangle could work'.[15] Although his supporters in Scotland remained passionately in favour of a Brown candidacy in the leadership election, it was precisely these connections that would have diminished his chances of victory. Two successive leaders form Scotland would not only have undermined Labour's dependency upon its Celtic and industrial heartlands, but would have given many potential Labour voters in England further cause to lapse into scepticism and distrust. Tony Blair lacked Gordon Brown's roots in the deep under-soil of the Labour party. As a consequence, it was Blair who was seen as the better candidate. Mr Brown might have been 'a more unifying figure with the party', but he was fatally 'lacking Mr Blair's popular appeal to uncommitted voters'.[16]

The fifth reason for Brown's decision not to run was the political calculation that he was unlikely to win. In two years, his political stock had fallen. He had been a long-established ally of John Smith's, but now that leadership was at an end. It was easier for Blair to appear to be offering something new, qualified by a due sense of continuity. The asymmetry was reversed with Brown. To make matters worse for the shadow chancellor, early opinion polls following John Smith's death showed a decisive lead for Blair. A poll of Labour party members on 15 May 1994 was particularly revealing. It showed that Blair was preferred as leader by 47 per cent of those polled. Gordon Brown, by contrast, received the support of only 11 per cent and trailed behind John Prescott with 15 per cent.[17] The momentum behind Blair had built up very rapidly. For Brown to resist it and to turn the party back around to him would require a divisive and probably highly negative campaign that would have split the party and undermined the movement for modernisation.

The accumulation of these factors made Brown's decision almost inevitable. Before allowing Blair a clear run at the leadership, Brown showed signs of examining a number of options to keep his possible candidacy alive. His supporters strenuously attempted to canvas opinion amongst the Parliamentary Labour Party and to mobilise trade union support on his behalf. Brown himself made a keynote address at the 1994 Welsh Labour Conference. It was described at the time as an attempt to 'reassert his credentials as the next Labour leader with a left-leaning revivalist speech designed to reassure both activists and union leaders that he has the inspirational vision and oratorical power to take the party into government'.[18] In the end, Brown became reconciled to discounting himself in the leadership election. Immediately after Smith's death, it had been difficult to fathom how such a close partnership would react to the situation. It was generally agreed that one would not stand against the other, but this understanding was qualified by the difficulty to 'believe it possible that either man could make that sacrifice, never knowing that he could have beaten the other to become the next Prime Minister'.[19] Ultimately, it was Brown who stood aside in the face of an imminent declaration of a Blair candidacy. The exact circumstances of Brown's deferral remain concealed by the privacy of the enduring relationship between the two men. It is known that resentments were created both by the speed and manner in which Blair had appeared to seize the initiative and to develop a momentum that effectively denied the shadow chancellor a free choice over the leadership. Gordon Brown and his supporters were particularly aggrieved over what they interpreted to be a betrayal by key individuals like Peter Mandelson, who were thought to have surreptitiously shifted allegiance from Brown to Blair at a critical stage. The circumstances surrounding Brown's displacement as a leadership contender have remained a source of controversy and a significant conditioning factor in the development and content of Blair's leadership.[20]

Without Gordon Brown in the field, Tony Blair had few challengers to his position as favourite and 'leader in waiting'. The possible challenges of Robin Cook and Jack Cunningham did not materialise mainly because they lacked support outside the party. This left Blair contending the leadership with Margaret Beckett and John Prescott. Beckett had been deputy leader under John Smith and was now acting leader in his absence. She promoted herself as a soft-left traditionalist with an eye towards electoral realism. She was a proponent of economic competence but retained a strong attachment to the trade unions and their rights to have a collective voice in the party. John Prescott was a hybrid figure of social Labour roots mixed with strands of modernisation and had a 'no-nonsense' attitude against European integration or against any dilution of Labour's commitment to full employment and redistribution. Although Prescott radiated working-class muscle and trade union power, he had an appreciation of the need for modernisation. He had played a pivotal role in securing conference support for John Smith's OMOV initiative in 1993. In contrast to Margaret Beckett, who proposed the abandonment of all trade union legislation passed by recent Conservative government, John Prescott proposed a far more discriminatory posture towards repeal.

Beckett and Prescott tried to confront Blair through encoded references and nuances, but it was difficult for either to make any inroads upon such a lead. There were serious concerns in the Blair camp that the public and media momentum behind him was so strong that it might provoke a backlash by a party traditionally resistant to outside pressure. The supporters of both his opponents sought to draw critical inferences from the lavish endorsements given to Blair by the Conservative press. But it was to no avail. The European elections and the five by-elections fought on 9 June just prior to the official start of the leadership election set a pattern that was never broken during the contest. At a time when Blair had already established a commanding lead in the polls, Labour won 62 of the 87 UK seats in the European parliament and registered an average Conservative to Labour swing of 18.42 per cent in the by-elections. In the view of Anthony King, the results demonstrated that Labour was 'now back, constituting a real electoral threat to the Tories for the first time since 1979'.[21]

On 21 July, the leadership election results revealed that Blair had won 57 per cent of the Electoral College. He achieved majority support in each of the college's three constituent parts (Figure 5.1).

Figure 5.1 Labour leadership contest 1994

Leader: % votes in different elements of Labour's electoral college

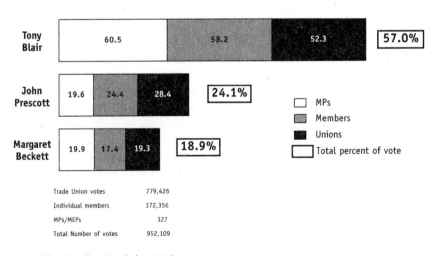

Source: The Guardian (22 July 1994)

In contesting the leadership in a responsible and supportive way, John Prescott had improved his chances of securing the deputy leadership. Partly because he was seen as not only the preferred candidate of the Blair team and partly because he fulfilled the role of 'old Labour' balance to Blair's innovative style, Prescott succeeded in defeating Margaret Beckett in all three elements of the electoral college. Blair and Prescott were widely feted as the dream team for the Labour party. The unity which John Smith had tried so hard to achieve and which was recognised as imperative for electoral effectiveness had been maintained and even enhanced – not least by the realistic prospect of future success. Upon being elected, Blair duly pledged himself to complete the process of Labour recovery: 'You have put your trust in me and I vow to you that I shall repay that trust ... I shall not rest until, once again, the destines of our people and our party are joined together again in victory at the next general election.'[22]

Themes, style and authority

Tony Blair was not only the youngest Labour leader, he was also the beneficiary of an idiosyncratic set of conditions, which converged to support and enhance his leadership. The impetus behind Blair was quite extraordinary and it allowed him to establish and then to develop an unprecedented degree of leadership authority in a conspicuously small time frame. In addition to the formal powers and privileges accorded to the leader of the opposition, Blair was able to inject several additional elements into his position. These were to have significant ramifications both to his leadership and, ultimately, to the entire framework of leadership politics within the British system.

First, Blair had risen to prominence with astounding speed. His very mobility struck a note of iconoclasm within a party that had traditionally reflected the British parliamentary conventions of institutional apprenticeship and graduated promotion. Blair had become a senior party figure with national recognition less than two years prior to becoming leader. In securing the great prize of a political career, Blair had suddenly overtaken more senior colleagues and those with arguably stronger claims in terms of experience, parliamentary presence or party links. Far from being the beneficiary of a closed order of preference, Blair's leadership was self evidently one that was based upon claims of overriding merit and aptitude.

A second foundation of personal authority was provided by the fact that Blair was neither born nor bred into the party. He was seen as not being instinctively part of Labour's social and traditional fabric. Blair turned this distance to his own advantage by claiming that it gave him the necessary critical perspective to see how the party appeared to those outside the organisation and how it could improve its reputation and appeal amongst the public.

109

In a party now disposed towards valuing electoral intelligence, market research and professional expertise, Blair had the credentials of a specialised consultant in public attitudes and political attachments. The progressive contraction of Labour's core vote made the party much more susceptible to a leader with the declared ambition of widening the party's appeal. While Blair's open cultivation of the wider electorate caused some anxieties within the party, they were more than overcome by his public appeal, which offered the prospect of electoral viability.

A third component of Blair's authority lay in the manner of his election. For an individual claiming access to contemporary currents of public opinion, Blair's position was enormously strengthened by Labour's reliance upon an electoral college in the process of leadership selection. The 1993 reforms had reduced the trade union element within the party conference from 40 to 33.3 per cent. They had also introduced an OMOV requirement which effectively abolished the block vote and, with it, the leverage of trade union leaders in the selection of the party leader. The candidates could legitimately assert that they were contending the leadership by appealing to an electorate of 4 million individuals in the largest democratic exercise that any political party had ever organised in this country. Blair, Prescott and Beckett operated separate campaign organisations, cultivated different appeals and issued *de facto* manifestos. They competed openly with one another in a series of debates, interviews and speeches, while polls tracked the individual strengths and weaknesses of each candidate.

The eventual winner of this intensive process could lay claim to a decisive affirmation of leadership, a mass-based mandate, an established position in the public arena and a huge disparity in status and leverage between the leader and any other figure in any other party. Such claims were further enhanced by Blair's sweeping victory in all three elements of the Electoral College. This was a particularly impressive performance against two such senior and established Labour party figures. For a party that had always prided self upon its democratic organisation, the reformed Electoral College embodied a different suffrage for a different kind of party and, with it, a different kind of Labour. Blair embodied the full implications of the change and also the irony involved in the transformation. The Electoral College had originally been established to shift the balance within the party from the right-wing elite to the left-wing activists based in the Constituency Labour Parties and the trade unions. The fact that such a device could produce unintended consequences first became apparent during the term of the first leader to be selected by the Electoral College. Securing the leadership through the Electoral College resulted in Neil Kinnock having a 'very clear mandate from party activists, much more so than any previous leader'.[23] Andrew Thorpe describes the ramifications of such a route to the top: 'Paradoxically, this fact would allow him, in the end, to push the party further to the right, in terms of policy and organization, than any leader since Gaitskell. The imprimatur of the electoral college, designed to be a guarantor for the left, was ultimately to be a weapon with which to beat it.'[24] Now with the onset of Tony Blair, the Electoral College had not only produced a right of centre leader, but one who was determined to use the democratic authority of the college to transform the party far beyond the parameters within which Neil Kinnock had to work during his leadership.

Blair's status in the party was further strengthened by a fourth component: namely that of personifying the real prospect of electoral victory. He had already translated his own polling leads in the leadership election into actual winning margins. Although Margaret Beckett had been acting leader of the party, it was Blair who headed the leadership rankings when Labour scored a resounding victory in the elections for the European parliament in June 1994. That election saw Labour achieve 43 per cent of the vote – i.e. 61 per cent of the combined two-party vote. It also revealed the first evidence that Tory voters in the South and East were prepared to switch to Labour rather than to restrict their dissent to the normal confines of the Liberal Democrat Party. Blair's succession to the leadership, together with his initial period as leader, coincided with high opinion poll leads for Labour. These added to the momentum of his drive to make the party even more receptive to the imperatives and disciplines of leadership politics in contemporary political engagement.

A fifth factor in Blair's authority as leader lay in his highly personalised interpretation of where the party needed to locate itself in the political landscape. Blair became not only the public face of the party but also the chief nerve centre and disseminating force of New Labour. It was Blair who redefined socialism into a selected blend of practical solutions and populist impulses. It was Blair who patented an ethical approach to social problems in the form of communitarian awareness of reciprocal obligation and social capital. And it was Blair who popularised the idea of a genuine 'third way' that avoided the pitfalls of both a state-centred command economy and a society based upon neoliberal dynamics and market values. The only agency that could hold these disparate and nuanced positions together into a recognised theme that approximated to a coherent rationale was the leader himself. Just as it was his self-proclaimed vision which provided the motivating force behind his leadership, so it was the public appeal of this vision which lent further weight to Blair's primacy in the party.

A final property of Blair's leadership authority was that most elusive ingredient which is savoured by all leaders – namely luck. Blair had the good fortune of being a rising star; one who had been uncompromised by previous government experience or by a close association with the 1992 general election defeat. He had exploited the licence of opportunity to good effect and was being widely cited as a future leader when John Smith died. In life and death John Smith was instrumental in unifying the party. Now Blair was set to benefit from the respect given to Smith by both the party and public, and from Labour's own appreciation of the functional value of unity at such a time. The leadership election proceeded on the basis of the need for harmony and the importance of rallying around a new leader. The gravitational force of Blair quickly pulled in John Prescott and Margaret Beckett to positions of only notional competitors. Blair also retained the closest support from Gordon Brown who remained a serious future contender for the leadership.

The outcome was a stable succession from Smith to Blair, which allowed the new leader to exploit the momentum generated by Smith's capacious leadership style and by the public sympathy over the party's loss. Within a few weeks of Smith's demise, a young leadership aspirant had been transformed into the heir apparent and, thence, to the leadership. The speed of the transition prevented any prolonged process of competition. The candidate's youth and the decisiveness of his victory facilitated a rapid and conclusive transition with little of the private rancour and suppressed frustrations that normally accompany the establishment of new leadership. Blair was fortunate that the party reunited so quickly following the death of a leader. He had the further good fortune to be made leader at the most propitious time when the cycle of political opportunity favoured Labour more substantially than at any other time during the previous thirty years.

The themes pursued by Blair were closely correlated with the aims and requirements of his leadership. One of the most significant was the need to give continual emphasis to the aggregate failures of successive Conservative governments. Blair was determined to keep John Major on the defensive by stressing the principle of accountability. After four Conservative administrations, the record of economic incompetence and social dislocation was persistently attached to Major and his government. The prime minister, in particular was targeted as the figurehead of a decadent party mired in allegations of sleaze and scandal, and subjected to deep splits in opinions and priorities. Blair deployed a series of populist devices designed to delegitimise the Major government. By exploiting public anxieties on issues like crime and the economy, and relating them to an asserted disenfranchisement of a silent majority, Blair could build up his claim that Labour was necessarily the people's party with the public interest as its guiding objective.

In addition to dispelling rumours that Blair was a closet Tory, these sustained assaults upon the Major administration helped to keep critical analysis away from his own party. They also provided the foundation to Labour's claim to governance: namely the need for national renewal. This theme of revival was both radical and conservative at the same time. It appealed to the need for change, but also to a concept of reform that would elicit traditional impulses and promote intuitive forms of constructive social behaviour. Blair wanted to revive political interest in the internal dynamics of individual actions and how

they related to a collective equilibrium. By providing a corrective to the dysfunctional properties of maximum self-advancement, Blair believed that a Labour
government could repair the social fabric and usher in a new community-
based order of interdependence and cohesion. 'We aren't simply people set in
isolation from each other, face to face with eternity', Blair observed. On the
contrary, we were 'members of the same family, the same community, the
same human race. This is my socialism.'[25] Blair wanted to divorce the meaning
of socialism from its old attachments to the state. Because the state was now
recognised as 'vested interest in itself, every bit as capable of oppressing
individuals as wealth and capital',[26] it was necessary to revive the full traditions
of a moral citizenship serving the community and a government making 'both
state and market subject to the public interest'.[27]

Blair's developed sense of Christian socialism was not limited to moral
injunction. It provided the basis to a range of wider policy initiatives designed
to protect personal freedom of action, whilst also recognising the equal status
of personal responsibility. Blair sought to popularise this vision as the
stakeholding economy or the stakeholding society. Proposed measures would
be intended to raise the public's consciousness of the value and functional
contribution of each individual holding a stake in social action. Policies would
also be intended to deepen and widen the scope of stakeholding responsibilities from organisations becoming more sensitised to the scale of their constituencies to individuals with an enhanced sense of a stake in the value and
operation of public goods. This concept was closely related to New Labour's
endorsement of a communitarian ethos. This acknowledged the role of the
individual but gave emphasis to the pivotal importance of the social fabric,
and the need for moral prescriptions relating to inclusion, cohesion and group
values. Communitarianism was seen as having 'provide[d] Blair and New
Labour with an antidote to Thatcherite individualism'.[28] It was regarded as
'Blair's rebuff to Old Labour'[29] and to its associations with state-centred categories of collective provision and universal entitlement.

In highlighting the ethical values and organisational potential of community, Blair demonstrated an attachment to another theme. This was the
appeal to one nation, which the Conservative party had long regarded as being
patented to it. Now Blair was prepared to appropriate it for himself. He pro-
claimed Labour as 'the party of one nation, rebuilding Britain as one nation'.[30]
Under a Labour government, Blair would ensure that it would foster 'One
Britain: the people united by shared values and shared aims, a government
governing for all the people'.[31] The corollary to this theme was that Labour
needed to be seen as a party which would govern in the interests of the whole
nation and not give any priority to one section over another. Labour had to
build on its popularity in order to present itself as the people's party pursuing
the public interest. New Labour would not be predisposed to one set of vested

interests over another. A New Labour government would not be the 'political arm of anyone today other than the British people'.[32] Instead of past dogmas based upon class strife, Blair pressed for a partnership of mutual benefit: 'Let us settle these arguments about industrial laws once and for good. There will be no return to the 70's … Forget the past. No more bosses versus workers. You are on the same side. The same team.'[33] As a result, the trade unions would be given the same access to government as employer and business groups. It was only by cultivating social unity that the party could create the impetus to renew the nation and to achieve its stated conjunction of 'New Labour, New Britain: The party renewed, the country reborn'.[34]

In seeking to build such a broad coalition by references to the nation and social morality, Blair was aware that the key underlying theme was the question of public trust. From the outset of his leadership, Blair underlined the party's need to recapture and cultivate a sense of trust. Even if he could persuade voters that the Conservatives had betrayed their trust, it did not necessarily follow that trust was simply transferred to the alternative party to government: 'The Tories have failed. But I will wage war in our party against complacency wherever it exists. The Tories have lost the nation's trust. But that does not mean we inherit it automatically. We have to earn it.'[35] To that end, the party had to demonstrate that it had undergone a genuine change, in order to justify its claim that it could transform the country. Before becoming the agency of renewal, Labour itself had to become the model of renewal.

This premise of a prior requirement gave the leader enormous leverage in advocating internal reform and in altering the public impression of the party. Especially close to Blair's heart in this respect was his enthusiasm to boost the party membership. This would not only diminish the position of the trade unions in the party, but invigorate the party by making it more representative of modern Britain, thereby giving it a stronger claim to act as a reference point for social reform: 'We have to represent communities and have roots in them. And we can't do that with a tiny membership base that is devoted solely to internal activities.'[36] In the leadership election, Blair drew attention to the need to use 'this opportunity to recruit many thousands of members'.[37] More members to Blair meant 'more activists and more activity – more people not just to be involved in local parties but to serve their communities'.[38] Blair used his own constituency of Sedgefield as a model for the party. By being proactive and imaginative at the local level, the party membership rose from 650 in 1983 to 2,000 in 1992. Perhaps more significantly, the membership became more a diversified and representative cross section of the constituency. Blair's own Sedgefield experience reinforced his belief in an expanded mass membership and in its capacity to strengthen the leader's assertions that Labour could be equated with a microcosm of society, with an expression of one nation, and with the embodiment of democratic vitality.

Tony Blair's leadership style was fused with his chosen themes and his strategic position within the party. The assessment of Labour's condition and the establishment of clear objectives for the party set the direction and tone of Blair's leadership. It was well known that Blair had been highly impatient with John Smith's relaxed and accommodating method of leading the party. Smith had lowered voices and decreased the temperature. His achievement was that he 'damped down activity and controversy to the point at which there was nothing to fall out about'.[39] His position had been one of successfully 'hovering above the party's internal disagreements, a leader for all factions'.[40] Blair appreciated the fact that Smith had induced a state of tranquility, but he felt that this would always be a temporary achievement. To Blair, the party was in limbo. It required drastic action to prepare it for an election campaign against a predictably resurgent Conservative party in the next general election. Given the precarious condition of John Major's parliamentary majority, it was likely that the general election would come in 1996 rather than 1997. For change to be established and to have an electoral effect it was necessary for modernisation to be pushed very hard and very early in the parliament. During 1993, Blair had become depressed and demoralised over not only the pace of reform but the lack of recognition of its vital importance. Too many difficult decisions were being deferred in the pursuit of unity and reconciliation. In the view of the modernisers, Smith had secured short-term stability by leaving the future direction of the party as an open question.

After Smith's death, it was clear that this question would no longer remain buried. This was partly because leadership contenders were expected to discuss their strategic plans for the party, and partly because both Blair and Brown were determined to pursue the modernisation agenda. But it was also because the suspension of hostilities under Smith was integrally linked to the idiosyncratic element of Smith's personal position in the party: 'His seniority, experience and ability put him in an unrivalled position of authority over his party. Through force of personality he had bound left and right after the bruising battles of the Kinnock years.'[41] Commentators recognised that while Smith's leadership strategy had been effective against the Conservatives, it was 'far from clear that it [would] work for anyone else'.[42] Hugo Young summed up the problem of any leader succeeding John Smith in 1994:

> Partly through Scottish provincialism, and partly with the caution of a leader quite content to be far ahead already, Smith was a master of the school of politics which teaches that the faithful must never be alarmed. His personal authority was a kind of substitute for a declared sense of direction.[43]

After witnessing the limitations of John Smith's leadership at first hand, Blair had no hesitation in running for the leadership in order to define and establish that new sense of direction which only a forceful leadership could organise.

The New Labour project was designed to change the identity of the party through substantive and transparent reform that would be driven, personified and publicised through a highly visible leadership. Once Blair had become leader, the party quickly began to resound to his priorities, his language and his criteria of leadership. Blair had a clear philosophy of a leader's function: namely to define a coherent set of objectives and to ensure that the organisation responds to those requirements in order to achieve them. He was determined that under no circumstances would his party suffer the indignities and embarrassments that the Conservatives had done under John Major. The Major administration became the ultimate deterrent. Blair would measure his own performance and the behaviour of his party by reference to the negative standards of the Major administration. Blair's leadership was designed and marketed as the counterpoint to Major's inability to prevent his party from disintegrating into sectarian and self-absorbing divisions. As a consequence, Labour's new leader emphasised the importance of discipline, the absence of weakness, and the presence of driving energy. In the quest to build public trust in the Labour party, Blair was insistent that his message should not be compromised by old doctrinal disputes. He sought to transcend ancient rifts through a language that diverted attention away from class conflict and social division towards themes of common appeal such as civic pride and universal moral values. The objective was to move Labour into a position where it could claim to represent the social need for consensus and the social potential for consensus. It could only achieve this position if Blair could demonstrate that his party was itself an exemplar of consensus, which had undergone such a genuine transformation that it was now a leader-centred organisation geared to public outreach.

The task Tony Blair set the party was one of an imperative motivated by rational calculation, common sense and moral certainty. He was perplexed by opposition and even by hesitation, or reservation. His vision was fuelled by individual will power and personal energy. He understood the need for consultation and negotiation in the construction of coalitions inside the segmented infrastructure of the party. But he was not prepared to be diverted or defeated by organisational inertia, or internal wars of attrition. In an interview with the *New Statesman*, Blair acknowledged that many in the party felt 'frustrated by the process of change' and especially about 'the lack of consultation'.[44] Nevertheless, he went on to point out in very robust terms that effective leadership often involved a centralisation of decision-making. The party either had to adjust to this type of leadership, or it could find another leader: 'With a modern political party you have to have effective ways of decision-making. My attitude has always been: if you don't like the leader, get rid of the leader and get someone else to do the job. But don't elect a leader and not allow him to lead. You can't do that in modern politics.'[45]

The missionary zeal that Tony Blair attached to the New Labour project, combined with his conviction in the value of leadership as a catalyst to integration and renewal, often drew him into conflict with his own party. The new leader did not flinch from such disputes. In many respects, Blair relished the confrontation. His personal crusade was conducted as much against his own party and its traditional constituencies as against the Conservatives. Friction was sometimes deemed necessary both to reassure the public that change was in progress and to provide visible evidence that the leader was actively reaching out to the public, not merely through the party but if necessary in opposition to it. This type of self-induced controversy with the party was typified in Blair's first Labour conference as leader in 1994. At what should have been an occasion to celebrate his new leadership, Blair chose to launch a campaign to replace Clause IV of the party's constitution.

To many in the party this surprise announcement was tantamount to heresy. Clause IV had been the animating principle of socialist philosophy in the British Labour party from its inception as a mass movement. The commitment to a 'common ownership of the means of production' in order to 'secure for the producers ... the full fruits of their industry',[46] had acquired almost mythical status in the movement. At the end of the twentieth century, Clause IV was generally recognised to be an outmoded objective in specific terms. Nevertheless, it retained its status as an anchorage point in the party's sense of itself and in its historical mission. It was precisely Clause IV's connection to Labour's identity and to the public's perceptions of the party that Blair found objectionable. Even if it was honoured in the breach and even if Labour politicians possessed a cultivated ability to work around it through obfuscation, the new leader regarded Clause IV as a constraint upon public understanding: 'We should stop saying what we don't mean and start saying what we do mean, what we stand by, what we stand for. It is time we had a clear, up-to-date statement of the objects and objectives of our party.'[47]

It was possible to view this move as unnecessary, risky and even reckless. The new leader would have to expend considerable political capital to wring any changes from the party. He had caused offence to many by identifying his opponents as not merely old Labourites but the 'Old Labour' party – i.e. the party left behind and marginalised by New Labour. Ultimately, Blair prevailed and the party adopted a new statement of aims and values in April 1995. The fact that Labour had been willing to retain an anachronism out of sentiment and inertia was intolerable to a leader like Blair. To him, the whole issue typified a culture that needed to be transformed from the top down. As a consequence, Blair risked his entire leadership and dared the party to undermine its key electoral asset in the Clause IV debate. His assault upon Clause IV and upon the relevance of Labour's history to the party's current requirements reflected the leader's approach of making the party more outwardly understandable even if this did risk internal disruption and division.

The Clause IV episode was symptomatic of the value placed by Tony Blair upon public demonstrations of leadership. By using and enhancing his authority to purse his chosen themes, the Labour leader was intent upon energising the party for a sustained electoral campaign. So great was the emphasis upon the central objective of achieving power that Blair and his team worked to arouse the party to a near permanent state of electoral preparedness. The abnormal cohesion of a campaign was now required as a normal condition for the party at all times. The leader's overriding aim was to secure not one but at least two general election victories. All other considerations were now regarded as secondary to the need for party discipline, public appeal and electoral viability. Accordingly, enormous resources were directed to the party's efforts to systematise and professionalise its relationship with the media, and to ensure ever higher standards of news management and effectively targeted public outreach.

Blair and his adopted role lay at the centre of all these efforts to elect a Labour government. The new leader was not prepared to front the party as a middle-class figurehead, or as an intellectual trustee for the vested interests of trade unionism. Neither was he prepared to be an apologist for, or a digression from, an outmoded socialist ideology. He wanted a genuine synergy between the leadership, the membership and the electorate. His role would be to provide a recognisable expression of views and beliefs with which large sections of the public could identify. To an increasingly atomised and individuated electorate, Blair would seek to offer a clear point of access to non-Labour voters and an imprimatur of the collective trustworthiness of New Labour. Just as his leadership had been a pivotal agent in the altered identity of the Labour party, so Blair himself became the personalised embodiment and defining symbol of the New Labour project.

Leadership contingencies and constraints

Blair had made a momentous start to his leadership. He gave the appearance of having transformed the political landscape by shifting the balance between the parties decisively and irrevocably in favour of a future Labour government. As Labour's lead in the polls widened to a gulf and as Blair further consolidated his position in the party, commentators and analysts competed in their use of superlatives to convey the sensational nature of Blair's impact upon the conduct and calculations of British politics. And yet, in spite of these plaudits and the associated projections of inevitable electoral victory, Blair's position was far from being unproblematic. Notwithstanding the extraordinary public reaction to his leadership, Blair was aware that he would have to contend with a set of circumstances that would make his entry into Downing Street far from certain.

One set of constraints related to his own party. Far from regarding the leadership election as the culmination of a modernisation process, Blair believed that the party was in dire need of a continuous and rapidly accelerating form of enforced change. The party's long-term decline and systematic deterioration needed to be arrested and reversed within a very short timescale. This would be difficult and provoke resistance from those who believed that they had a closer proximity and a better understanding of the party's traditional heartlands. Many on the left were demoralised but they remained unconvinced by Blair's New Labour project. Others had attributed Labour's defeat in the 1992 general election to an excessive emphasis upon presentational values and bland policies. The vocal sceptics represented a strong undercurrent in the party that gave notional support to Blair but retained reservations over the price of his leadership. In his first speech as leader to party conference in 1994, Blair addressed the source of this unease: 'Some of you support me because you think I can win. But it is not enough. We are not going to win despite our beliefs. We will only win because of them. I want to win not because the Tories are despised but because we are understood, supported, trusted.'[48] The problem for Blair was that in many quarters of the party he was neither understood nor trusted. Some thought he was a closet Tory. Worse still, others believed that he was trying to establish a SDP Mk II, located this time within the Labour party. Blair was an outsider; namely a convert to the party. As a consequence, he was thought to be largely devoid of an intuitive knowledge of its traditions and rhythms. This was exacerbated by his unclubbable behaviour, by his cultivation of media elites, and by his presumption in personally reapplying Labour principles to modern conditions. Blair also antagonised those with a more traditional disposition by his view that the party was backward and complacent, and therefore in desperate need of urgent attention.

Sceptics and waverers were prepared to tow the line because they thought he could win. Nevertheless, they were also aware that the modernisers were not a social movement but a disproportionately small and narrowly based grouping dependent upon the continued acquiescence of the party's power brokers. Blair for his part was determined to reconfigure the Labour party as a non-socialist but progressive electoral force. He was intent upon squeezing the institutional privileges of Labour's structural components in order to widen the party's appeal to those with middle-class aspirations and with concerns for social cohesion and public services. As long as Blair and his team were able to lead the party into such impressive levels of public support, complaint and distrust remained muted. But Blair was fully aware that party unity was a perishable commodity and that a balance needed to be constantly refined between modernising iconoclasm and political caution. He always risked being too far out in front of his party and, as a result, he had to be attentive to the ever-present threat of a damaging backlash.

Public opinion constituted another set of considerations for the Blair leadership. Although the record polling leads that coincided with Blair's succession to the leadership provided a potent impetus to his authority, the new leader was always wary of the distortions that could lie within such large margins in Labour's favour. For over fifteen years, Labour had been beset with an apparently irremovable association with economic incompetence, high taxes, stagflation, industrial strife, nationalisation, trade union militancy and social disorder. It was unlikely that all such concerns could have been resolved so quickly in Labour's favour. On the day that the leadership election result was declared, a MORI/*Times* poll revealed that while Labour had a 28 per cent lead over the Conservatives in voting intentions, it had not achieved corresponding levels of public estimation. In fact, the party's reputation in a range of categories had actually fallen in comparison to its position in February 1989 when the Conservatives were in the lead on voting intentions. In July 1994, more people now thought Labour would raise taxes and fail in keeping its promises and in improving living standards. *The Times* concluded that the 'findings may depress Mr Blair [b]ut they also give him the ammunition in his fight to persuade the party that the modernisation conducted by Neil Kinnock and John Smith was inadequate in so many ways'.[49]

Another MORI poll in October 1994,[50] reaffirmed that still over half the public thought that Labour 'should not be so closely linked to the trade unions'.[51] Another problem was specified in the preference given by two-thirds of the respondents for increased tax cuts and by 90 per cent who wanted a reduction in VAT on domestic fuel. Even though Labour had become attached to a minimalist programme, a majority of voters remained convinced that tax would be higher under a Labour government. This reflected a residual distrust of the party: '[V]arious questions on the party's image show that a significant minority of those who now say they will vote Labour still have reservations about the party'.[52]

Even though the polling showed that Labour's image had improved and that the Conservative core vote had been diminished, Blair was aware of the probability that Labour's popularity was both unsustainable and artificially inflated. The high support level was in part an expression of Tory unpopularity and mid-term protest, rather than a sign of genuine conversion. Blair and New Labour were enjoying a honeymoon period that could not last in its initial form. The leadership had to be wary over the consequences of false security and complacency. The Conservatives had repeatedly swept back into contention nearer the period of general elections. Moreover, it was John Major's government that would determine the timing of the next general election and it would do so in order to take full advantage of any movements of opinion. Blair had to retain the integrity of Labour's core vote whilst maximising the appeal to floaters and ensuring that new supporters remained at ease with the party. This was more difficult than it appeared because Labour's wider support was also its softest support. One study showed that as many as three-quarters of those who had voted Conservative in 1992 and who were now intending to vote Labour had weak attachments to the party. Riding high in the polls, therefore, was something of a mixed blessing for Blair. It generated high expectations that would be difficult to sustain. The inflated leads were the product of voter volatility that could rebound upon the leadership when the economy recovered sufficiently for disenchanted Conservative voters to switch back to a position of safety first.

Another more specific influence that conditioned Blair's leadership was the Liberal Democrat party. Concerns amongst New Labour strategists that the party might peak too early and become the victim of a late Conservative resurgence prompted interest in the Liberal Democrats. To win power, Labour was already confronted with the need to secure a swing from the Conservatives of at least 4.3 per cent which would represent the biggest swing to Labour since 1945. A swing of such magnitude seemed highly uncertain. A more likely outcome was a hung parliament in which some form of cooperation between Labour and the Liberal Democrats would be essential. Even to achieve the limited outcome of a hung parliament, Blair needed to maximise the anti-Tory vote, especially in the South and West where the Liberal Democrats were not only strong but very often constituted the chief challenge to Conservative seats. Since the splits in the two national parties opposed to a fifth Conservative administration threatened the New Labour prospect, efforts were made to shift the Liberal Democrats away from their stated position of 'equidistance' between the two main parties.

Blair achieved this objective and set out to develop it much further. He engaged in private negotiations with Paddy Ashdown over how the two parties could cooperate as participants in a common cause. The Liberal Democrats had little to lose as they were already being squeezed in the centre ground by New Labour. Under Blair, the Labour party was now more congenial and less threatening to voters in Middle England. Labour's rise in acceptability made it less likely Paddy Ashdown and his party would be portrayed as fifth column-ists for a trade union dominated party of high taxation and nationalisation. On the contrary, it would open up the possibility of more Liberal Democrat seats by means of a decline in Tory resistance and an increase in tactical voting to the detriment of Conservative incumbents. The danger for Blair was being seen to court a party that provoked deep hostility amongst local Labour organisations and which represented the partial remnant of the disgraced SDP. Because of the historical enmity between the two parties, Blair had to keep the nature and scale of the negotiations on cooperation confined to the respective leaderships of both parties.

The main object of attention for Blair and the conditional factor that required the closest attention and the most careful assessment was the Conservative party. John Major and the Conservatives constituted Blair's core adversary. They would determine the extent to which his leadership would succeed or fail. The Conservatives were the focus of New Labour's positioning, planning and campaigning. In many respects, the Conservative party was the *raison d'être* of New Labour and the force that had precipitated the various reforms put in place by the modernisers. To a large degree, the Major administration had been responsible for the revival of the Labour party not only as an opposition force, but also as an electable alternative government. By the same token, whatever benefits the Conservative government had provided to the opposition could always be diminished or even possibly withdrawn.

The Conservatives had shown in the past an extraordinary ability to recover from poor polling positions in order to retain their governing status. Bair was conscious that his predecessor had seen substantial leads melt away under the pressure of a Conservative campaigning machine whose reputation had become one approximating to invincibility. The problem for Blair was that even though the Conservatives were in disarray and divided on Europe, they remained in government with all the powers of incumbency and with the choice of election timing at their disposal. As the general election approached the Conservative government might well benefit from an economic recovery and a rise in the 'economic optimism index'. As it had done in the past, the government would also rely upon a partisan tabloid press that could revive negative images of Labour, set a political agenda critical of Labour and create anxiety and a sense of insecurity over change. Labour planners could not forget that the polls had misinterpreted public opinion in the 1992 general election and had not predicted the scale of a Conservative revival that saw the party amass a record number of votes.

Like all leaders of the opposition, Blair's options were conditioned and constrained by the party in power. He had carefully exploited the opportunities for opposition to stitch together a loose coalition of disaffection that might take the party into power. But much would depend upon the government's powers of recovery and in particular upon its ability to rise above its own internal preoccupations and to turn its critical energies fully upon the opposition. Blair used the threat of a Conservative resurgence as a constant stimulus to his party to avoid complacency and to remain united and vigilant. Nevertheless, there was serious concern amongst party managers that the Conservatives would resort to a sudden and radical response to New Labour which would disrupt party planning and threaten Labour's position in the profile of public support. The reaction they had in mind was a repetition of the 1990 strategy when the Conservatives reversed their fortunes with a change of leadership.

Considerable speculation over John Major's future had already built up in 1993 and it was known before John Smith's election that Conservative dissidents were planning to move against the prime minister in June 1994. The party's predicted performance in the European elections would be the catalyst to a leadership challenge later in the year. When John Smith died in May 1994, the pressure upon John Major's leadership was immediately eased. Michael Heseltine noted that the 'momentum for a change of leadership of the Tory Party that had taken such hold that spring subsided like a pricked balloon. Within a matter of weeks the focus of attention had shifted.'[53] The demise of John Smith was a source of quiet relief to many Conservative MPs. Smith's gravitas and authority had been perceived as a serious threat to the Major administration. However, this initial relief was short-lived. Very soon a 'growing number of Ministers and Tory backbenchers agreed that if Labour did elect Tony Blair as leader, the Conservative leadership crisis would be worse than ever'.[54] Ironically the opportunity to remove Major in 1994 came to nothing because of the consequences of Smith's death. To have immediately moved against the prime minister would have looked like political desperation and an act of tasteless manœuvring in the wake of a public figure's demise. Furthermore, for the Conservative party to respond effectively to Labour's new leadership it needed first to know the person's identity. Labour's long selection process in effect constituted a hiatus for the Conservatives as well. By the time it was possible to make a political assessment of Blair's leadership in 1994, it was effectively too late for a leadership challenge.

In 1995, however, the landscape was different. Blair had not only settled in, he had become a formidable figure who transfixed the Conservatives as much as Labour supporters. By the middle of 1995, the gulf in the poll rankings between Labour and Conservative showed no signs of contraction. As the estimated swing from Conservative to Labour since the 1992 general election reached 17.5 per cent,[55] increasing numbers of Conservative MPs saw their seats enter the column of vulnerable marginals. New Labour was threatening the Conservative heartlands and the party's hold over those sectors mostly closely associated with Conservative support: 'What is most remarkable about the Labour recovery is its consistency across the electorate … [I]t is the intention of women to vote in a Labour government, as it is for the elderly, the middle class and the south to end the Tory hegemony.'[56]

Blair now risked becoming the victim of his own success. His own position reflected the critical value placed in a party's capacity to devise strategies of leadership projection and public appeal. Blair had provided graphic illustration of a leader's influence upon party image, identity and reputation. The dynamics between the leader's individual authority, prestige and leverage, and the collective benefits accrued by the Labour party were not lost on their opponents. The Conservatives could appreciate the need to respond in kind in order to regain some of the initiative ceded to Blair in the accelerating politics of national leadership. The concern for the Labour leader was the form in which such a response would be made.

Notes

1 Quoted in Cal McCrystal, 'Those mild, mild days of youth', *Independent on Sunday*, 22 May 1994.
2 McCrystal, 'Those mild, mild days of youth'.
3 John Rentoul, *Tony Blair*, rev. edn (London: Warner, 1996), p. 54.
4 The Conservative candidate won 29.2 per cent of the vote and the Alliance candidate secured 22.6 per cent of the vote. Blair's share of the vote increased to 56.0 per cent in 1987 and to 60.5 per cent in 1997.
5 MORI/*Sunday Times* 22 September 1991.
6 See Andy McSmith, *John Smith: Playing the Long Game* (London: Mandarin, 1993).
7 Philip Gould, *The Unfinished Revolution: How the Modernisers Saved the Labour Party* (London: Little, Brown, 1998), p. 162.
8 Gould, *The Unfinished Revolution*, p. 161.
9 'Bury the Past', *The Economist*, 16 January 1993.
10 'Bury the Past', *The Economist*.
11 Quoted in Gould, *The Unfinished Revolution*, p. 178.
12 Eric Shaw, 'The Wilderness Years 1979–1994', in Brain Brivati and Richard Heffernan (eds), *The Labour Party: A Centenary History* (Houndmills: Macmillan, 2000), pp. 137–8.
13 Tony Blair, 'The right way to find a Left alternative', *The Observer*, 9 May 1993.
14 Tony Blair, *Leadership Election Statement 1994: Change and National Renewal* (London: Centurion Press, 1994), p. 15.
15 Angela Lambert, 'After you, Tony', interview with Gordon Brown, *The Independent*, 16 August 1994.
16 Peter Riddell, 'But this isn't a one man race', *The Times*, 16 September 1994.
17 Gallup/BBC poll. BBC 1, *On The Record*, 15 May 1994.
18 Patrick Wintour and Seumas Milne, 'Brown makes pitch to left', *The Guardian*, 23 May 1994.
19 Anthony Bevins and Andy McSmith, 'Rivals for Smith's bequest of unity', *The Observer*, 15 May 1994.
20 For an exhaustive analysis of the nature and implications of the Blair–Brown relationship, see James Naughtie, *The Rivals* (London: Fourth Estate, 2001).
21 Anthony King, 'The real winners came second at Eastleigh', *Daily Telegraph*, 11 June 1994.
22 Quoted in Patrick Wintour, 'Blair pledges triumph in return for trust', *The Guardian*, 22 July 1994.
23 Andrew Thorpe, *A History of the British Labour Party*, 2nd edn (Houndmills: Palgrave, 2001), p. 199.
24 Thorpe, *A History of the British Labour Party*, p. 199.
25 Tony Blair, 'The Young Country', Leader's speech to the Labour Party Conference 1995 in 'New Labour, New Britain', in Tony Blair, *New Britain: My Vision of a Young Country* (London: Fourth Estate, 1996), p. 62.
26 Tony Blair, 'Forging a New Agenda', *Marxism Today*, October 1991.

27 Blair, 'Forging a New Agenda'.
28 Stephen Driver and Luke Martell, *New Labour: Politics After Thatcherism* (Cambridge: Polity, 1998), p. 167.
29 Driver and Martell, *New Labour*, p. 29.
30 Quoted in Anthony Bevins, 'Crown prince stakes claim to rule', *The Observer*, 5 June 1994.
31 Blair, 'The Young Country', in Blair, *New Britain*, p. 72.
32 Leader's speech to the Labour Party Conference 1996, *The Independent*, 2 October 1996.
33 Leader's speech to the Labour Party Conference 1996, *The Independent*, 2 October 1996.
34 Blair, 'The Young Country', in Blair, *New Britain*, p. 72.
35 Tony Blair, 'Accepting the Challenge', Leader's speech accepting the leadership of the Labour Party in 1994 in Blair, *New Britain*, p. 29.
36 Quoted in Peter Hetherington, 'Blair method modelled on pit village success', *The Guardian*, 28 May 1994.
37 Blair, *Leadership Election Statement 1994*, p. 19.
38 Blair, *Leadership Election Statement 1994*, p. 19.
39 Senior Labour party source quoted in Bevins and McSmith, 'Rivals for Smith's bequest of unity'.
40 Andy McSmith, 'Life and soul of the party', *The Guardian*, 13 May 1994.
41 Stephen Castle and Paul Routledge, 'Which one will it be?' *Independent on Sunday*, 15 May 1994.
42 Castle and Routledge, 'Which one will it be?'
43 Hugo Young, 'Plain speaking required from Mr Blair and Mr Brown', *The Guardian*, 26 May 1994.
44 Quoted in an interview with Ian Hargreaves and Steve Richards, *New Statesman*, 5 July 1996.
45 Quoted in an interview with Ian Hargreaves and Steve Richards, *New Statesman*, 5 July 1996.
46 Clause IV of the Labour Party constitution committed the party to 'secure for the producers by hand and by brain the full fruits of their industry and the most equitable distribution thereof that may be possible, upon the basis of the common ownership of the means of production and the best obtainable system of popular administration and control of each industry and service'.
47 Blair, 'New Labour, New Britain', Leader's speech to the Labour Party Conference 1994 in Blair, *New Britain*, p. 49.
48 Blair, 'New Labour, New Britain', Leader's speech to the Labour Party Conference 1994 in Blair, *New Britain*, p. 48.
49 'Blair the Victor', *The Times*, 22 July 1994.
50 MORI/*Economist* poll. *The Economist*, 1 October 1994.
51 'Striding clear', *The Economist*, 1 October 1994.
52 'Striding clear', *The Economist*, 1 October 1994.
53 Michael Heseltine, *Life in the Jungle: My Autobiography* (London: Hodder and Stoughton, 2000), p. 475.
54 Anthony Bevins, 'The Conservatives', *The Observer*, 15 May 1994.
55 Robert Worcester, 'Blair beats the blues', *New Statesman and Society*, 28 April 1995.
56 Worcester, 'Blair beats the blues'.

6 Keeping up with Blair: the 1995 Conservative party leadership contest

Tony Blair was not responsible for the basic problems of John Major's premiership. Nevertheless, Labour's new leader succeeded in throwing the full scale of the prime minister's deterioration into high relief. Blair exacerbated the difficulties of the prime minister. He offered a conspicuous model of strong party leadership at a time when such a phenomenon was often considered to be unviable in a post-ideological era. He also openly competed for public and national leadership credentials, which under normal conditions would be more closely associated with the premiership. Major was already beset by misfortunes and challenges emanating from his own party and government. Tony Blair's dramatic accession to the Labour leadership, combined with his campaign to reorganise, relocate and redefine the party from the top served to accentuate the chronic nature of Major's predicament. As the polling position of the Conservative party continued to fall in the aftermath of John Smith's death and the election of his successor, so Major's position within the party became increasingly strained.

A prime minister *in extremis*

From 1979, Conservatives had grown accustomed to prevailing over Labour in terms of leadership competence, party management and electoral effectiveness. Notwithstanding high profile Labour leaderships, personalised appeals, professional campaigns and even the incidence of economic downturns, the Conservative Party had become conditioned to the prospect of Labour squandering its electoral potential through party mismanagement and ideological rigidities. Now Tony Blair and his New Labour project threatened to disable the opposition's traditional contribution to the Conservative hegemony. Labour's new leader was not merely intent upon winning the next general election. He advocated a realigning partnership with the Liberal Democrats and a programme of constitutional reform that would create the possibility of forming a centre-left coalition to squeeze the Conservatives into a minority and marginal position.

John Major and his advisors were aware of these threats, but in order to confront them the prime minister had first to attend to his own power base within the Conservative party. Just as Blair had set out to give his party a course of electric shock treatment in 1994, so Major followed suit in 1995 with an audacious attempt to energise his party by suddenly subjecting it to an unheralded and unprecedented leadership contest. Major's sense of leadership politics impelled him towards a strategy designed to reduce the deficit between himself and Tony Blair. Major opted for the only device available to him that offered the prospect of galvanising the party around his leadership. In doing so, he hoped to secure a revised claim to a personal mandate and to provide a decisive break with the recent past. Accordingly, on 22 June 1995 the prime minister announced he would be resigning his position as Conservative party leader, in order to trigger a leadership contest in which he himself would be a candidate.

John Major felt he had been forced into a position where in order to resolve the problems of the Conservative party and his government, he would have to give public recognition that a leadership crisis existed. In doing so, the prime minister in effect reaffirmed that the difficulties confronting his administration were reducible to leadership and could be resolved by a cathartic injection of leadership authority. Major had become increasingly frustrated over the level of indiscipline in the party and over the way that this incoherence had generated deep undercurrents of internal opposition and persistent rumours of impending leadership challenges. The Major adminis- tration had almost become conditioned to civil strife as a permanent feature of government. Even in the spring of 1993, the prime minister had had to endure the threat of a possible leadership election in the following November. Stories of a leadership challenge in November 1994 formed part of the poli- tical backdrop over the succeeding twelve months. By 1995, it was clear to Major and his advisors that a challenge to his leadership would finally occur in the autumn of that year. It was evident that a leadership election in November 1995 would in effect constitute the final chance for the party to change leaders prior to the next general election. It was precisely the forthcoming campaign that John Major had most in mind when he confronted the leadership issue in June 1995.

Conservative party strategists believed that, despite being over 25 points behind Labour, the next election was there to be won. The government could emerge from its mid-term slump to take advantage of an improving economy and a projected rise in the 'feel good factor'. However, the party would need to alert itself to the threat of New Labour and to the struggle ahead to remain in government. The whip's-eye view of John Major recognised the realism of a prime minister having to tolerate dissent and unpopularity in the mid term of a government and especially a government that constituted the fourth successive Tory administration. Nevertheless, he also believed that the luxury of indiscipline should be subordinated to the imperatives of political survival when a government neared a general election. He and his team were, therefore, irritated not only by the continuing disarray within the party but by the lack of any sign that the disorder would moderate as the next general election approached. To Major, the corrosive atmosphere of fragmentation, leaks and plots was worsening rather than improving. It was subverting his premiership and placing the continuity of the Conservative government in jeopardy: 'All the optimism, all the shine of 1992 had long gone; there was no feeling that people were marshalling strength for a general election, which might come within a year; no sense of arming ourselves for the fight. Instead it was barely possible to turn on the radio or television without hearing someone discussing whether or not I would be challenged for the leadership of the party.'[1]

According to the prime minister, there were three options in addressing this problem. The first choice was to sit out the storm and prepare for a probable November leadership contest. In the meantime, the party might restore itself to unity and revive its appreciation of a prime minister dedicated to keeping the party together. The second choice was to resign from the premiership and allow the party to appoint a successor. The third option was to stand down as party leader and precipitate a leadership election at a time of the prime minister's own choosing. The latter course appealed to John Major, but carried a number of risks. Not the least of these was that he could be defeated, or forced out either by a 'stalking horse' challenge, or else by a large abstention rate that would allow senior figures to compete for the leadership in the second and succeeding ballots. Despite the uncertainties, Major opted to bring the election forward by five months.

When the prime minister unexpectedly resigned from the leadership, he did so on the basis of calculation. By forcing the issue out into the open and opting for a quick election, Major believed that he would save the party precious extra time to regroup for a general election without the distraction of a summer and an autumn of internecine factionalism. He also recognised the tactical value of surprise in his choice of action. He would be seen as having taken the initiative and to have created a challenge to those whose campaigns had not yet matured into organisations capable of competing with a prime minister for parliamentary support. Injustice was another factor in the decision. Major remained aggrieved that despite winning the 1992 general election against the odds, he felt that he had not been accorded the same degree of respect that his recent predecessors had enjoyed. He still sensed that he was treated as if he were an interim prime minister positioned between Margaret Thatcher and another party heavyweight waiting to assume the crown from the caretaker figure of John Major. To him, the level of insubordination he had to endure had been discourteous and unwarranted. To the extent that this had been fuelled by or exploited by clandestine leadership rivals, then Major's dramatic challenge would serve to incommode them by forcing them prematurely out into the open, or by humbling them into silent retreat. Finally, personal exasperation also played a significant part in the prime minister's decision.

The daily difficulties of leadership had become a permanent distraction to the prime minister and to the public at large. The position was exacerbated by the fact that the public strains of leading the Conservative party occurred at precisely the time when Tony Blair was consolidating his position and the New Labour project within the Labour party. Major was infuriated that the leader of the opposition had in his view been given an easy ride in the media both directly in terms of supportive interest and indirectly by the concentrated attention given to Conservative divisions, splits and speculations over the leadership. The public disarray within the Conservative party amounted to a constant distraction to the leader's time and energies. Because of it, Major had lost opportunities to attack the New Labour leadership and to make political capital over the revision of Clause IV. Opportunities to publicise government plans and achievements, and to establish a clearly defined position on policy, had also been squandered by the continual references to the plight and performance of the Tory leadership. Major found this to be personally debilitating. He remarked at the time on the role that exasperation had played in the decision to step down.

> What was really in my mind was the sheer frustration that for weeks we had tried to set a proper political agenda, and that political agenda was just being drowned out by this background noise ... The cacophony was deafening, so I was very fed up ... There is a great deal of malevolent political chatter that is complete nonsense. The trouble with professional politicians is that a high amount of ignorant nonsense is traded as commonsense.[2]

Later, he would recall that the thankless task of trying to hold the party together was becoming so 'intolerable to me personally'[3] that if someone else could do it then he or she should be given the opportunity to do so: 'I decided to give the parliamentary party the opportunity to replace me, taking from my shoulders the responsibility of keeping the Conservative Party together.'[4]

Major's short speech of resignation to the press in the Downing Street garden echoed all the constituent components of what was a highly unconventional course of action. He pointed out that he had been prime minister for nearly five years and that over the past three years he had been 'opposed by a small minority'[5] in the party. He implicitly linked this source of dissent to the phenomenon of 'repeated threats of a leadership election'.[6] In the event, no challenge had ever materialised, but still the destabilising rumours of an imminent leadership challenge had persisted. He complained that the 'same thing [was] happening in 1995'[7] and asserted that this time action needed to be taken: 'I am not prepared to see the party I care for laid out on the rack like this any longer.'[8] In order to 'remove the uncertainty',[9] Major announced that he had resigned as Conservative party leader and as a consequence a leadership election would have to take place. He made it clear that he would be a candidate in the ensuing election:

> If I win, I shall continue as prime minister and lead the party into and through the next election. Should I be defeated, which I do not expect, I shall resign as prime minister and offer my successor my full support. The Conservative Party must make its choice. Every leader is leader only with the support of his party. That is true of me as well. That is why I am no longer prepared to tolerate the present situation. In short, it is time to put up or shut up.[10]

In a private meeting with executive officers of the 1922 Committee prior to his public declaration, the prime minister was even more succinct: 'If I win I expect the party to behave itself ... If I lose, so be it.'[11]

Scenarios, calculations and projections

At the outset, Major achieved his immediate objective of surprise. He had seized the initiative from his critics and prompted a leadership contest on his terms and at a time that suited his purposes. The boldness of the prime minister's stroke was quickly acknowledged by the Conservative press, which, like the Conservative parliamentary party, had also been caught off guard. The *Daily Express*, in a front-page splash entitled 'So who says he's wet now?'[12] reported that the prime minister had in one stroke confounded those 'critics who claimed he lacked courage or leadership qualities'.[13] The editorial was even more glowing:

> John Major said that he would one day surprise us all by dictating his own political destiny. He has proved as good as his word. His decision to relinquish the Tory helm to precipitate a leadership contest is a gamble. But this is not the most outstanding aspect of his decision. It is the boldness. In one daring move, the prime minister has confirmed all the qualities of shrewdness and toughness that friends knew lurked beneath that apparently grey and cautious exterior, but which have rarely been evident in public.[14]

The *Daily Mail* was more guarded but acknowledged that when the prime minister 'sensationally quit as party leader' Major had 'finally roared his defiance at the Tory critics'.[15] The *Daily Telegraph* accepted that the resignation amounted to a 'powerful surprise not least to those Tories who were planning a long campaign to unseat him in November'.[16] *The Times* agreed that Major had staged a 'coup de theatre' in the Downing Street garden, which rose to the level of 'a drama'.[17] The *Sunday Times* was left in no doubt that the prime minister had done something wholly unexpected: 'John Major has mounted the most dramatic challenge in British politics since Margaret Thatcher declared war on the Tory establishment 20 years ago. His demand that the Conservative party re-elect him leader without delay or fight the next election under new management is electrifyingly bold. We are witnessing an attempted prime ministerial coup'.[18]

Notwithstanding the effectiveness of the prime minister's stage management in resigning from the leadership, both he and those who professionally analysed his actions were acutely aware that this move represented an enormous gamble on his part. In many ways, the resignation was an act of public humiliation in which the prime minister openly conceded that he could not control his own party. It was an admission of weakness. Courage in these circumstances could be construed as 'courage born of desperation' after having been 'tormented beyond endurance'.[19] The risks that were generated by placing the leadership in such an exposed position were considerable.

- Major could lose the initiative and be defeated. This would lead to political turmoil, a vote of no confidence, and a general election held in conditions wholly unfavourable to the Conservative party.
- The process of leadership selection could become prolonged and further undermine public confidence in the Tories' will and competence to govern. Labour could press for a vote of no confidence and trigger a general election and political defeat for the Conservative party.
- Major might achieve a 'technical win', the marginal nature of which could deepen his leadership problems prompting the possibility of a cabinet revolt.
- Major might be replaced by a right-winger like Michael Portillo producing an immediate split in the party.
- Major might be replaced by a progressive pro-European candidate like Michael Heseltine who would also divide the party.
- In order to win, Major might have to make concessions to the right wing on Europe and on public expenditure. Alternatively he could be forced to make accommodations to the left wing by relaxing fiscal and monetary constraints and by moving to a more pro-European position. Both courses of action threatened to destabilise the party and his role as a consensus-building leader.

A further risk that the prime minister would not have recognised as being a threat lay in the prospect of Major not being challenged at all. The prime minister probably hoped that he would be restored to the leadership, if not by acclamation, then at least by a general realisation that the party's interests were best served by his continued presence as the point of equilibrium. Major had calculated the difficulties of anyone challenging him in so short period for preparation, and in conditions where any successor would in all likelihood go down to defeat in a general election. By assuring himself of the support of all the key members of his cabinet, the prime minister's plan was to allow the party to give its judgement upon his record without ever having to campaign for support.

Commentators and analysts, however, were quick to point out that the logic of a leadership contest implied an element of competition and in this case the opposition should be as testing as possible. The demand that Major's challenge be taken up was particularly strident in many of those newspapers which were traditionally Conservative in their allegiances. For example, the *Sunday Telegraph* thought that a failure to challenge the prime minister would send out the wrong signal to the public on the state of the party: 'For now that he has chosen this unwise course, Mr Major must be challenged. The Conservative Party would lose public respect if it pretended to unanimity at such a juncture. The prime minister has decided to ask his MPs an important question, and they should give him an honest answer.'[20] The paper also thought that it was necessary to respond to Major's intention to seek re-election on the basis of his achievements as leader. In the view of the *Sunday Telegraph*, the prime minister's decision to stand on his record was in itself a sign of incompetence because it was precisely 'his record which [had] caused the trouble'.[21] As there were 'real doubts about his competence, his electability and his European policy', the paper believed that 'Mr Major deserve[d] to be challenged.'[22]

Peter Riddell in *The Times* observed that John Major needed a serious rather than a merely nominal challenger. In the absence of a real challenger, Major's campaign was already 'drifting' and 'the tactical initiative that Mr Major won' through his surprise resignation risked 'being lost'. 'In order to rally the waverers', Mr Major required 'someone he [could] portray as a real threat'.[23] Riddell claimed that party unity needed a strong visible opponent to the prime minister: 'Mr Major has to mobilise the mutual antagonisms of his possible successors. For that he needs a strong challenger now. The damage to Cabinet unity has already been done ... So he will be more convincingly able to claim a victory, however pyrrhic in the long term, if there is serious alternative than if the challenger is a nonentity.'[24] Simon Heffer in the *Daily Telegraph* also added his imprimatur to the proposition that the prime minister should be confronted in an actual leadership contest. He believed that the dissenting voices in the party needed to respond to the opportunity of a contest, in order to retain their legitimacy as internal critics: 'He has shrewdly taken the fight for the future of the Conservative Party back to his opponents; if they cannot find a candidate to run against him, their credibility will be shot to pieces until after the general election. It would be an admission that all the carping and hectoring of recent weeks and months had no underpinning of principle.'[25]

The absence of an immediate challenger reflected the fact that the political risks of a leadership contest were not confined to the prime minister. Those with leadership ambitions, and with the experience and parliamentary teams to support such objectives, had to be cautious in such circumstances. Serious challengers were only ever likely to emanate from the cabinet, and yet collective responsibility generated the expectation that cabinet ministers would support the prime minister – at least in the first round. It was also difficult for any senior figures to claim that their leadership would unite the party when their candidatures would almost invariably serve to exemplify party divisions. For Michael Heseltine, the charge of betrayal against Margaret Thatcher was sufficient to keep him from any sign of disloyalty against her successor. Michael Portillo was the rising star of the right but there was a widespread perception that he was not yet ready for the leadership. Portillo also had to consider the merits of waiting until after the next general election and for a less damaging leadership election in opposition. Moreover, like Heseltine, Portillo had already pledged himself to supporting the prime minister. The only way of minimising the personal damage of a leadership challenge and of securing a release from the prior commitments to prime ministerial loyalty would be a 'stalking horse' opponent to enter the first round. Such a device could act as a register of disaffection and an incitement to abstention, sufficient to cause the prime minister to withdraw from the process. This would allow the entry of other more serious contenders into the contest. In 1995 Barry Field and Norman Lamont were cited as possible stalking horse contenders. In the end, the challenge came from elsewhere. The ambiguity of the event was compounded rather than diminished by entry of a candidate who was neither a stalking horse nor one of the party heavyweights.

John Redwood's candidacy was unexpected. A little known and junior member of the cabinet, Redwood was an intellectual figure on the right wing of the party. He had been one of the very few cabinet ministers that Major had not been able to inform of his sudden intention to precipitate a leadership contest. After the prime minister's announcement, Redwood had been conspicuously out of contact until he too opted for the shock tactic of declaring his candidacy. Redwood made it clear that he had not entered the contest as a stalking horse. He was competing to win the leadership. Under the campaign slogan 'No Change; No Chance', Redwood launched his own manifesto. This was a mix of general statements on the need to cut taxation and reject outright all plans to abolish the pound, combined with populist gestures over the retention of local hospitals and the Royal Yacht *Britannia*.

Although it was generally acknowledged that Redwood would have very little chance of ever becoming leader, his candidacy injected real uncertainty into the eventual outcome. It generated a profusion of scenarios in which the disaffection of the Conservative party might be turned in a number of different directions. For example, supporters of Michael Heseltine could calculate that if Major was sufficiently damaged in the first round to withdraw from the contest, this would give their man one final chance of the leadership in the second round. In order to achieve such an outcome, there would have to be a sufficient number of Redwood votes, or abstentions, to force Major to stand down. Portillo supporters were faced with the same calculations. Both the Heseltine and Portillo teams were acutely aware of the danger of Redwood acquiring a first round momentum that could confound all expectations and see him propelled into the leadership in the same way that Edward Heath and Margaret Thatcher had been in 1965 and 1975 respectively.

In these circumstances, tactical voting could lead to a preferred outcome, but it could also lead to an outcome least favoured by those engaging in the practice. John Redwood supporters attempted to maximise the right-wing vote by claiming that Michael Heseltine supporters could not be relied upon to abstain and that Heseltine himself had already reached a pro-European accommodation with the John Major. By the same token, they encouraged the Heseltine team to vote for Redwood, in order to remove Major and to trigger a second ballot. The danger for the backers of both Heseltine and Portillo was that Redwood could act as a stalking horse for either team, but that in doing so he might succeed in outmanœuvring both sides. In sum, Redwood might become the beneficiary of a false consensus producing a leader that very few Conservatives had either envisaged or wanted.

The complexity was particularly aggravating for the right wing of the party. Its dissent had provoked the leadership contest. Two of its champions – Peter Lilley and Michael Portillo – had considered a challenge at this primary stage. Michael Portillo's team had even made contingency plans for a campaign headquarters. Multiple phone lines had already been installed in preparation. But both ministers pulled back from the brink. The Portillo team believed that it could afford to await the initial outcome, or even to delay a leadership challenge until after the general election. When it became evident that John Redwood's supporters were intent upon seizing the leadership of the Conservative right, divisions grew between them and backers of Portillo who had come to expect all right-wingers to rally around Portillo when the time was propitious to do so. The Redwood challenge demonstrated that such an assumption no longer held. In a section of the party that claimed to value the attachment to principle above that of expediency, Redwood's conspicuous courage in the face of a defiant prime minister provided a damaging contrast to the prudent caution of Portillo. John Redwood's political adviser Hywel Williams later observed that it was Redwood who had 'given focus and energy to the causes of Tory discontent'.[26] Moreover, it was Redwood who had for a brief period 'taken the political battle out of the nerveless hands of the profess-ional political class'.[27] To Williams, this represented a significant improvement on what Portillo had to offer to the party or to the public.

It was no idle boast ... for Redwood to respond to one question at a press conference that his chief intellectual influence was the British people. Portillo, by contrast, was the consummate professional politician bred within the bone of his Party's political machine. That accounted both for his appeal within his party and for a wider public suspicion. Redwood might not be the alternative, but he had shown that the British public found its political class arrogant, second-rate and stuffy – especially in its Conservative form.[28]

Whether John Major had foreseen this outcome or not, he certainly possessed a reputation for astute infighting and political gamesmanship. He may have been initially disappointed to be challenged for the leadership, but he was aware that there were advantages in having Redwood as a rival: 'I knew that if I was to have an opponent, he was the ideal one – beatable, Eurosceptic, and a Cabinet colleague whose defeat would settle things beyond doubt.'[29] In many respects, it was preferable to have a challenger if only to limit the damage that could be incurred by extensive abstentions. Any abstentions in a contest without a challenger would have been interpreted as a vote for anyone but John Major. Now dissenters would either have to vote for John Redwood, or else abstain in which case the parliamentary party would look even more divided and less likely to agree on a replacement for the prime minister.

Fighting leadership

The prime minister had a strong core of support. John Major also knew that it would be difficult for Redwood to become an ecumenical rallying point for diverse dissent and delayed ambition. Nevertheless, the incumbent was aware of the dangers of miscalculation and of the unpredictability of tactical voting. Many MPs wanted to wound Major to the extent of forcing a second round, but not to the extent of setting in motion a Redwood victory. Major also knew that the entire objective of prompting the contest was to achieve a vindication of his leadership and to increase his authority over the parliamentary party. The scale of the Redwood vote and the abstention rate would be highly significant in this respect. The view amongst analysts at the time was typified by the *Guardian's* assessment of how much registered disaffection the prime minister could withstand in the contest (Figure 6.1).[30]

In his autobiography, Major reveals that he had set himself a floor of 215 votes as the minimum level of support for him to continue as prime minister. For him, a minimal numerical win would be unacceptable in these circumstances: 'Unless I had a decent majority supporting me, I would have no true authority. Too many MPs would have openly shown their dissatisfaction. The party wouldn't bind. Better a new leader who might enjoy a fresh surge of goodwill and have no baggage from the recession or the disputes over Europe.'[31]

In order to achieve this minimum standard and surpass it, Major put to

Figure 6.1 Estimated implications of different voting distributions in the first ballot

Major	Redwood	Abstentions
250 plus	40	20–40

- PM vindicated! Home and dry until next election

Major	Redwood	Abstentions
230	35	65

- Should be safe provided he doesn't botch instant Cabinet reshuffle

Major	Redwood	Abstentions
210–230	30–35	60–80

- Touch and go whether Major survives as abstentions rise. Eased out in favour of new contestant

Major	Redwood	Abstentions
200	60	70

- Resignation looms within days as Cabinet grows restless. New contest

Major	Redwood	Abstentions
190 or less	60	80

- Major set to quit immediately.
  Heseltine/Portillo to join second ballot, Gillian Shephard as compromise?

Source: The Guardian (3 July 1995)

full use the campaigning resources of his position. For example, he pressured the 1922 Committee to review the rules on leadership challenges, in order to ensure that there would be no opportunity of another contest in November, or at any other time prior to the next general election. He drew on the support of the party's constituency associations, which reported a 90 per cent rate of support for the prime minister on the eve of the leadership ballot.[32] In addition, Major offered the prospect of a substantial cabinet reshuffle following the contest. Its scale and, therefore, its potential to appease either the left, or the right, or both wings of the party was further enhanced by the retirement of Douglas Hurd from the position of Foreign Secretary. The Secretary of State for Northern Ireland played his part by issuing a public warning over the way that criticism of the prime minister was threatening the peace process in Northern Ireland. Patrick Mayhew alluded to the need for 'a stable political base'[33] to continue the negotiations: 'The prospects for an enduring peace in Northern Ireland would be seriously damaged by instability at the top of British government.'[34] Mayhew warned that to 'throw him over' would be a 'tragic wayward act of panic'[35] with very serious repercussions: 'Much damage has already been done, but it can still be repaired. Any more of this commotion against the prime minister, however, and that may cease to be the case.'[36]

The main thrust of Major's case remained the danger of the unknown combined with the needlessness of change. He and his team defended the record of the government. Major drew attention to the centrality of his position as the balance wheel of the party and the person who could stave off a general election long enough for the economy to recover. His campaigners stressed the need for caution and warned against the counterproductive consequences of leadership experimentation. In their view, there would be no point in voting against Major if the only consequence would be to damage still further his authority as prime minister. This would undermine the party's efforts either in retaining power after the general election, or in limiting the size of the defeat in preparation for the party's return to government after a parliament in opposition. Major's team pointed out to the Eurosceptics that anything, which jeopardised the security of the government, would make the election of a Labour government even more likely, and with it an administration more sympathetic to the European Union. If the threat of a New Labour government was insufficient, Major's supporters relied upon the prospect of an internal civil war should either Heseltine or Portillo be elected leader.

John Major could also point to the opinion polls for comfort. A MORI/ *Times* poll on June 29 showed that the leadership contest had boosted support for both Major and the Conservatives to their highest levels for two years.[37] A MORI/*Economist* poll revealed that Tory loyalists clearly favoured Major over Redwood. In response to the question of whether the candidates boosted or damaged the Conservative party, Redwood's score was −13 (i.e. the percentage boost minus the percentage damage) while Major was ranked as +53 per cent. The same poll confirmed that in a general election with Redwood as leader, the Conservatives would suffer an adverse swing of a further 2.5 per cent to that which they would be projected to experience under Major. The additional swing was equated to an expected loss of a further 64 Conservative seats (i.e. to a total parliamentary representation of just 79 seats).[38] In an ICM/*Daily Express* poll, the following question was posed: 'Putting aside your party preferences, who would you most like to see as Conservative Party leader?' The result again revealed a clear preference amongst Conservative identifiers for Major (52 per cent) over Redwood (15 per cent). In the electorate as a whole, Major (36 per cent) was shown to be more popular than Redwood (11 per cent) by a factor of three to one.[39]

Notwithstanding these impressive levels of comparative support, John Major's position was not as secure as it initially appeared. First, although the leadership election had raised the level of Conservative support, that level remained at a conspicuously low level. The MORI/*Times* poll, for example,

Figure 6.2 Projected electoral effect of candidates and possible contenders (1) (% swing to Tories from current voting intentions)

Q: How would you vote if there was a general election tomorrow under these leaders?

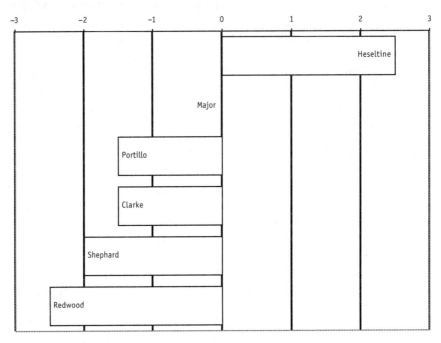

Source: MORI/*Economist* (1 July 1995)

showed a 7 per cent increase in Conservative support, which lifted the level from 22 to 29 per cent. In similar vein, those satisfied with Major's performance as prime minister also rose by 7 points from 21 to 28 per cent, but this had to be put in the context of a dissatisfaction rating of 64 per cent.[40] Second, sudden boosts of support in such circumstances could often be a reflection of increased publicity. When news agendas returned to their customary priorities, the enhanced support levels might well be shown to be soft and unsustainable. Third, when the polls widened the choice available to respondents, then Major's position was not so impregnable as it appeared in the head-to-head competition with John Redwood. For example, in the MORI/*Economist* poll on voting intentions under different leaderships (Figure 6.2), Major's lead over Redwood (i.e. 2.5 points) was the same margin as the prime minister's deficit in relation to Michael Heseltine.[41] Fifty-two Conservative MPs who would have lost their seats under Major could be expected to save them under a Heseltine leadership. A Gallup/*Sunday Telegraph* poll on the weekend prior to the Tuesday vote asked who, in the event of a second ballot and with an injection of new candidates, would make the better Conservative party leader (Table 6.1). The result again showed a clear preference for Michael Heseltine.[42]

Table 6.1 Second ballot preferences (%)

Q: In the event of a second ballot, with more people involved, which of these do you think would make the better leader of the Conservative party and prime minister?

Kenneth Clarke	8
Michael Heseltine	25
John Major	17
Michael Portillo	11
John Redwood	7
Gillian Shephard	6
None of these	26

Source: Gallup/*Sunday Telegraph* (2 July 1995)

An ICM/*Daily Express* poll, which had reported Major as having a 36–11 per cent preponderance over John Redwood in the voter preferences for the position of Conservative Party leader, also revealed a more ambiguous picture in the detailed polling of personal characteristics (Table 6.2).[43]

Table 6.2 Public assessments of personal characteristics (%)

Q: Which politicians do you think have the following qualities?

	Major	Heseltine	Portillo	Clarke	Redwood
Tough	20	**41**	23	23	16
Extreme	6	20	**32**	15	30
In touch with ordinary people	**36**	15	7	10	16
Arrogant	13	30	**41**	28	26
Charismatic	11	**36**	21	5	11
Capable	**48**	39	22	20	23
Caring	**50**	14	4	8	10
A vote winner	**35**	**35**	14	6	14

Note: Highest rankings in bold
Source: ICM/*Daily Express* (4 July 1995)

Here Heseltine was level with Major in voter appeal. But he was ahead on charisma and toughness at a time when political commentary and discussion were placing a premium upon such attributes. But perhaps the most disturbing results came in that part of the MORI/*Economist* poll, which addressed which of the candidates boosted or damaged Conservative prospects (Table 6.3). When the respondent sample was widened to include 'all voters', Michael Heseltine was shown to have a lead of 32 points over the prime minister.[44] John Major had other reasons to be disconcerted by this poll. It revealed another weakness in a key sector of public support – namely those who had voted Conservative in the 1992 general election but who no longer intended to support the party in the next general election. It was this cohort of voters upon whom Conservative recovery was most dependent. Their responses to the question of which candidates helped or hindered party prospects demonstrated a disturbing hostility to John Major.

Table 6.3 Projected electoral effect of candidates and possible contenders (2) (% boost minus % damage)

Q: On balance, do the following boost or damage the Conservative party?

	All voters	Tory loyalists*	Ex-Tories**
Heseltine	+25	+38	+24
Shephard	+9	+21	+5
Lang	−4	+7	−4
Redwood	−7	−13	+6
Major	−8	+53	−30
Clarke	−8	+17	−10
Rifkind	−9	+14	−17
Howard	−12	+16	+7
Portillo	−13	+9	−17

* Those voting Tory at 1992 general election and intending to vote Tory at the next election
** Those voting Tory at 1992 general election but who no longer intend to vote Tory
Source: MORI/*Economist* (1 July 1995)

In this section of the poll, the prime minister was registered behind every one of the nine named senior figures including John Redwood by 36 points and Michael Heseltine by an alarming 54 points.

A fourth source of concern for Major lay in the open hostility of much of the conservative press. Columnists and leader writers had already had extensive experience of analysing the failures of John Major's premiership. Now they drew upon their own prior judgements to reach a conclusion which, in most instances, was one of condemnation and the need for change. Andrew

Neil in the *Sunday Times* typified the approach of many in his response to Major's assertion that his record as prime minister would constitute a manifesto for his leadership campaign. To Neil, it was precisely Major's record in government that was the problem.

> [T]here is nothing in Mr Major's make-up or track record to suggest he has the ability to re-invent himself or his government. The hallmark of the Major years has been a squandering of the Thatcher legacy and even his own surprise election victory in 1992 ... His has been a government ... that has lurched from folly to gaffe to crisis, buffeted by events beyond its control under a limp leadership that has allowed squabbling nonentities to fill the vacuum left by an absence of firm government ... The Tory party is in dire need of a prime minister who offers a fresh start, new inspiration and strong, determined leadership.[45]

The Times alluded to the prime minister's claim that he called the election to clear the air. But in the paper's opinion, were he to win, the 'air [would] be more acrid still'.[46] He could have taken the opportunity to alleviate some of the problems of party management, but he had failed to do so. A vote for Major, therefore, was a 'vote for disunity and defeat'.[47] It was the prime minister who had 'divided his party and lost election after election'.[48] As a result, there would be 'no escape route without a new leader'.[49]

The Times was also noteworthy for providing the platform for William Rees-Mogg's long-standing indictment of John Major's leadership. In the columnist's view, the prime minister's decision to call a leadership election, combined with the standard of his subsequent campaign, had succeeded merely in exposing the deficiencies of his leadership to the full. The election would not 'resolve the question of John Major's temperamental weakness as a leader' or 'his underlying weakness ... in the direction of national policy'.[50] Under Major's leadership, 'British policy ha[d] been adrift during his five years in Downing Street'.[51] For Major to stand on his record and to decide 'not to make any new policy statement to justify his re-election' meant in effect that he was 'a candidate without a manifesto'[52] and therefore a leader offering no strategic direction for the country. In Rees-Mogg's view, to re-elect him under these circumstances would be a pointless act of blind faith that would not make any contribution to resolving the serious policy disputes within the party: 'The country does not know where the Conservative government is heading.'[53] If Conservative MPs were to elect John Redwood, then the position would at last be clear and the 'Conservatives would have some real chance of winning'.[54]

There was to be no respite for Major in either the *Daily Telegraph* or the *Sunday Telegraph*. For example Simon Heffer in the *Daily Telegraph* asserted that it would be in the party's best interests if it failed to rally behind the leader's call for a vote of confidence: 'The evidence of Mr Major's weaknesses is plentiful; the concatenation of crises and scandals ever since the summer of 1992, when the pound came under pressure in the ERM, have shown him to be a poor prime minister ... It would be best for his party, in my view, if it replaced him now, for there is nothing to suggest that he will govern more effectively in the future.'[55] On the day of the vote, the *Daily Telegraph* editorial was unambiguously against the continuation of John Major in office:

> The business of government may be carried on for another year or 18 months, but every poll and statistic suggests that an administration led by John Major would have an appointment with the undertaker by 1997. A new leader might indeed find the party ungovernable, might even find himself forced into an early general election by lack of a Commons majority. But he would open the possibility of a sea-change, a revival in Tory fortunes ... It is time for Major to go, and give another leader the opportunity to save the Tories, not least from their own divisions.[56]

The *Sunday Telegraph* could offer little relief with references to 'real doubts about his competence' and to his increasing incapacity of 'settling the issue that splits his party, or leading his government and his country'. The paper conceded that history would probably be kinder to Major than his critics had been, 'but it [was] nevertheless to history that he should be consigned'.[57] It was not merely that *The Times*, the *Sunday Times*, the *News of the World*, the *Daily Telegraph*, the *Sunday Telegraph*, the *Daily Mail*, *The Sun*, all adopted positions against Major in the leadership election,[58] it was that they did so without knowing who his likely successor might be. In effect, it was an indictment against Major to the extent of implying that any replacement at any cost would be preferable to the prime minister's remaining in office.

John Major was clearly vulnerable as the day of the vote approached. He knew it would be difficult to continue as leader and prime minister if a third of the parliamentary party voted against him or abstained. He was aware that the rank and file Conservative supporter had not been sufficient to save the leaderships of Edward Heath in 1975, or Margaret Thatcher in 1990. John Redwood would not win the contest, or at least not on the first ballot, but his support was sufficient for Major to make a number of overtures to the right prior to the vote. For example, he made it known unofficially that he would promote a leading right-winger to the post of foreign secretary; rule out participation in a European single currency in 1999; commit the government to a referendum if it were ever to propose abolishing the pound; and put in place immediate measures to cut income tax.[59]

The prime minister's final plea came in an article on the eve of the poll. In it, Major played on the fear of the unknown by issuing a dire warning to the party: 'The Conservative Party has looked into the abyss. Tomorrow, it has a clear choice. It can jump into the abyss. Or it can finish this business and get on with working for a better future for our country and turn the spotlight on Labour.'[60] The abyss referred to by Major meant a result that could unleash a civil war within the party and lead to the destruction of any hopes of electoral victory either then or in the foreseeable future. *The Times* for one was unimpressed by the scare tactic. The paper concluded that John Major represented something of an abyss himself. At the eleventh hour, it sought to reverse the metaphor back onto to the prime minister: 'Now, when Tory MPs are offered a new escape route, they are threatened with a new abyss', but in effect there was 'no escape route without a new leader'. Front page splashes in the *Daily Mail* ('Time to ditch the captain'[61]) and in *The Sun* ('On your bike John'[62]) sought to convey the message in more succinct terms.

A victory of sorts

In the event, Conservative MPs as a whole did not choose the abyss. The prime minister was returned as leader in the first ballot.

John Major	218
John Redwood	89
Abstentions	8
Spoilt Ballots	12

Despite securing an outright win, it was clear that a substantial minority of the party had indeed chosen the abyss. Major had publicly lost the support of a third of his colleagues and had only exceeded his private threshold of 215 by three votes. He was relieved that the gamble had paid off but it was not an emphatic reaffirmation. In his words, it was 'less than I had hoped for, but more than I feared. It was a "grey area".'[63]

On the one hand, Major's position had been strengthened and his leadership was now secure at least until the next general election. As members of the cabinet and his campaign team rushed to hail the victory and guide perceptions of a decisive deployment of prime ministerial authority, Major could prepare for his grand restructuring of the cabinet through which he would reinvent his government. On the other hand, the position of the dissidents in the party, especially on the right, had also been improved. Their mobilising force had been visibly demonstrated. They had a new champion in the form of John Redwood. They also had justifiable expectations that the prime minister would now have to defer to the right in policy and personnel. As the prime minister asserted that there would be no recriminations and that the party could unify now that the poison had been drawn, the contest had in fact legitimated an open and explicit hostility to Major and his team. In effect, the leadership competition had ensured that the disaffection would continue and would do so with uninhibited vigour. Now that the leadership was no longer in question, dissidents could not be accused of attempting to bring down the leader. For all practicable purposes, Major was no longer removable.

The ambiguity of the result was compounded by a number of other contradictions. For example, the dramatised nature of the prime minister's resignation and subsequent claims for renewal and change sat uneasily with the prosaic nature of his campaign that implied either no change or an unarticulated change that would become apparent after the contest. Another disjunction was evident between the apparent boldness of the measure and the objectives implied in the manner of its implementation. On the one hand were the positive and proactive characteristics associated with a leader engaged in an electoral ordeal of his own choosing. On the other hand was the reactive and defensive nature of the prime minister's conduct during the campaign when the main aim became one of neutralising other potential leaders in the party. A tension also existed between the gravity and long-term implications of a leadership election at that time, and the abrupt nature of its inception together with the brevity of the campaign. A process of reflection, renewal and restored unity was identified as necessary, but it was followed up with a deliberately abbreviated campaign in order to maximise the chances of the prime minister's survival.

A further contradiction was apparent in the contrast between the public character of Major's exposed appeals for support and the private brokering and clandestine accommodations that secured victory. In part, when a process of leadership selection is limited to MPs it ensures that support is always to some extent developed by private negotiation and coalition building. Notwithstanding this characteristic, Major had a reputation for manipulative scheming which the leadership election of 1995 did little to diminish. After the result was announced, rumours swept Westminster that the prime minister had been saved by a group of about twenty supporters of Michael Heseltine who had made a late switch from abstention to John Major. Heseltine had had a long meeting with Major on the morning of 4 July – the day of the first ballot. In his autobiography, Major strenuously refutes that any deal took place that secured Heseltine's support in exchange for becoming deputy prime minister with a base in the Cabinet Office and chairmanships of several cabinet committees. Major insists that a meeting with Michael Heseltine prior to the leadership contest had already established the principle of the change in his responsibilities. According to Major, any discussions regarding Heseltine's promotion related to the earlier meeting and not to events unfolding at Westminster. Many MPs found this very difficult to take at face value. A simple deal was widely assumed to have occurred once Major's canvassers confirmed that the prime minister was short of votes. Norman Lamont's view is that the prime minister's arrangement with Heseltine was far more manipulative than a simple deal: 'I suspect that the prime minister used his subtle personal skills to finesse Michael Heseltine out of the contest without him ever realising it. By offering him the post of Deputy Prime Minister some time before he told him there was going to be a leadership election, he had locked him in to supporting him. The only way Michael could ever become leader was by being totally loyal to Michael.'[64] However accurate or inaccurate such deductions were, John Major's victory was pervaded by suspicions of tactical gamesmanship that undermined his claims of strategic leadership.

Out of this profusion of contradictions, probably the most significant tension lay in the arguably illogical nature of Major's decision to precipitate a leadership election at all. In resigning, Major complained of previous threats to his leadership, which had proved to be 'phoney' and the factional specula- tions of a 'small minority'. The extreme nature of his action did not seem proportionate to his own reasons for the news of a leadership election: '[I]f all this is true, why pay much attention to it? And if it is not true, why take the risk of proving its untruth?'[65] Underlying the episode was a paradox of leadership – namely a leader in a position of weakness embarking upon a course of corrective action, which would have the effect of exposing the very weakness at the centre of the problem. By making leadership the centrepiece issue, Major reaffirmed that it was his leadership, which amounted to being at one and the same time both the problem and the solution. Forcing a leadership election was a sign of a lack of leadership resources, which was unlikely to be reversed simply by prevailing in a contested election. The state of the Major premiership reflected deeply rooted problems in the party that were not susceptible to the easy fix of a re-elected leader.

John Major hoped that by calling a leadership election and prevailing in the subsequent competition, he would provide a technical solution to the short- term problems of his leadership and, through this, a resolution to the electoral problems of the party. But the party was too fragmented on principles and convictions to be united around a damaged leader offering the remote possibility of electoral security. In this context, it was very unlikely that the party would bind together around the prospect of more of the same – namely a continued succession of highly contested party positions portrayed by the leader as consensus-inducing balances. To John Major, parliamentary divi- sions were almost frivolous compared to the *fundamenta* of party unity and electoral security. But to many in the party, Major's excursion into leadership solutions was equally superficial in its disregard for genuinely held differences on policy and strategy. In such a context, Major's choice of an agency of party integration appeared to be wholly insufficient to achieve its objectives. If calling a leadership election was a sign of a lack of leadership, then winning it by a calculation of divide and rule was equally an indication of a leadership in name only. The exposure of Major's predicament would not and did not resolve the problems inherent in such a leadership.

This theme of a 'no win' leadership was repeatedly alluded to and analysed in numerous reports following Major's success on 4 July. Simon Heffer, for example, remained thoroughly unconvinced by the nature of the prime minister's victory: 'Mr Major will lapse once more into indecision, procrastination and prevarication. Malcontents (and not just the 111 who did not vote for him yesterday) will mumble about him being back in his old ways.'[66] The leadership contest had merely denied the dissidents of any salvation for the rest of the parliament. 'Nothing, except the votes of the British people at the ballot box, can remove him from office. MPs have had their chance, and chose not to take it.'[67] *The Sun* concluded that Major had 'achieved nothing with this mid-summer madness'[68] other than to reveal the size of the dissent against him: 'What else would the Grey Man do but saddle his party with a grey result? … Major said he wanted the leadership election to clear the air. Instead it has left a nasty smell still hanging there.'[69] Simon Jenkins described the challenge facing the prime minister as 'nothing less than the wholescale reconstruction of a shattered administration, and a fairly shattered party'.[70] In Jenkins' view, this amounted to a 'giant task of leadership, the lack of which was the central charge against Mr Major in the contest. The charge stuck, indeed was validated by the contest itself.'[71] *The Times* reacted strongly against Major's description of his victory as 'clear cut'.[72] The paper agreed that it was 'clear cut but only in the sense that a forest is "clear cut" by loggers: The Tory landscape is littered by broken stumps and will remain so for years'.[73]

The leadership issue may have been settled for the duration of the parliament, but very little else had been resolved. The boost in the ratings for the government, the Conservative party and the prime minister did not herald a long-term recovery (see Figure 7.1 on p. 160). Major continued to run ahead of his party but more on the basis of the least worst leadership option. In this way, the 1995 leadership contest revealed the depth of the Conservatives' leadership crisis. Major's ratings as prime minister continued to be very low but they remained higher than the government's own level of approval. The former continued to be viewed by commentators and analysts to be more a consequence, rather than a cause, of the latter.[74] The Conservative party still harboured hopes that a new leader would reverse its fortunes but the leadership contest demonstrated that in contrast to 1990, no alternative leader had the potential to secure an electoral recovery. The Conservatives were locked in with a leader who not only characterised but exemplified leadership failure. Major's continuation in the premiership underlined the Conservatives' systemic failure to replace him with anyone who might draw the party out of its public obsession with leadership dysfunction.

The leadership contest also gave graphic illustration of the extraordinary lengths to which a leader would go not merely to maintain the leadership but to enhance its internal and public reputation. In Major's own judgement, it was necessary to test himself against other potential or actual claimants to his position. It was not possible for him to carry on as a leader without this public and private review. The problem for Major was that in flagging up the pivotal significance of leadership, he raised the stakes of the leadership contest and what it could achieve. By winning unconvincingly, he effectively held the leadership issue in stasis until after the general election. His chief rivals were now effectively ingested into the Major administration for the duration of the parliament. Michael Heseltine had become deputy prime minister in charge of policy presentation and media relations. Michael Portillo also suffered from mixed fortunes. He had been promoted to the one post he had always coveted – namely the Secretary of State for Defence. But he had lost ground within the party. To many, John Redwood was the only beneficiary of the contest. He was now the talisman of the right. Moreover, from his position on the backbenches, he was liberated from government responsibilities and collective inhibitions. Michael Portillo's position was at once both enhanced and also diminished. *The Times* concluded that he was now trapped: '[I]f he is content to serve on under a prime minister he so recently intended to fight, his claim on the high ground of politics, pointedly made over the past twelve months, cannot so easily be made again. He will have to serve in a cabinet which is predominantly hostile to his views. He will be less able to dissent – even in code.'[75] In addition to being trapped, Portillo was also relatively more isolated after a cabinet reshuffle that was widely seen to have been a rebuff to the right: 'The right believed that their labours and votes had served Major, and that he had now betrayed them.'[76] Major had raised their expectations, but had not fulfilled them.

The leadership election did not foster the tranquility which Major had hoped for. It reaffirmed that leadership was a central issue and an integral requirement of political engagement, but the election had not provided the sweeping endorsement that Major needed to give his leadership renewed authority. As the prime minister was later to acknowledge, the achievements wrought by the election were largely negative in substance: 'It was probably decisive in saving my leadership, for to have drifted on into the autumn, at the mercy of speculation about when my enemies would spring a contest on me (as opposed to my springing one on them), could hardly have added to the 218 votes I received in July. I firmly believe that my re-election as leader postponed – and, I hope, saved the party from – an irrevocable split over European policy.'[77] Once again, John Major was placed in a position where he had to underline what his leadership had averted rather than what it had gained. His position within the party was now more secure than it had been. He was free at last to turn his attention fully towards the Labour party and in particular to his main tormentor and chief adversary. The 1995 Conservative leadership election ensured that the collision course between Major and Blair would continue on track and reach a point of culmination. But before the climax of the next general election lay nearly two years of sustained campaigning that would centre upon the merits of the two leaders and on the value of political leadership for effective government.

Notes

1 John Major, *The Autobiography* (London: HarperCollins, 1999), p. 609.
2 Quoted in 'Ready to fight for his political life', John Major interviewed by Robert Preston, *Financial Times*, 1 July 1995.
3 Major, *The Autobiography*, p. 616.
4 Major, *The Autobiography*, p. 616.
5 Resignation speech, *Daily Telegraph*, 23 June 1995.
6 Resignation speech, *Daily Telegraph*, 23 June 1995.
7 Resignation speech, *Daily Telegraph*, 23 June 1995.
8 Resignation speech, *Daily Telegraph*, 23 June 1995.
9 Resignation speech, *Daily Telegraph*, 23 June 1995.
10 Resignation speech, *Daily Telegraph*, 23 June 1995.
11 Major, *The Autobiography*, p. 625.
12 'So who says he's wet now?' *Daily Express*, 23 June 1995.
13 'So who says he's wet now?'
14 'Why the Tory Party must rally around this courageous man', *Daily Express*, 23 June 1995.
15 David Hughes and John Deans, 'Major's great gamble', *Daily Mail,* 23 June 1995.
16 'Shock tactic', *Daily Telegraph*, 23 June 1995.
17 'Coup de Theatre', *The Times,* 23 June 1995.
18 'A brave start', *Sunday Times*, 25 June 1995.
19 'Last chance for the Tories', *Daily Mail*, 23 June 1995.
20 'Who governs Britain?' *Sunday Telegraph*, 25 June 1995.
21 'Who governs Britain?'
22 'Who governs Britain?'
23 Peter Riddell, 'The challenger Major needs', *The Times*, 26 June 1995.
24 Riddell, 'The challenger Major needs'.
25 Simon Heffer, 'John Major is right to fight but he ought to go', *Daily Telegraph*, 23 June 1995.
26 Hywel Williams, *Guilty Men: Conservative Decline and Fall 1992–1997* (London: Aurum,1998), p. 119.
27 Williams, *Guilty Men*, p. 119.
28 Williams, *Guilty Men*, p. 119.
29 Major, *The Autobiography*, p. 633.
30 *The Guardian*, 3 July 1995.
31 Major, *The Autobiography*, p. 643.
32 See Philip Webster, 'Major fights to win over the waverers', *The Times*, 3 July 1995.
33 Patrick Mayhew, 'Why he is the best man for the job', *Daily Telegraph*, 29 June 1995.
34 Mayhew, 'Why he is the best man for the job'.
35 Mayhew, 'Why he is the best man for the job'.
36 Patrick Mayhew, letter to *The Times*, 22 June 1995.
37 *The Times*, 29 June 1995.
38 *The Economist*, 1 July 1995.

39 *Daily Express,* 4 July 1995.

40 *The Times,* 29 June 1995.

41 *The Economist,* 1 July 1995.

42 *Sunday Telegraph,* 2 July 1995.

43 *Daily Express,* 4 July 1995.

44 *The Economist,* 1 July 1995.

45 Andrew Neil, 'Don't flunk it – Major is a loser and must go', *Sunday Times,* 25 June 1995.

46 'Change or decay', *The Times,* 3 July 1995.

47 'Change or decay'.

48 'Major's abyss', *The Times,* 4 July 1995.

49 'Major's abyss'.

50 William Rees-Mogg, 'Ahead but still adrift', *The Times,* 23 June 1995.

51 Rees-Mogg, 'Ahead but still adrift'.

52 Rees-Mogg, 'Ahead but still adrift'.

53 Rees-Mogg, 'Ahead but still adrift'.

54 William Rees-Mogg, 'The revolution Major should but cannot stop', *The Times,* 3 July 1995.

55 Simon Heffer, 'John Major is right to fight but he ought to go', *Daily Telegraph,* 23 July 1995.

56 'Time for a change of leadership', *Daily Telegraph,* 3 July 1995.

57 'A vote for change', *Sunday Telegraph,* 2 July 1995.

58 Only the *Mail on Sunday,* the *Evening Standard,* and the *Express* newspapers remained loyal to the leadership.

59 See David Wastell and Toby Helm, 'Major in last-minute ditch to woo Right', *Sunday Telegraph,* 2 July 1995.

60 *Daily Telegraph,* 3 July 1995.

61 *Daily Mail,* 4 July 1995.

62 *The Sun,* 1 July 1995.

63 Major, *The Autobiography,* p. 645.

64 Norman Lamont, *In Office* (London: Warner, 2000), p. 446.

65 'Who governs Britain', *Sunday Telegraph,* 25 June 1995.

66 Simon Heffer, 'Only one way to heal wounds', *Daily Telegraph,* 5 July 1995.

67 Heffer, 'Only one way to heal wounds'.

68 'Chickens hand it to Blair', *The Sun,* 5 July 1995.

69 'Chickens hand it to Blair'.

70 Simon Jenkins, 'Now for the hard part', *The Times,* 5 July 1995.

71 Jenkins, 'Now for the hard part'.

72 'The Real Victor', *The Times,* 5 July 1995.

73 'The Real Victor'.

74 This outlook reflected a judgement that had become established since 1994. See John Curtice, 'Failures that will outlast a change of face', *The Independent,* 6 April 1994; Ivor Crewe, 'Sacking leaders cuts no ice with voters', *The Observer,* 10 April 1994; Anthony King, 'Better the PM you know', *Daily Telegraph,* 11 June 1994; Anthony King, 'Dropping Major may hit Tory election chances', *Daily Telegraph,* 12 May 1995.

75 'The Real Victor', *The Times.*

76 Anthony Seldon, *Major: A Political Life* (London: Phoenix, 1997), p. 590.

77 Major, *The Autobiography,* pp. 646–7.

7 The long presidential campaign

Head to head: John Major

The prime minister's leadership problems were already well established prior to the death of John Smith. When the Labour leader died, the *Sunday Telegraph* commented acidly that the plight of the two parties were comparable: 'At present the Labour Party has no leader, and the Conservative Party acts as if it had none. Labour's contest should help to fill the Tory vacuum as well.'[1] Major was already besieged by a party and a government in turmoil. Splits on Europe, taxation and the sphere of the state were compounded by an eroding majority of seats, the positioning of rival leaders, a profusion of leaks and the continual ridiculing of the prime minister as weak, ineffectual and gauche. These problems were considerable but they were not as significant as the emergence of Tony Blair as the new Labour leader. At a stroke, Blair appeared to exacerbate all his other difficulties. Blair's youth and good looks, his style, media appeal and articulate evangelism immediately placed the prime minister at a disadvantage. In 1990, John Major had been the youthful option. At that point he had the distinction of being the youngest prime minister of the twentieth century. He had injected new blood into the party and effectively rejuvenated the government. Now, within four years, he was confronted by an opposition leader ten years his junior and one who was making his party and his administration look grey, outmoded and worn out. At the very time when Major needed to redeploy his own claims to innovation and fresh beginnings in order to resuscitate the party, Blair suddenly appeared to trump Major's credentials and decisively assign the prime minister to the properties of his own caricature.

John Major was deeply resentful of Tony Blair. On a personal level, he found him uncongenial and distant. Initially, the new leader had caught the prime minister off guard. Blair's rise had been so fast that Major was unsettled by the lack of previous personal contact with the new Labour leader. In parliament's 'clubland', the two men had been strangers to one another. Now they were expected to form a working relationship. Party leaders not only have to attend a profusion of public events, but are required to meet privately to discuss issues of state on Privy Council terms. With John Smith these private meetings were often relaxed social occasions, accompanied at times by glasses of whiskey and good humour. Meetings with Blair, however, were far less sociable and were more in the nature of formal briefings. It was reported that Major found Blair to be cold, clipped and supercilious.

It is likely that the prime minister's personal distaste for the Labour leader was fuelled by another cause of resentment. Major had always been sensitive to being patronised from above. Now he was confronted by a curious role reversal by being challenged by a Labour leader who was socially superior to Major. The prime minister's class reflexes were strongly aroused by Tony Blair's education at public school, Oxford and the Bar. Major would have suspected that Blair's rapid ascent had been facilitated more by privilege than achievement. Major was irritated by what he saw as the pretension and self-possession drawn from inherited position and advantages. To the prime minister, 'Tony Blair looked and sounded like a middle-of-the-road Tory.'[2] He was adopting Conservative positions and could almost be seen as challenging for the Conservative leadership from outside the party. The position was further exacerbated by the evident popularity of Blair amongst many Conservative voters and MPs. Just at a time when Major needed to mobilise the parliamentary party and to galvanise the Conservatives in the country, he was challenged by a Labour leader who in many quarters of the Conservative party was more socially acceptable than himself. Blair not only stimulated class prejudice in Major, he did so within the Conservative party as a whole.

The social status of the leader of the opposition represented a considerable threat to Major. The prime minister was immensely proud of his own background and of the role he attributed to his personal will in the now legendary journey from Brixton to Downing Street. It was a rags to riches story that made him into the living embodiment of the social mobility associated with the Thatcherite revolution. Nicholas Wapshott described him as 'more the sort of meritocratic leader that the Labour party might have produced'.[3] John Major's story had become the branded embodiment of his political message. His background and his advancement to the premiership was the model of his own governing ideal of a classless society. Tony Blair reawakened the old images of an establishment and the hierarchy of signs, symbols and nuances that went with it. Just as Major's closest allies in the party tended to be drawn from the ranks of self-made men, so the strongest complaints of Major tended to come from high Tories. Boris Johnson observed the frustration of the latter with a prime minister whose social inadequacies in their view rendered the party effectively leaderless. It was these Conservatives in particular who felt 'a sense of national shame' whenever they saw Major 'representing this country abroad, beaming his stitched-on, capped-tooth smile'.[4] Far from being a prime minister to look up to, Major was an embarrassment – 'an anti-Cicero, a style vacuum, a cultural black hole'.[5] Major returned the criticisms with references to 'New Labour; old school tie'[6] and to Blair's inherent incapacity to comprehend the nature of poverty, or to understand the Conservative instincts of the lower middle class, or to grasp the dynamics of private enterprise.

Tony Blair's heavy usage of high rhetoric in his appeals to values and emotion represented another source of resentment to John Major. The prime minister recognised that language and argument were the main weapons of any opposition, but in his view the Labour leader's verbal assaults were excessive and unwarranted. The accusatory style, combined with the level of political denigration and the imputed moral superiority on the part of the opposition, were constant irritants to the prime minister. Major found Blair's blend of articulate intellectualism, sophisticated oratory and noisy self-belief to be distasteful. In particular, he objected to the way that Blair sought to use social piety and moral judgement as a medium of populist politics. He regarded this kind of appeal as self-serving and bogus. A close ally of Major commented that Blair's leadership style touched a raw nerve: 'Major finds Blair unbelievably sanctimonious. He presents himself as a shining perfect figure as opposed to the cynical and corrupt politicians opposite him. Meanwhile Labour is playing politics as dirtily as ever. John Major feels that there is a dissonance between image and reality.'[7]

Nevertheless, the chief problem posed to the prime minister by Blair's leadership style was the way it cast further public doubts upon Major's own capacity for leadership. In effect, Tony Blair's flamboyant leadership distracted attention away from the prime minister's more reserved outlook upon the role and practice of political leadership. John Major's conception of leadership had evolved within the responsibilities of government where the emphasis necessarily lay with negotiation and compromise. In his words, he did not disparage the 'vision thing' but he believed there was more value in the 'action thing' and the 'practical thing'. He continued: 'By all means listen to a politician when he tells you what he plans – but ask, too, how he will do it. Take it from me. The devil is in the detail.'[8] Major was a practising politician who had direct experience of the underlying complexities and limitations of government. The act of governing meant attending to a profusion of cross-cutting conflicts that could not be resolved by 'windy rhetoric, pious clichés or ad-man's speak'.[9] Major's only concession to a guiding vision was a personal commitment to extract the maximum potential for accommodation from the political process. Referring to the qualities required of a prime minister, Major made it clear that vision and purpose were synonymous with more practical virtues. In his view, prime ministers needed a 'clear vision of what they are doing, a consistency of purpose, a capacity not to be panicked out of that consistency of purpose, and a clear inclination both to hear and to understand what people's concerns are and to try and mould policy to deal with them'.[10]

Leadership to Major was embedded in realism rather than oratory: 'My politics was quiet politics. I disliked brash populism. I distrusted conflict. I was at ease with the knitting-up of conciliation. It may have been boring to some; it may have been seen as grey, but it had its points.'[11] In Major's view, this kind of leadership was highly effective. It may have been derided by some but he remained firmly committed to the style that had marked his rise to promin- ence: 'I am not going to change. I listen a lot. I reflect a lot. I make decisions when I have listened, weighed up the facts and decided what the objective is and whether it is achievable.'[12] He was annoyed with Blair in the way that he tried to transmute the inevitable accidents and setbacks of government into either intentional acts, or as products of negligence or incompetence. What Labour was 'so adept at distorting', he complained, 'were often the everyday happenings of government: the choices, disappointments and mistakes that always take place'.[13] To the prime minister, this was a naïve view of politics. It overlooked the impact of quiet negotiation and concealed the subtle successes of such an approach:

> Take care not to confuse oratory with practical concern. Look for the achieve-
> ments of government not always in bold plans or crude conflicts, but some-
> times in mended fences too, and sometimes in the accretion of small steps
> whose pattern takes time to become clear.[14]

To Major, this was the real measure of political effort. Conciliation and aggre- gation were integral features of leadership within a democratic system. The prime minister was infuriated not only by what he saw as Blair's inability to grasp the interior subtleties of leadership but also by the opposition leader's refusal to acknowledge that political leadership always involved the balancing of groups and opinions within a party.

To make matters worse for Major, Blair even took to criticising the prime minister in public on precisely these grounds:

> [T]he moment any leader starts to play with factions within his own party,
> rather than lead it, then it is only a matter of time before the factions make the
> party disintegrate. Labour took a long time to learn that lesson. Mr Major
> may be learning too late.[15]

In the prime minister's perspective, drawing critical attention in such a way to the normal processes of party management and political leadership was tanta- mount to professional hypocrisy. To Major, it typified Blair's whole approach to politics which the prime minister believed was superficial and irrespon- sible. Major's irritation with the way that Blair persistently equated careful conciliation with poor leadership was dramatically revealed in a Prime Minister's Questions on the BSE crisis. In response to Blair's indictment of 'weak and ineffectual leadership',[16] Major angrily responded in the following terms:

That really was one of the most trivial series of comments – utterly trivial. This is a matter of great interest to British agriculture. Scientific changes are important to that industry, but the right hon. Gentleman does not understand them, does not enter into any research on them, deliberately distorts what little he does know, ignores the reality of what is happening to the British beef industry, and moves – as he does on his third question every Tuesday and Thursday – into a carefully pre-packaged, pre-prepared piece of irrelevant, juvenile sloganising.[17]

Given that Labour had been out of power for so long, it was perhaps understandable in Major's view that its leadership should be so out of touch with practical politics. To a prime minister thoroughly conditioned to a Conservative hegemony and to the virtues of pragmatic leadership, Blair's claims to leadership were themselves a sign of Labour's own protracted isolation and inexperience.

John Major could claim that Tony Blair was ignorant of what he did not know. He could assert that New Labour only existed at the level of rhetoric. Nevertheless, the challenge to the prime minister and the Conservative party was that his adversary and the project he sponsored were highly effective. The immediate inroads that Blair had made into Conservative territory had not been the short-lived achievement of a honeymoon period. Far from being quickly reversed, the momentum behind Blair had increased. Within six months, the Labour leader was in the process of changing the rules of engagement on the very issue of leadership itself. He was establishing different priorities and evaluative criteria that were to the detriment of John Major. By pouring so much emphasis and public attention upon the virtues of vigorous and radical leadership, Blair was devaluing the incumbency advantages of the premiership. The Labour leader was also threatening the classic game plan of Conservative electioneering – namely to draw Labour out into the open space of public inspection where their divisions, irresponsibilities and incoherence could be exposed. Under Blair, Labour was already out in the public and being fêted by a receptive media for its integrity, trustworthiness and leadership. Major remained confident that he could engineer a repetition of the 1992 general election surprise. He was reassured by three key premises. First, that the Conservatives had won the battle of ideas; second, that the party had a formidable campaigning organisation; and third, that Labour neither would not, or could not, ever change. Labour or New Labour would always revert to its inherent nature. Its apparent harmony and unanimity would implode under pressure. It was Major's role as leader to exert that pressure.

Head to head: Tony Blair

Tony Blair was a leader with a mission. He was also a man in a hurry. This was due in part to his natural impatience with opposition and to his limited tolerance of the time-consuming properties of political negotiation. His emphasis upon speed, however, was in the main drawn from the knowledge that both he and the Labour party had the one remaining opportunity to prove itself as a co-participant in Britain's version of a two-party system. The political circumstances now favoured Labour but the party had a track record of self-generated instability. It also remained an object of distrust and suspicion. As a consequence, the nearer it came to power, the more intense and aggressive the scrutiny would become. In many ways, this was unfair on a patient opposition. The Major administration had amassed a large and growing record of conspicuous incompetence that under normal circumstances would render it beyond hope of re-election. Even so, Blair had to proceed upon the assumption that the critical analysis of Labour would be comparable to any indictment of the Conservative party. His realisation that Labour had been given an historic opportunity to make a breakthrough filled Blair with a nervous anxiety over the need to realise the potential of a Labour victory. Donald Macintyre observed that even with opinion poll leads in excess of 25 per cent, Blair remained haunted by the spectre of defeat.

> [F]or the Labour leader, every hostage given to a Tory press, every extravagant spending promise, every needless posture struck about issues ... threatens the shattering of ... the renewed hopes of British social democracy. So prevalent is the belief among politicians of all parties that Labour will win the general election that scarcely any of them confronts the historic meltdown it will mean for Labour if he fails to do so.[18]

Blair was equally concerned over another form of defeat: namely the inability of a Labour government to retain power. The new leader was not prepared to form an interim government between two Conservative administrations. His role would not be one of ushering in a Labour administration for the party to indulge in its fissiparous tendencies once in office. The objective for Blair was not simply to rein in the party, but to reconfigure it in order to make it congruent with contemporary society. For Blair, this would not be a makeover; it would be a genuine transformation from the top through leadership and from the bottom through an expanded membership responsive to a plurality of communities and social positions. The appeal would be one of competence, responsibility and electability in order to relieve a public and its governance of Conservative fatigue. But it was also more that. Driven by a visionary leadership, it called for the kind of shift in political attachment, which would ensure Labour of at least two full terms of office. Electability, therefore, demanded long-term discipline and cohesion. It required a leader-centred party and a leader with the will and capacity to energise the party and mobilise new sectors of Labour support.

Labour's leader was a highly astute politician who knew his strengths and weaknesses, and who appreciated the need to cultivate support from a broad range of bases. Unlike many Labour politicians, Blair had little time for deal making and fixes within the enclosed world of party elites and machines. He appreciated the need to work within the structures and rhythms of the party but he was not willing to be confined by them. As a result, Blair could be seen as unsociable, distant, direct and intolerant towards the costs of extended negotiation. His seriousness and commitment to long-term measures could give the impression of a person who did not place enormous value upon personal relationships. Anthony Giddens noted this side of his political intensity at an early stage: '[H]e doesn't have much of a sense either of playfulness, or even emotional warmth. He doesn't seem the kind of leader who is going to be loved by his supporters within his party or among the wider population.'[19] Philip Gould recognised some of these characteristics but regarded them more favourably as the concomitants of strategic vision.

> He sets contemporary politics into a vast sweep of history that goes back to the Liberal-Labour split and forward into the next century … He will follow his instincts whatever the consequences, leading sometimes to stubbornness and inflexibility … He has a sense of the destiny of the nation, and of the pulse of the people. In this he is like Margaret Thatcher.[20]

The allusion to Thatcher became a common reference point and it was a theme which the Labour leader actively fostered in projecting himself as the counterpoint and antidote to John Major and his administration.

The leader of the opposition was known to have a very low opinion of John Major both as an individual and as a leader. The prime minister's cultivated mediocrity and self-styled ordinariness was lost upon Tony Blair. His own self-belief, intellectualism and personal magnetism were both confounded and irritated by the presence of Major in Number 10. To the leader of the opposition, John Major's premiership represented an open contempt for the principles of meritocracy to which Blair was personally committed. Blair's whole parliamentary career had been confined to the largely anonymous world of opposition politics where frustration and futility are never far below the surface. John Major, by contrast, had had a highly privileged political background. From the beginning, his career had been based within the governing party. He had no conception of political life outside the comfort zone of the Conservative hegemony. Like many in the party who had become accustomed to government status, serious politics was assumed to be confined to the division of opinion and support within the Conservative party. To those on the outside, this exclusive sphere represented a permanent source of irritation.

Tony Blair was not alone in regarding John Major as a particular product of his political milieu. According to this perspective, the prime minister had achieved a position beyond his ability by a combination of careful positioning and disarming guile. To make matters worse, Major had acquired the leadership not through an open electoral process but through a party competition restricted to MPs. Since 1990, he had retained his position through a leadership style that sought to ameliorate divisions through ambiguity and a continual balancing of factions. This was not Blair's modus operandi. From the outset, he was the 'kind of leader who expect[ed] his party to revolve around *his* instincts and *his* requirements'.[21] To a figure like Blair, the prime minister was a weak and an equivocal camp follower of the New Right who could effectively play upon people's fears of Labour to continue the neo-liberal hegemony. He had led the fabled Conservative come-back in the 1992 general election through an exceptional performance in arousing popular anxieties over the consequences of Labour's policies on taxation and constitutional reform. Blair knew that, irrespective of Labour's opinion poll leads, Major's skills in negative campaigning remained as formidable as they were in 1992. John Major, therefore, was not merely the political target and chief adversary of Tony Blair. He constituted a significant threat to New Labour and represented a nightmare vision to Blair of a pathology of leadership that the leader of the opposition might well fall victim to in government.

The certainty of a Conservative revival in the approach to the general election made the issue of Labour's location in the political landscape a matter of continued significance. New Labour strategists had to make every effort to ensure that their position would be as resistant as possible to Major's personal campaign to arouse public distrust of Labour. The main countermeasure for Blair was to fix public attention on himself and on his appeal to a new politics that transcended the old fixtures of left and right in favour of a responsible and ethics-based attention to the dynamics of social change. This was a leadership-based amalgam of high civic aspiration and fiscal caution; a 'new binding moral imperative to replace the dying embers of collectivisation'[22] mixed with a realistic set of policies that could be delivered; in other words, a hybrid of animating idealism and reassuring pragmatism.

Blair was intent upon moving Labour firmly into the Conservative heartlands. He openly engaged the Conservative government on the Middle England agenda. He was sensitised to the issue of tax; he understood the importance of personal aspiration; he addressed the problems of law and order; and he steered Labour into a convincing recognition of the value and legitimacy of business and market-driven enterprise. In particular, the Labour leader cultivated the theme of middle-class anxieties. These included a concern for the infrastructure of public institutions and services, and the criticism that Britain's development within the European Union was being jeopardised by the increasingly polarised and dogmatic divisions within the Tory party. These middle-class issues also included the disquiet over the deterioration in social and family structures and a reaction to the onset of middle-class insecurity through economic recession and global trends. Blair even termed those in the middle as 'the anxious class. People insecure about their jobs. Afraid that public services will not be there when they need them. Struggling to pay mortgages and new charges. Prompted to opt for private pensions and now finding that they get very little in return.'[23] In addressing such issues, the Labour leader not only claimed an intuitive understanding of the middle class fusion of aspiration and insecurity, he could personify the syndrome.

In contrast to his recent predecessors, Blair could communicate effectively with this conservative constituency. He was evidently more at ease with its dispositions and concerns than either Neil Kinnock or John Smith. John Rentoul observes that the distinction between Kinnock and Blair was based upon the wider horizons of the latter.

> Curiously, for Blair is the Christian socialist and Kinnock the non-believer, Kinnock's roots were in a socialism of Original Sin, holy war and salvation. The world was tainted by the wickedness of capitalism, and only those who had a change of heart – preferably through the heroism of workers in struggle – could be saved. Whereas Blair was a relativist, seeing good and bad in everyone, Kinnock had been a fundamentalist. If profit and nuclear weapons were morally wrong, then most of the electorate were condemned. It was his past moral absolutism combined with his insistence on winning which opened the way for Kinnock's changes of mind to be seen as opportunist, rather than the product of sincere reflection.[24]

John Smith was, like Tony Blair, a middle-class lawyer. But unlike his junior colleague, Smith was embedded in the Protestant ethos of guilt. His social conscience compelled him to enter into public service within a Labour organisation that possessed its own belief system and structure of social norms. The Labour party to both Kinnock and Smith was synonymous with a civic religion. In this context, Blair was a genuine heretic. He had sincerely held views that were at variance with the accepted orthodoxies of the Labour movement. In effect, they amounted to alternative convictions. Blair's endorsements of the virtues of the free market, enterprise culture, and fiscal and monetary stability were not merely for effect or advantage. They were central beliefs emphatically declared and joyously reiterated. To Hugo Young, the contrast between Blair and his predecessors was stark. Blair had 'exceptionally clear ideas, painful to many sentimentalists, about how the Labour Party should deal with its past, and make itself a new future.'[25] Kinnock and Smith had both advanced the cause of modernisation, but in doing so they were never able to 'transcend the impression that they were doing what they did for reasons of expediency. They were painted, sometimes unfairly, as men defining their party to comply with opinion polls.'[26] Young perceived that Blair was 'critically different' in the way that he converted 'Labour's talk of markets and opportunity, of community and competence, into language from the heart of socialism'.[27]

Labour's leader was intent upon galvanising the party into a pivotal campaign in which under his leadership it would become once again a party of government. Blair's leadership would be the catalyst for, and the agency of, a new identity for the party without which it was destined in his view to deteriorate into a minor force in British politics. The guiding objective of the New Labour project was to disrupt political boundaries, to dislodge prior attachments, to achieve a realignment of the left; and even to change the form of British governance through a programme of constitutional reform. In this respect, Blair was openly engaging in the style and aims of transformative leadership. He wanted nothing less than a renewal of Britain. Self-proclaimed radicalism, however, was mixed with the calming reassurance of familiar landmarks and values. The message of one-nation classlessness, the ideals of community obligation and social cohesion, and the traditional liberalism of rights, inclusiveness and opportunity were welded together to support the theme of consensus leadership. New Labour appeared to be sponsoring change and changelessness at the same time.

The tensions and even contradictions implicit in such a hybrid, however, were largely superseded by the figure of Blair. It was the leader that provided the logic to the New Labour project. It was his persona and his vision that animated the party, widened its appeal and suspended the disjunctions. It was the force of Blair's insistent message that change could be equated with security that led to a marked receptivity to the corollary of insecurity being defined by a continuity of Conservative government. Tony Blair raised the stakes of political leadership. It was not just that his leadership marked a sea change in the Labour party, or that his conception of leadership had become a governing priority of the party. It was that Blair's leadership was motivated and guided by the need to counteract the Conservatives' chief electoral asset. More significantly, it was Blair's intention to displace those claims to national leadership that had become such a central component of the Conservative hegemony.

Anti-leadership strategies

The chief advantage and most immediate asset that Blair possessed in this conflict over leadership claims lay in his rapidly acquired pre-eminence in the polls.

Figure 7.1 shows the pattern of public satisfaction with the performance of the two main party leaders. Even though Blair was young and inexperienced, and had risen to the leadership very suddenly, the new leader of the opposition moved rapidly from an approval level in the mid-30s to a satisfaction rating that often exceeded 50 per cent. While his better-known predecessor, John

Figure 7.1 Satisfaction with John Major, Tony Blair and the Conservative government (August 1994–March 1997)

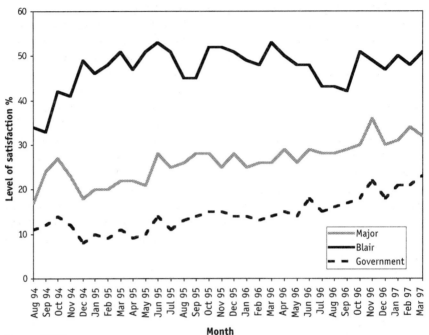

Source: MORI

Smith, achieved an average level of satisfaction of 35.9 per cent, Blair's average was conspicuously higher at 47.2 per cent. For John Major, it was clear that the prime minister ran well ahead of his own government in the public's estimation. It was also a source of some comfort that the level of satisfaction in his performance as party leader improved during this period. Nevertheless, these positive features were more than counterbalanced by the fact that his ratings began at a very low level and remained on average 21 points behind Blair.

When the question posed was one relating to the standing of the party leaders as an actual or potential prime minister (Figure 7.2), a similar pattern was revealed. John Major may have been expected to excel in this kind of poll not only because of his status as prime minister but because Gallup's question asked which of the party leaders would make the *best* prime minister. But in this tighter poll, which forced respondents to make a definite choice amongst the three leaders, Blair remained dominant. The main casualty in this kind of poll is normally the leader of the third party. The polls covering this period proved to be no exception. The average level of public satisfaction with Paddy Ashdown as a party leader was 41.3 per cent. His position in the poll for the best prime ministerial candidate, however, averaged only 13.7 per cent. John Major did

160

Figure 7.2 'Who would make the best prime minister?' (July 1994–April 1997)

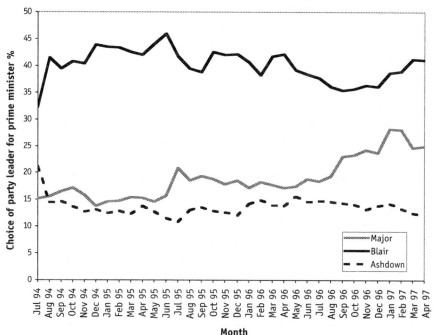

Source: Gallup

manage to improve his performance in this poll. In the first six months of 1995, the gap between Blair and Major was on average 28.5 points. In the last four months before the general election, the deficit had narrowed to 13.5 points. Nevertheless, the trend line shows a remarkable consistency with Blair always well in front, averaging 40.1 per cent to the prime minister's average of 18.9 per cent.

Given his prevalence in leadership polls and the chronic nature of John Major's problems with the Conservative party, Tony Blair had little cause to engage directly in anti-leadership strategies. The highly exposed difficulties of the prime minister meant Blair could relinquish much of the task of criticising his adversary. In effect, he could leave that to the corrosive talents of leader writers, cartoonists and disaffected Conservative MPs and ministers. The leader of the opposition benefited enormously from the crises of government that were increasingly diagnosed as derivatives of a dearth of leadership. Blair's chief task was to maintain the momentum of this critical framework. He continually addressed the Conservative government's disarray in terms of a leadership deficiency. He maintained a public agenda of prescribed leadership through a language dominated by references to leadership solutions. Tony Blair urged the prime minister to 'get a grip'; he repeatedly pointed out the inconsistencies in the prime minister's positions; he excoriated what were described as John Major's 'climbdowns'; and he persistently alluded to the damage being inflicted upon the country's interests by the lack of clear leadership and personal vision. The climax to one Prime Minister's Questions typified the message, which Blair was intent upon establishing in the minds of the voters. He asserted that there was 'one very big difference' between the two leaders: 'I lead my party, he follows his.'[28] In the context of direct leadership confrontation, Major later conceded that this 'wounding jibe [was] the best one-liner he ever used against me'.[29]

The Labour leader was assisted in this muted anti-leadership strategy by a succession of crises relating to the Conservative government or to the Conservative party. These ranged from disclosures that parliament and the public had been misled to cases of financial conflict of interest; and from incidents of personal and sexual misconduct to the succession of European policy reversals, along with the breaches of cabinet confidentiality and collective responsibility that accompanied the party's civil war of European integration.[30] These 'local difficulties' could, and were, exploited to depict a lack of leadership both in the origins of the crises and in the way they were subsequently handled. Blair was also helped by the destabilising influence of the Thatcher precedent. Blair even risked instability in his own party by explicitly seeking to associate his leadership with that of Margaret Thatcher. He actively encouraged parallels to be drawn between them and openly acknowledged her achievements in demonstrating the positive effects of leadership operating on clear principles and convictions. By fostering a renewed appreciation of Margaret Thatcher and even an affectionate nostalgia for her, the Labour leader sought to maintain critical pressure upon the prime minister. The intention was to subject John Major's subtle yet opaque style of leadership to the intense glare of dramatised leadership drawn from the past and the present.

Under Blair, Labour had come to value and to promote leadership as a political instrument and even a programme in its own right. This allowed the focus of attention to remain upon the Conservative party's disunity in general and upon the ascribed personal failings of the prime minister in particular. It was exactly this position which represented Blair's preferred outcome: namely a persistently weakened prime minister locked into a syndrome of disaffection that fell just short of an acute condition. The retention of John Major's disabled premiership was the priority of Blair's anti-leadership strategy. Major had to be kept in power but at the same time stripped of his leadership.

The static pattern of the Conservatives' deficit in the polls that had become established in 1995, together with Labour's strategy of leadership inflation, forced Major into playing for time. Although he did not rule out a date in 1996 for a general election, this became an increasingly remote possibility. The required rate of political recovery remained too high to be achieved in an early election. The only solution to the problem of running out of time was to extend the parliament to its maximum length. This option risked the appearance of a government lacking confidence and even legitimacy, but it at least allowed time for economic recovery, for Conservative relaunches, and for a rallying of the core vote around the government and especially the leader. To party strategists, the latter would be the key to the Conservatives remaining in power.

The public's continued trust in John Major's individual honesty and integrity offered the party its best hope of corporate salvation. The prime minister provided a point of access to public opinion, which could be employed to neutralise, or at least to marginalise, the negative associations of the party and the government. John Major was an accomplished and enthusiastic campaigner. If he could revive the spirit of 1990 in his leadership and the spirit of 1992 in the government, then even in such adversity the Conservative hegemony might remain intact. The task for John Major was to reiterate the virtues of his leadership and to raise as many questions as possible on the meaning and the value of Tony Blair's leadership.

From the inception of Blair's leadership, Major had tried to discover ways of challenging the new leader that would be effective in terms of both reducing Blair's appeal and enhancing the prime minister's own claims to leadership. Initially, John Major sought to use the tragedy of John Smith's sudden death to raise the standard of political engagement in such a way that his successor would be conditioned by a new atmosphere of mutual respect and restraint. Major asserted that the loss of a valued colleague reminded everyone that there are 'things higher than politics and across all the divisions, common bonds of humanity that unite us all'.[31] Major went on to underline the presence and importance of 'friendship' and 'decency' in politics: '[T]here are private relationships across all parties, there is principle and there is respect and understanding for the beliefs and convictions of others.'[32] The prime minister said he had 'little taste for the politics of point scoring or for belittling others … If people who attack the policies of others could respect their motives then politics would have a fresher feel than it does today.'[33] He reflected upon the cross-party consensus of the war years and the creation of the welfare state and drew an unfavourable comparison with contemporary politics: 'Sometimes I feel … that there is too much knocking, too much carping, too much sneering. If politicians fight, in party and across party, like ferrets in a sack on every issue, is it surprising if the public turns away?'[34]

In making such an appeal, John Major was adopting a prime ministerial role in giving expression to national sentiments at a time of public loss. He was also drawing attention to his maturity and experience in being able to take the long view and provide a conciliatory perspective above the normal rancour of politics. Although many interpreted his injunction as a challenge to his own divided party, it was primarily a gesture to the opposition and became part of a more general strategy of restraint in attacking Labour's new leader during his first few months in office. Whether Major's prescriptions were genuinely meant or whether they proceeded upon the premise that they were unsustainable in a parliamentary context, he was nevertheless irritated by Blair's refusal to be patronised by prime ministerial guidance. The first few sessions of Prime Minister's Questions with Blair as leader of the opposition set the pattern for the ensuing relationship. For example, in their very first question time on 18 October 1994, the following exchange took place:

> *Mr Blair:* Last Thursday on BBC television, the Chancellor of the Exchequer specifically ruled out a referendum on a single currency. Did he speak for the Government?
>
> *The Prime Minister:* First, may I congratulate the right hon. Gentleman on his new position. It carries with it very great responsibilities, and I wish him well in those responsibilities for as long as he holds them … As for the right hon. Gentleman's substantive question, at the moment no one knows what may be at issue in the intergovernmental conference in 1996. The question of a referendum on any issue does not arise and very probably will not arise.
>
> *Mr Blair:* With all due respect, the Chancellor specifically ruled it out and therefore he thought that it did arise. Is not that the problem: that the Chancellor takes one view on Europe, the Employment Secretary takes another view and the Prime Minister hovers between the two? Does he – *[Interruption.]*
>
> *Madam Speaker:* Order. The House will come to order.
>
> *Mr Blair:* I repeat: he hovers between the two. Does he agree that a divided Government is a weak Government, and a weak Government is no good for Britain?
>
> *The Prime Minister:* The right hon. Gentleman has already said that, were he to form a Government, it would be a weak Government, and that is precisely because he said that his Government would not be isolated in Europe. Irrespective of the issue, irrespective of the British interest, irrespective of the views of the House or the Members of the House, and irrespective of the views of his colleagues below the Gangway, the right hon. Gentleman would follow slavishly whatever Europe says. That is not a credible position for any Government in this country.[35]

In the following week, the prime minister found Mr Blair even less receptive to a new spirit of mutual respect and collegiate constraint.

> *Mr Blair:* Now that today we have another report by the Cabinet Secretary exonerating another Minister, can we make ourselves clear about the basis on which the Prime Minister is running the Government? A week ago, he said that there were unsubstantiated allegations against his Trade Minister and insisted that he stayed. A few days later, there were allegations that were supposed to be unfounded, as he called them, and he insisted that the Minister concerned went. Now there are new unsubstantiated allegations against the

Chief Secretary to the Treasury, and he stays. What is the basis on which the Prime Minister decides to retain or dismiss his Ministers – the truth of the allegations or merely the number of them?

The Prime Minister: I had understood that when the right hon. Gentleman became leader of the Labour party we were going to see a new style in politics. I had not expected to see the right hon. Gentleman step down into the gutters of public life quite so soon. ... Now there is no doubt. We now know where we are with the right hon. Gentleman and we know precisely what way he plans to play his politics. The right hon. Gentleman says to the House that he does not believe that the allegations are substantiated, yet he is still prepared to peddle them in here ... Despite the fact that the right hon. Gentleman does not believe the allegations and does not believe that there is anything substantial in them, he still wants to see them examined in public. People will ask for what party political reason he wants to see them established in public. If that is to be the new, clean politics, let us have the old, dirty politics from Labour that we have been used to.[36]

Major quickly came to realise that the stalling device of prime ministerial *noblesse oblige* would do little to resist the ominous advance of Tony Blair in the competitive politics of national leadership. It was time to move to other counter-leadership strategies.

In his own sudden rise to prominence John Major had had the advantage of being difficult to define and, therefore, difficult to target as a political actor. Now he was confronted by a leader who was even more mercurial and elusive than Major had been when he entered Number 10 Downing Street. The Conservatives' first assault upon Blair centred upon his evident inexperience. Attempts were made to attach significance to his evident youth and to the fact that he had risen too far too fast. Blair had not been blooded as a senior politician. He had suffered neither setbacks and failures, nor political crises. The Conservatives needed to counter the impulse that it was 'time for a change' by raising questions over what that change might produce. To the prime minister, Tony Blair was a political parvenu, who had no understanding of the multi-dimensional character of government. He had served no apprenticeship within government. Unlike John Major who had grafted his way up through the hierarchy of Conservative administrations, Blair now threatened to enter government at the highest level with an alarming absence of hands-on experience.

The chief problem with this line of attack was that Major himself, and the leadership crisis which surrounded him, were in many ways responsible both for the appeal of Tony Blair and for the fact that he had not been tested by character-building crises. Moreover, in criticising Blair's inexperience, the Conservatives merely underlined the extensive scale of their own longevity in office. The logic of the case for experience also carried with it an implied antidemocratic argument: namely that the longer the Conservatives remained in office the greater their claim was to government power. Ultimately, a leader of the opposition was bound to occur who had had no experience of government office. And yet at this precise point, when the dynamic of a two-party system was already in doubt, the 'experience argument' appeared to support its permanent suspension. In the event, the ambiguities of this argument remained unexamined. The charge of inexperience was left as a background theme that carried implications of social prejudice and hegemonic presumption. On these grounds, John Major could appeal to Thatcherites like Andrew Neil who duly voiced concerns over the qualifications of Tony Blair and his shadow cabinet for high office: 'Barely one has ever held down a real job in the market economy, ever created a single new job through their own endeavours, ever had to compete in the marketplace, ever raised wealth-generating investment, ever had to meet a payroll.'[37] Major himself continued to emphasise the theme even after Blair had been leader of the opposition for two years. In his final rallying address to the Conservative party conference in October 1996, Major sought to put down his rival by reference to his junior status: 'Sorry, Tony. Job's taken. And anyway, it's too big a task for your first real job.'[38]

A related theme to inexperience and one that was deployed extensively against Blair and the New Labour project was the superficiality of the opposition party. It was claimed that Blair's leadership was necessarily more apparent than real. Such vaunted leadership could only be achieved at the level of style and presentation. This was particularly so in such an open-textured and segmented organisation as the Labour party. Blair's leadership, therefore, was shallow in content and designed with the explicit intention to deceive the public. To Major, Blair was merely an exponent of 'soundbite politics,'[39] which remained deficient in substance: 'Blair doesn't ask me questions about anything that is of serious interest. It's whatever is the soundbite issue of the day.'[40] According to this perspective, Blair's leadership had a bogus quality to it. Set as it was in a circular relationship with New Labour, Blair was depicted as an ambiguous front man for an ambiguous product but one that had been cleverly marketed 'with everything pre-determined and pre-packaged as though you were selling a soap powder.'[41] Its market penetration had been immediate but Major claimed that it had no basis for survival: 'As for this new biologically improved Labour Party, it may wash blander but I would give it a shelf life of under three years.'[42]

The generalised appeal and superficiality of Tony Blair was at first seen to be almost benign in nature – a product of the leader's naiveté and Labour's unlikely state of internal peace. At first, the Conservatives' response was one of pointing out how such a state of affairs was incapable of being sustained. There were simply too many tensions and contradictions within the New Labour project. Tony Blair was renamed 'Tony Blur' with the intention of highlighting the imprecision of intent and priorities embedded in the project.

While Labour had endeavoured to jettison unpopular policies and negative associations, in order to create a broad coalition of support, it was at one level merely a beneficiary of dissent. Major sought to point out that stagecraft leadership was no substitute for a programme of government: 'When does he [Blair] ever have a policy? He sets up a commission, or a discussion group, or a commission to examine what the discussion group said, or a discussion group to examine what the commission said. What about making some hard decisions? It's hard-edged, this world. You have actually to decide something and then do it.'[43] Blair was simply taking advantage of Conservative disarray. Just as New Labour was criticised as a fictional party, so Blair had failed to substantiate his credentials for the premiership.

The Conservatives' early response to Blair had been to equate his governmental inexperience with flawed ambition and youthful hubris. As such, it was thought that he would inevitably overreach himself and precipitate the predicted collapse in public appeal and party support. Blair was characterised as 'chancer' but one who amounted to a provocative irritant. Nevertheless, it was believed that both he and New Labour would in the end be exposed as temporary aberrations. It was not until June 1996 when the Conservatives showed few signs of ever closing the gap on Labour that Blair was reconfigured into an altogether more threatening entity. The decision to make Tony Blair the target of highest priority for the Conservative campaign reflected both the need to challenge Labour through its leadership and the length of time required to do it. The clear emphasis upon negative campaigning also demonstrated the extent to which the Conservatives had had to give up fighting on the government's own record. The imperative now was to concentrate upon the risks and threats posed by Labour.

The strategy was exemplified by the 'New Labour, New Danger' campaign, which at first featured a pair of red eyes looming from a red curtain and then the same eyes staring from the shadows of a half-open purse. They were intended to convey the impression of a hidden menace waiting to spring forth with unabated ferocity. It played upon the theme of a socialist subversion and an unsuspecting public. The campaign reached its climax when this theme of threat was fused with the image of Tony Blair. With the addition of a mask and the overlay of a pair of leering eyes, the 'New Labour, New Danger' device now became an attempt to use the image of the Labour leader against itself. With a year to go before the general election, the Conservatives were intent upon undermining Blair in support of their own leadership investment. The counterpoint to John Major's honesty, propriety and trustworthiness would now be switched away from the prime minister's own party and directed towards Blair himself. The impact of Blair's individuality was to be turned against its progenitor by transposing the already ubiquitous icon of a smiling Blair into the embodiment of a demonic conspiracy. The guiding message was that his leadership should be questioned and even feared. The further subtext was that the very notion of strong leadership itself should be a cause for concern.

Although the advertisement had an immediate impact and achieved high levels of recognition, there was little in the way of follow-through by Major or senior ministers. The prime minister was not only sensitive to the dignity of the office, but also to the religious objections to the imagery. But an even more significant concern to Major was the integrity of his conception of consensus leadership and its relationship to his assumed roles of 'honest John', likeable prime minister and national conciliator. John Major was aware that this was a high-risk venture that could rebound upon him. Peter Mandelson, for example, had been quick to seize upon its possible value to the Conservatives, but also upon its capacity to shift the focus back upon the government. He made a comparison that was guaranteed to sting Major into reconsideration: 'There has never been … any sort of political communication like it in Britain before now. Not even the Conservatives under Norman Tebbit would have would have dreamt of placing advertisements like this. It is something which the prime minister should condemn and take steps to disown.'[44] The 'New Labour, New Danger' campaign had more negative slants upon Tony Blair in preparation but by the end of 1996 the theme had effectively been abandoned as excessively direct and personal. The electoral U-turn was unfortunately resonant with the Conservatives' reputation in government. More significantly still, the promotion and withdrawal of the 'New Labour, New Danger' theme was symptomatic of a far deeper disarray amongst Conservative strategists over how to counter a resurgent Labour party that appeared to be more of a phenomenon than a political organisation.

At the heart of the problem was the Conservatives' long-standing difficulty in establishing a focus and a direction to combating Blair and New Labour. From the very beginning of Blair's leadership, Conservative strategists could not ascertain the optimum strategy for defining and then condemning the Labour opposition. As Hywel Williams explains, the Conservatives quickly discerned two main ways to challenge Blair but then could not decide which one to choose.

> By autumn 1994 it was clear that the Conservatives could use one of two tactics against Blair. He could be a socialist wolf, red in tooth and claw but dressed in Bambi designer-chic, or he could be an opportunistic closet Tory who was stealing Tory policies. But he could not be both. Having chosen one version, the Tories would have stick to it, day in, day out for three years. But in endless political Cabinets Major was irresolute, wavering between the attractions of each thesis. His uncertainty infected every other Minister; the confusion about the Tory view of Blair was never resolved.[45]

There were problems with both strategies. If Blair was depicted as having moved Labour to the centre where it had endorsed the principles of the free market and the enterprise culture, then it was difficult to attack New Labour without subjecting the Conservative government to criticism. The logic of what was known in Central Office as the 'Coke strategy' centred upon the idea that the Conservatives represented the 'real thing' – i.e. the original and genuine flavour of Thatcherite revolution. This being so, it would clearly be preferable to any second-rate substitute. However, the appeal to discriminating consumers could lead to a fine market outcome with 'Pepsi' being the preferred choice. Acknowledging that Labour had undergone a genuine transformation under Blair carried the risk of making Labour less threatening to the voters. On the one hand, this positioning allowed the Conservatives to claim that there would now be no point in voting for an opposition, which was indistinguishable from the government. On the other hand, it also proffered the prospect of voting against the Conservative government with safety.

The other main strategy was to portray Labour as an unreconstructed party of socialist aspiration. Notwithstanding Blair's leadership, Labour would remain the sinister force of unremitting class antagonism in a slightly altered form. The chief problem with this depiction was that it flew in the face of public opinion. It also ran up against the evident middle-class nature and business-friendly ethos of Blair's leadership. The use of virulent imagery and polarising language drawn from the cold war of industrial warfare would leave the Conservatives looking out of touch and buried in the past. It would make them appear negative and also reactive. They would be seen to have lost the initiative to New Labour and to have resorted to disproportionate and even recidivist responses. Nevertheless, Conservative strategists retained a strong attachment to the fear factor which had been so effective in previous campaigns against Labour.

The problem in resolving the tensions implicit in these two strategies generated interest in compromise positions. The 'head and body' critique, for example, attempted to aggregate both Labour's changes and its retained traditions. Instead of emphasising the distinctions between the parties, this tactic stressed the gap between Blair and the rest of the party. This could be used to explain the appeal of New Labour, while at the same time it provided a way of criticising it as a bifurcated phenomenon. By October 1995, one noted analyst concluded that Conservative strategists had had no choice but to fight on these grounds: '[T]he Major administration understands that it cannot win any competition with Blair which hinges on issues of personality and leadership. It has therefore adopted as its central strategy against Labour the attempt to decouple Blair from his own party.'[46] Although this tactic had the potential to shift attention towards a genuine source of strain within the Labour party, it suffered from three significant drawbacks. First, it was difficult to sustain because of Labour's impressive closure of ranks around a leader whose electoral college victory had transformed the party and the shadow cabinet into a state of quiescence. Second, John Major himself was running what was in essence a 'head and body' campaign in which he was seeking to differentiate himself from the rest of the Conservative party. Third, if Blair could be shown to be out in front of his party this would only serve to substantiate his own claims to a Thatcher model of leadership that would be to the detriment of John Major.

The other main compromise position was the 'New Labour, New Danger' campaign. This too was plagued with conceptual and operational difficulties. At one and the same time it conceded that Labour was 'new' but that it was also still dangerous. Once again, Major was faced with the problem of Labour's 'newness' being based upon an assimilation of Conservative values and policies. According to this logic, New Labour was implicitly safe, or at least harmless. But at this juncture, New Labour was then equated with danger, which not only created confusion but helped to subsidise Labour's message: 'The Conservative Party spent millions of pounds advertising the fact that Labour was new. It then sought to counter that impression by showing that this novelty contained danger – not hope ... But what were the new dangers? Here the problems started.'[47] On some occasions, the dangers were policy based at which point they seemed minimal. On other occasions, the dangers remained undefined and lapsed into an undifferentiated sense of dread that seemed insubstantial. An additional problem remained with the 'New Labour, New Danger' hybrid: 'Ministers did not understand it. They frequently slipped back to bad old artful ways and described Labour as unreconstructed Socialists beneath the artful veneer.'[48] At other times, the attack slipped the other way. Butler and Kavanagh refer to one acrimonious exchange in the House of Commons when 'Major accused the Labour leader of being a jack-daw – stealing Conservative policies.'[49] When the prime minister's aides reminded him later that he was off-message, Major rebuked them: 'I am the message,'[50] he retorted. This confusion, even at the top, merely underlined the mutable and contested nature of the message itself.

The anti-leadership strategies of John Major and Tony Blair were markedly different from one another because they were based upon the separate needs and positions of both candidates. Major had to fight a rearguard battle against a leader who had been well received by the public and who had opened a durable lead in a range of attributed leadership properties. Being both short of time and deficient in leadership resources, the Conservative leader had to engage in direct, critical and sometimes personal attacks upon the leader of the opposition. John Major had to risk not looking prime ministerial in order to maximise his chances of retaining the premiership. In effect, he had to induce the public to compare Tony Blair unfavourably with the incumbent. By subverting Blair's claims to be an alternative prime minister, Major hoped to destabilise the leader-centred project of New Labour in its bid to constitute an alternative government.

In contrast to the prime minister, Blair was able to look less desperate and more statesmanlike. The public's affection for John Major and its respect for the premiership meant that Blair needed to be indirect and discriminating in his critiques of Major's leadership. Accordingly, he would target the Tories rather than John Major, but in doing so he would leave the critical conclusions to be drawn by inference and association. Blair concentrated very effectively upon establishing a positive model of strong leadership and then allowing commentators and the public to make their own comparisons between New Labour and the Conservative party's disarray. By openly employing Margaret Thatcher as a frame of reference and as an evaluative standard, Blair was able to subject the prime minister to a form of elliptical criticism that further compounded his problems within the party of government.

Both candidates for the premiership had to be cautious over the explicit usage of anti-leadership strategies. This is because such devices carry the risk of diminishing the leadership credentials of those who employ them. In essence, they can be seen as destructively negative in content and a sign of weak leadership on the part of those who adopt them. The risk is compounded by the political danger of asserting the need for higher standards of leadership in an opponent, which the critic is then unable to satisfy within his or her own organisation. Notwithstanding these provisos and limitations, Tony Blair experienced a clear advantage over John Major in withstanding anti-leadership strategies. This was due in the main to his position in being able to substantiate and to cultivate his claims to leadership. In effect, Blair was able to supplement his activities in the politics of leadership competition with a capacity to outperform Major in defending his leadership from other sources of complaint.

Keeping it together

A central feature of any leadership is the ability on the part of the leader both to strengthen and to sustain the integration of the organisation upon which the leader depends and through which the leader seeks to impose a set of priorities on a wider constituency. The deep leadership crisis that afflicted the Conservative government from 1993 to 1997 meant that John Major's political resources were mainly directed to resisting any further erosion of authority. Prime ministers are expected to maximise the level of party unity in order to compete effectively in general elections. For John Major, the dissonance within the Conservative party was so deeply rooted that his main task became the more minimal objective of establishing some form of electoral viability, which could be built upon in an ensuing election campaign. The objective was not so much a matter of keeping the party together but of limiting the consequences of having failed to retain its unity. Even this limited aim represented a prodigious task. Apart from the aggregate effects of years of leadership speculation within the party and the Conservative press, Major had been besieged with a succession of political scandals that either had a direct leadership connection, or were invested with a leadership dimension to the detriment of the prime minister. As the parliament progressed, the government's majority became increasingly tenuous under the pressure of by-election defeats and the defection of Conservative MPs to other parties.[51] By November 1996, the Conservatives' fragile majority no longer existed.

This sense of decline was further exacerbated by a sharp reduction in party donations and electoral resources at a time that coincided with the emergence of a lavishly financed new party. The Referendum party was pledged to contest any seat where none of the existing candidates had prescribed holding a national referendum on Britain's future in the European Union. By intruding so simplistically into the highly complex and divisive issue of Europe, the Referendum party threatened to weaken still further the Conservatives' base in southern marginal seats. It opened up yet another front for a Conservative government already confronted by New Labour, the Liberal Democrats and the nationalist parties in Scotland and Wales. Although Major had the power to select any election date that might serve his party's interests, he found that his discretion in this choice was largely without value. The conditions and projections were so dire that he had no real alternative other than to delay the election. However, this only strengthened the impression that he was simply hanging on to office and postponing defeat for a demoralised government.

To make matters worse for Major, he was increasingly surrounded by leadership rivals. The most prominent contenders were Michael Portillo, Michael Heseltine, John Redwood, Kenneth Clarke, Stephen Dorrell, Malcolm Rifkind and Gillian Shephard. Against the background of almost inevitable electoral defeat, aspiring leadership successors and their respective factions manœuvred for position. Even in January 1996, the intensity of leadership rivalry and the fatalism of electoral defeat had become a palpable combination at Westminster: 'The sheer number of potential runners in a post-election leadership race makes Major's task of holding the party together even harder. Neither Major nor Thatcher were frontrunners before they won the leadership and some senior Tories advise a flutter on a dark horse.'[52] The loss of government had even become a prior condition in the calculations of different factions. The right claimed that the left had already written off the election in its preoccupation to prevent the emergence of Michael Portillo as an heir apparent. In similar vein, the left claimed that 'many on the right [saw] defeat as their best hope of seizing control of the party'.[53] John Major's leadership in electoral defeat, therefore, had now become a requirement in the long-term planning of many of his most senior colleagues.

John Major sought to resist further disintegration and to reverse trends that were to the Conservatives' disadvantage. He made repeated appeals to the party for unity but to his continued dismay the divisions remained even when he placed the party on election readiness. Increasingly, Conservative strategists came to rely on the figure of Major himself as the centrepiece of the party's electoral appeal. For example, the prime minister inaugurated a series of presidential press conferences designed to wrest the initiative in media attention to themes selected by the party leader. Major also instituted what was described as an unprecedented consultation exercise within the Conservative party to discuss policy priorities for the next Conservative government. The exercise, entitled 'Our Nation's Future', was Major's answer to Blair's Clause IV campaign. Major hoped it would succeed in rallying the party together around a leader-centred process of mass participation. By actively engaging with the party outside Westminster, the prime minister hoped not only to re-energize the Conservatives' organisational base and its core vote, but also to place the publicised divisions at Westminster within a larger context. In essence, he hoped to portray the indiscipline as being confined to a quarrelsome minority.

The prime minister's efforts in unifying the party from the bottom up were, however, regularly subverted by the strident nature of Conservative politics at the centre. Major continued to face revolts and rebellions. His cabinet ministers maintained their practice of leaking against one another. Margaret Thatcher kept up her indictment of one-nation Toryism and the dangers of a European superstate. And aspiring leaders still repeatedly positioned themselves within a deepening matrix of Conservative factions. While newspaper editors demanded cabinet sackings and successive reshuffles, party dissenters pressed Major to establish 'clear blue water' between the party and New Labour. In this fractious atmosphere, Major maintained his role of trying to keep the party together through balancing groups and opinions. For example, he achieved agreement to a referendum should a Conservative government ever propose that it was in Britain's interests to join the single European currency. Major hoped that this compromise position would 'ease the tensions within my own party'[54] and close the issue down for the remainder of the parliament. These hopes proved to be ill founded. As neither side was satisfied, the briefings and counter-briefings continued unabated.

The chronic nature of the Conservatives' divisiveness and incoherence prompted Major to intensify his disengagement from the public face of his party and to make a virtue of his own isolation. To an ever-increasing and more conspicuous extent, the prime minister marketed the party around his persona. Major's individual qualities and credentials were made synonymous with the achievements of the government, the integrity of the premiership, and the underlying spirit of the party at the grass roots. The strategy of accentuating the positive through the character traits and professional experience of the prime minister led to a progressive diminution in the collective expression of the party. In November 1996, for example, he published a defence of his government's record and an outline of its future plans without ever once mentioning the Conservative party.[55] By the time the election was formally called, John Major had become an almost iconic metaphor for the party and the government. This process was exemplified by the party's manifesto. Its cover carried a full-page close-up of the prime minister's face. No other politicians were pictured in the document. The prime minister had no inhibitions in claiming the manifesto to be wholly his own. Since he provided the corporate embodiment of the party, it seemed wholly appropriate for the manifesto to be publicly equated with his principles and temperament. 'It has my imprint upon it,' he said. 'It is my manifesto, not just to my constituents but to the whole of the country.'[56] As Major increasingly distanced himself from his party, he even issued a separate statement of his government's record and reasons for re-election. *The Times* published the statement under Major's chosen title: 'My personal manifesto'.[57] In spite of being vilified for years over his alleged lack of leadership, John Major's brand of reassuring consensus building was now given prominence. It was allocated the task of drawing upon the pragmatic impulses of Middle England voters and of supplanting a party identity with a personal depiction of trust. This populist dissociation of leadership from its immediate base at the national level constituted the optimum strategy for maximising the Conservative vote in 1997.

For Tony Blair, keeping everything together looked to be a far simpler task than that which faced his chief adversary. The Labour leader headed a party unified by the first real prospect of electoral success for over twenty years. Moreover, as the parliament neared its full term that prospect became increasingly imminent. Blair also benefited from a broad coalition of non-partisan support garnered from the public's long-standing dissatisfaction with the Conservative government. And yet in spite of the factors in Labour's favour, party history ensured that Blair remained acutely conscious of the potential for failure. It was this prospect of underperformance and underachievement that continually drove Blair to seek ever greater assurances of electoral viability and organisational integrity. The price of prospective government became eternal vigilance.

New Labour strategists remained preoccupied with the dangers of complacency. Survey evidence showed that public perceptions, or fears, of party disunity had twice the negative effect on voting intentions where Labour was concerned in comparison to any evidence of disunity on the part of the Conservative party.[58] Polling also revealed that much of Labour's support was volatile and, therefore, susceptible to late swings against the party. Blair remained anxious that Labour's poll position was not only inflated and unsustainable, but might conceal a process of having already peaked at an underlying level.

He continually guarded the party against the perils of operating on the premise that governments won and lost elections. New Labour remained under inspection from a wary electorate and public trust remained the key issue.

The fragility attributed to the coalition, together with the historic opportunity to establish a basis for a left of centre government, impelled Blair to continue the crusade to minimise Labour's negative connotations and to maximise its appeal outside the party's core constituencies. Under Blair, the party was repeatedly pushed towards a centrist and unprovocative position on the economy. Labour now accepted that public spending levels were 'no longer the best measure of the effectiveness of government action in the public interest'.[59] It acknowledged that government could not 'solve all economic problems or end the economic cycle'.[60] In this context, Labour was pledged to refrain from raising income tax rates during the first five years of a Labour government. New Labour also promised to adhere to the Major administration's own spending limits for the first two years of a Blair administration.

Exceptional though these assurances were, Blair's appetite for consolidating support remained far from satisfied. As a result, trade union activity and history continued to be diminished in the composition of Labour's new identity and in the public presentation of the party's platform. New Labour's organisational emphasis turned increasingly to the news management and information-processing resource at Millbank. Whether it was market research, private polling, telephone targeting or focus group technologies, Labour's communications headquarters acquired a reputation for being incapable of relaxing its grip on the development of the party's message and on the prosecution of its electoral strategy. Millbank was also directed to the party itself. It was the chief action agency of a leadership intent upon keeping the party at large 'on message'. Through phones, faxes, modems and pagers, shadow spokespersons and candidates were continually informed of the party's line in the public arena. Millbank was part of a prodigious corporate campaign designed to exert discipline and to prevent the emergence of inconsistencies and incoherence that could undermine the party's news priorities.

At the same time that new technologies were transforming the scale and style of central coordination, Blair was making considerable efforts to achieve a rapprochement with the proprietors and editors of Conservative media outlets like *The Sun* and the *Daily Mail*. The policy and culture shift that embraced an endorsement of the enterprise culture, an active engagement with business, the abandonment of Clause IV and a set of approving allusions to Margaret Thatcher's leadership methods provoked a measure of serious unease in the party. The dismay and discomfort in some quarters were further exacerbated by Blair's sustained commitment to reduce the influence of the party conference and the NEC. There were other sources of anxiety. At the same time that Blair was openly pushing for constitutional change in the Labour party, it was also known that he was engaged in private negotiations with the Liberal Democrats on the issue of reforming the British constitution. A commitment to constitutional reform, and especially to a form of proportional representation, would in his view maximise the chances of a centre-left governing coalition. However in doing so, it also risked a new electoral regime that would be achieved at the direct expense of Labour's parliamentary representation.

The projection of political leadership had been used by New Labour as an instrument of opposition to the Conservative government. Now the implications of such leadership were deployed by those elements in the Labour party who were most concerned about the direction in which it was being taken. To his critics, Blair's leadership was synonymous with substantive changes in policy and in the movement's overall objectives. Consequently, encoded references to the nature and value of the Labour leadership became a medium of complaint. Some of the criticism took the form of objections to the price being paid to achieve electoral viability. To many of those associated with the egalitarian fundamentalism of 'old Labour', the big opinion leads did not suggest a need for caution so much as an implicit mandate for Labour to follow its radical principles. Blair's leadership, therefore, was being misdirected. There was no need to consider pacts and anti-Tory coalitions with the Liberal Democrats. Roy Hattersley, for example, strenuously objected to any leadership deals with the Liberal Democrats not only on the grounds of what Labour would have to offer on constitutional reform, but because to him the Liberal Democrats were untrustworthy and opportunists. 'For a party of principle, it is impossible even to contemplate negotiating away its programme for … the allegiance of minority parties.'[61]

Other criticism related less to the leadership engagement with Middle England politics and more to the people who surrounded the leadership, and whose advice and guidance appeared to carry disproportionate influence. Particular animus was directed to pollsters, market researchers and media consultants who were often collectively regarded as an unacceptable and largely concealed elite. In a well-publicised interview for the *New Statesman* in August 1996, Clare Short exemplified this genre of leadership opposition in a critique of Blair's advisers: 'I sometimes call them the people who live in the dark. Everything they do is in hiding. We go to the shadow cabinet. We go to the National Executive Committee. Everything we do is in the light. They live in the dark.'[62] She thought that such an elite distorted and detached the leadership from the party. They were in the forefront of a modernisation campaign that risked losing touch with the reality of the party's presence and its history.

> These people are making a terrible error. They think that Labour is unelectable, so they want to get something else elected, even though really it's still the Labour Party. This is a dangerous game, which assumes people are stupid. It gets to the point where you are ashamed of your own past … [W]hat they are

now doing is allowing the Tory propaganda version of Labour to be the reality.[63]

Such public critiques of New Labour from within the party's ranks were rarely heard. Commentators and analysts, however, were not so reticent. Many of them raised questions over the foundations and sustainability of Blair's leadership. A common theme was that the leader had marched out ahead of a bemused party whose tolerance was only as elastic as Labour's opinion poll advantage. The party not only lagged well behind the leadership, it remained largely unreconstructed from the model, which Blair was committed to transforming out of recognition. Blair had to 'educate and win over his party'[64] but this would remain difficult in a party traditionally resistant to leadership direction. Initially, Blair had based his appeal on capacious values and uncontested ethics. In time, these generalised norms came under closer scrutiny for what they might signify in terms of policy choices.

Some critics claimed that the prescription for a stakeholding community represented a political replacement for standard policy options: 'New Labour needs a moral imperative because there is no magic wand which a fiscally cautious Blair government can wave.'[65] Others asserted that Blair's value-based vision lacked the kind of content that would give Labour the anchorage and rallying point to win an election. *The Times*, for example, thought that Blair's redefinition of socialism posed more questions than it answered: 'Mr Blair's social-ism is so common-place as to be almost meaningless. The sense of community – from the local neighbourhood to the nation state – play a central part in Conservative traditions. And it is not clear whether Mr Blair has anything distinctive to add to these values.'[66] Even sympathisers on the left recognised that for all of Blair's apparent radicalism, his project bore a close similarity in policy terms to Labour's 1992 election campaign: namely, to 'put before the electorate a small number of carefully costed, cautious policies for immediate implementation',[67] but in contrast to 1992 there would be no linkage to any increases in income tax. In September 1996, Martin Jacques recognised that Blair had transformed the Labour party but he remained unconvinced that vision of Labour's leader could be translated into social change: 'He as a project for the party, a project to get elected, but not a project for the country – a challenge of a totally different order … The truth is that Blair is deeply ambitious when it comes to changing the party and deeply unambitious about changing the country. He is pessimistic about what can be achieved.'[68]

Whether Blair wanted to settle his appeal at the diffuse level of values, or relate those values ultimately to a coherent programme of government, it was widely believed that with either strategy he would encounter problems of increasing severity from a largely uncomprehending party. The modernisers' solution of boosting the party membership in order to reduce Labour's dependency upon the unions had yielded quick results. By the end of 1994,

Blair was 'less dependent on union general secretaries (many of whom tried to block his election) than any of his recent predecessors'.[69] Nevertheless, the heavy reliance upon the soft and non-institutional support of new members was thought to be a high-risk strategy that could rebound upon the leadership when it required the support of the party's heavy machinery.

In sum, Blair's leadership was widely admired but it was also seen as an achievement with a doubtful prognosis. It was often referred to as a product of suspended internal politics that would erupt with renewed factionalism after the temporary respite. It seemed highly probable that Tony Blair's reputed authoritarianism would at some point provoke an equal and opposite reaction amongst the rank and file. Even if the party's discipline were to hold until after the election, it was thought likely that it would rapidly break down once Labour had achieved office. At the very minimum, Blair's conspicuous leadership would continue to raise doubts over the degree to which there existed a trustworthy correlation between 'the head and the body'. Even when the election was imminent, *The Economist* reported that 'the one-man-band question [was] still the one the leader's intimates fear[ed] most' because it could 'cost them the election'.[70]

The leader was well aware of the democratic instincts and fissiparous properties of his party but in the main Blair saw these as reasons for continued discipline rather than as a case for any relaxation in the momentum. To Blair, Labour's recidivism was far more of a threat than any reaction to central direction. In April 1995, Philip Gould reported to him that with the election possibility only a year away, New Labour was 'still a party in transition',[71] requiring further extensive modernisation. Gould continued the indictment and defined his solution.

> New Labour does not have the flexibility, adaptability, capacity for innovation ... that is the hallmark of a successful political organisation ... Labour does not yet have a political project that matches the Thatcher agenda of 1979, nor will be able to sustain Labour in government and transform Britain ... Labour must replace competing existing structures with a single chain of command leading directly to the leader of the party. This is the only way that Labour can become a political organisation capable of matching the Conservatives.[72]

The impetus had to remain with the process of leadership-centred modernisation. New Labour strategists pressed ahead with the negotiations for a Labour-Liberal Democrat framework document on constitutional reform. The prospect of Liberal Democratic cooperation to defeat the Conservatives in key southern marginals overrode reservations from party traditionalists. Further reform to the party structures and procedures were prepared to enhance the public cohesion and campaigning integrity of Labour.[73] As far as the leadership was concerned, the benefit of any doubt would lay with what-ever succeeded in focusing public attention upon the selected priorities and policy agenda of the New Labour project.

Blair's attitude towards his own party was captured by his succinct reaction to one of the Liberal Democrats' more nuanced documents giving oblique approval to dropping the party's pre-existing policy of 'equidistance' between the Conservative and Labour parties. According to Paddy Ashdown, the private view of the Labour leader was that the Liberal Democrats had been altogether too guarded. Blair said that he would have taken a much more direct approach: 'From my experience, you have to take your party members and shove their faces in it before they really understand.'[74] Blair's attitude to Labour party dissent and division was similarly robust. Occasionally, it was even expressed in public. In September 1995, Blair responded to a question on opponents within the party in the following robust terms: 'I'm a politician, not a psychiatrist, but if people seriously think that by going back to where we were 10 or 12 years ago to win power, then they require not leadership, but therapy. We've got to smash that complacency out of the system.'[75] In July 1996, a question on the same theme provoked the same kind of response: '[A] lot of people on the left have tended to define radical politics by reference to a whole lot of Labour positions that were not really radical or very sensible politically ... Many of them are stuck in a time warp as to what radical politics actually mean today.'[76]

The Labour leader's primary aim was to secure power but an objective of comparable significance was to govern as New Labour and not to allow the party, as it had done in the past, to turn against a Labour government. It would serve little purpose to form a Labour administration only to see it disintegrate, thereby allowing the Conservatives to return to power for another extended period in office. A minimum of a second full-term Labour government became the driving commitment behind the campaign to win the forthcoming general election. With this in mind, Blair continued to press for reforms to tighten party discipline, to manage the party conference and to limit the capacity of the National Executive Committee to become an alternative power centre to that of a future Labour government. Blair's commitment to maintaining coher-ence was typified by his move to hold a party referendum on a draft manifesto in 1996. It was seen not only as another way in which the leadership had circumvented and marginalised the party hierarchy, but as an insurance device against later claims that a Labour government had betrayed the party.

Blair was looking ahead to the future problem of keeping it all together: 'There's no doubt that a vote of all individual members will give the manifesto a legitimacy within the party that it has not enjoyed before – which will make it difficult for anyone to complain because a Blair government hasn't done what it never promised to do in the first place.'[77] Blair wanted to make it quite clear that at the very outset he had a minimal and responsible programme for government. He did not want his administration to be judged either against a standard set in an earlier era of industrial strife, or against a set of amorphous ideals. The intention was to implicate the party as a whole into the responsibility of government. In effect, Labour's plebiscite was part of a concerted campaign on the part of Blair 'to join ... principles to practice, the party's activists to its supporters in the country, and himself to the party – or, as he would term it, the head to the body'.[78]

As the campaign entered the formal period of electioneering, there were very few discernible differences in tone or content between the general election and the previous three years of concerted leadership competition. Tony Blair continued to remind voters of the failures of the Conservative administration and of New Labour's competence for government, together with the security provided by his leadership and his personal guarantees of performance. He maintained the now long-established theme that Major and his administration had hung on to office beyond its natural life span and that the Conservatives had no objective other than that of mere survival. Blair dismissed the Tories as 'a degenerate party' and described John Major as a prime minister who was 'always fighting for a job, never fighting for a vision'.[79]

For his part, John Major reiterated the familiar message that Labour could not be trusted with the economic recovery and that Old Labour remained in existence waiting to 'tax and spend' in government. He underlined his commitment to a classless Britain and raised questions over whether Labour could ever adjust to a more mobile society with its emphasis upon opportunity and choice. Major's prejudice against socialism in general and Blair's social status in particular gave an increasingly strident edge to his attacks. Major insisted that New Labour was a dangerous chimera concealing a 'secret army'[80] of socialists that would, under the new leader, usher in an illiberal regime of central coercion. He recognised the 'smug "we know better" tone in all they do – the sheer arrogance' and deplored 'their bossiness, their fussiness, their pushiness'.[81] According to Major, Tony Blair was a symptom of Labour's extended period of opposition and of its extreme ambition: 'Eighteen years in opposition have left Labour ravenous for power. They mouth the words they are given, wear the right suit and tie, smile when told to do so.'[82] Major continued to question the purpose of such atypical coherence. 'What lies behind the smile?'[83] The *double entendre* was deployed to underline what was portrayed as a Labour message of double-dealing. As the Conservatives launched a poster campaign featuring a diminutive Tony Blair sitting submissively in Chancellor Kohl's lap, John Major also attempted to depict Blair as a threat to the nation's sovereignty. In essence, Blair was accused of being soft on the issue of the European Union: 'Unlike the Labour leader, I will retain our vetoes. If it is right for Britain, I will keep my feet on the brakes. Mr Blair would go to Amsterdam and put his foot on the accelerator to a federal Europe. This is the clear choice on May 1.'[84]

The threat of a European superstate was compounded by a warning that Labour's collaboration with the Liberal Democrats on constitutional reform would lead to an assault upon the British constitution and to the disintegration of the United Kingdom. The prime minister insisted that the election was 'literally a battle for Britain'[85] because Labour did not have the experience to grasp the consequences of its reckless agenda: 'A thousand days of Labour government could ditch a thousand years of British history.'[86] In the final week of the campaign, Major played upon the consequences of replacing experience with an untried and untested novice in the premiership. His warning was drawn from the insights of a seven-year premiership. The inference was that only Major's personal skills and strategic grasp of the issue could protect the nation's security. These warnings against Labour's 'siren voices of change'[87] did not have the same leverage that they had had in 1992. The long campaign failed to shift the general pattern of opinion, which had originally been formed in the aftermath to the Exchange Rate Mechanism episode in 1992. Blair and New Labour had succeeded in holding the mid-term levels of support through to the election period. Some slippage occurred in the final period but in the end Labour prevailed with dramatic effect. The New Labour project secured an advantage of 43.2 to 30.7 per cent in the popular vote and a landslide majority of a 189 parliamentary seats.

The events of 1 May 1997 did not simply mark the end of the Conservative government. They represented the culmination of an extraordinarily protracted leadership crisis that had had a profound effect upon the conduct and development of British politics. John Major had finally lost the premiership. He immediately announced his intention to resign the leadership of the Conservative party. The landslide defeat had undermined the Conservative hegemony but at the same time it also marked the revival of the ethos of strong leadership. Blair's victory was not merely characterised by his leadership. The requirements of the victory were engineered and driven through to completion by the forces surrounding the Labour leader. Consequently, the commitment to leadership virtues in service to a personal vision of national renewal and social restoration became the main animating principle of the new administration. The nature of Major's long defeat and of Blair's extensive preparations for Downing Street dramatically revealed the contemporary dynamics of leadership politics in Britain. They also demonstrated the existence of an accelerating trend towards a leadership-centred system of political engagement. The collision course of John Major and Tony Blair had produced an impact of seismic proportions in the role of leadership both in the calculations of political parties and in the operation of politics in the public sphere. An analysis of these leadership features, together with an appraisal of their significance and implications, are provided in the concluding chapter.

Notes

1 'The right to choose', *Sunday Telegraph*, 15 May 1994.
2 John Major, *The Autobiography* (London: HarperCollins, 1999), p. 592.
3 Nicholas Wapshott, 'John Major: Who I am and whence I came', *The Observer*, 2 December 1990.
4 Boris Johnson, 'The young contemptible', *Daily Telegraph*, 5 December 1994.
5 Johnson, 'The young contemptible'.
6 Leader's speech to the Conservative Party Conference 1994, *The Times*, 15 October 1994.
7 Quoted in Stephen Castle, 'This time it's personal', *Independent on Sunday*, 3 November 1996.
8 Leader's speech to the Conservative Party Conference 1994, *The Independent*, 15 October 1994.
9 Leader's speech to the Conservative Party Conference 1994, *The Independent*, 15 October 1994.
10 Quoted in an interview with Stephen Fay, *Independent on Sunday*, 25 November 1990.
11 Major, *The Autobiography*, pp. xxii–xxiii.
12 Quoted in an interview with David Wastell, *Sunday Telegraph*, 25 November 1990.
13 Major, *The Autobiography*, p. 731.
14 Leader's speech to the Conservative Party Conference 1994, *The Independent*, 15 October 1994.
15 Tony Blair, 'Britain is crying out for strong leadership', *Daily Telegraph*, 8 December 1994.
16 Hansard, House of Commons, 31 October 1996, col. 781.
17 Hansard, House of Commons, 31 October 1996, cols 781–2.
18 Donald Macintyre, 'Steady, Tony, it could still fall apart', *The Independent*, 4 July 1996.
19 Anthony Giddens, 'What's he up to?', *New Statesman and Society*, 24 February 1994.
20 Philip Gould, *The Unfinished Revolution: How the Modernisers Saved the Labour Party* (London: Little, Brown, 1998), pp. 192–3.
21 Andrew Marr, 'Someone old, someone new', *The Independent*, 28 July 1994.
22 'New Labour, new stakeholders', *The Guardian*, 9 January 1995.
23 Tony Blair, 'Battle for Britain', *The Guardian*, 29 January 1996.
24 John Rentoul, *Tony Blair*, rev edn (London: Warner, 1996), pp. 184–5.
25 Hugo Young, 'Only Blair dares to admit that the good old days are gone', *The Guardian*, 16 June 1994.
26 Young, 'Only Blair dares to admit that the good old days are gone'.
27 Young, 'Only Blair dares to admit that the good old days are gone'.
28 Hansard, House of Commons, 25 April 1995, col. 656.
29 Major, *The Autobiography*, p. 607.
30 For example, see David Leigh and Ed Vulliamy, *Sleaze: The Corruption of Parliament* (London: Fourth Estate, 1997); Gerald James, *In The Public Interest* (London: Warner 1996); *First Report of the Committee on Standards in Public Life, Volume 1: Report, Cm 2850–1* (London: HMSO, 1995).
31 Quoted in Stephen Bates, 'Major plea for less "sneering" in politics', *The Guardian*, 14 May 1994.
32 Quoted in Bates, 'Major plea for less "sneering" in politics'.
33 Quoted in Bates, 'Major plea for less "sneering" in politics'.
34 Quoted in Bates, 'Major plea for less "sneering" in politics'.
35 Hansard, House of Commons, 18 October 1994, col. 139.

36 Hansard, House of Commons, 27 October 1994, cols 1003–4.
37 Andrew Neil, 'Cracks in the facade of Blair's Potemkin village', *Sunday Times*, 14 April 1996.
38 Leader's speech to the Conservative Party Conference 1996, *The Times*, 12 October 1996.
39 Quoted in an interview with Michael Jones, *Sunday Times*, 30 April 1995.
40 Quoted in an interview with Michael Jones, *Sunday Times*, 30 April 1995.
41 Quoted in an interview with Michael Jones, *Sunday Times*, 30 April 1995.
42 Leader's speech to the Conservative Party Conference 1994, *Sunday Telegraph*, 16 October 1994.
43 Leader's speech to the Conservative Party Conference 1994, *The Times*, 15 October 1994.
44 Quoted in Colin Brown, 'Major challenged to disown the "demon"', *The Independent*, 12 August 1996.
45 Hywel Williams, *Guilty Men: Conservative Decline and Fall 1992–1997* (London: Aurum, 1998), p. 69.
46 John Gray, 'Divide and rule', *The Guardian*, 2 October 1995.
47 Williams, *Guilty Men*, p. 143.
48 Williams, *Guilty Men*, p. 144.
49 David Butler and Dennis Kavanagh, *The British General Election of 1997* (Houndmills: Macmillan, 1997), p. 40.
50 Butler and Kavanagh, *The British General Election of 1997*, p. 40.
51 Emma Nicholson and Peter Thurnham defected to the Liberal Democrats. Alan Howarth switched to the Labour party.
52 Andrew Grice, 'They're behind him … but can he trust them?' *Sunday Times*, 14 January 1996.
53 Grice, 'They're behind him … but can he trust them?'
54 Major, *The Autobiography*, p. 687.
55 See John Major, 'What's right with Britain', *Daily Telegraph*, 11 November 1996.
56 Quoted in Arthur Leathley, 'Cast your doubts aside and trust me, pleads Major', *The Times*, 24 April 1997.
57 John Major, 'My personal manifesto', *The Times*, 9 April 1997.
58 See 'Flattened by Blair', *The Economist*, 6 July 1996.
59 'New labour, because Britain deserves better', Labour Party Manifesto 1997, p. 11.
60 'New labour, because Britain deserves better', Labour Party Manifesto 1997, p. 11.
61 Quoted in Michael White, 'Hattersley warns against compromise', *The Guardian*, 18 June 1994.
62 Interview with Clare Short, *New Statesman*, 9 August 1996.
63 Interview with Clare Short, *New Statesman*, 9 August 1996.
64 Peter Riddell, 'Marching out in front', *The Times*, 24 October 1994.
65 'New Labour, new stakeholders', *The Guardian*, 9 January 1995.
66 'What's in a name', *The Times*, 16 September 1996.
67 Paul Anderson and Nyta Mann, *Safety First: The Making of New Labour* (London: Granta 1997), p. 45.
68 Martin Jacques, 'His project for the party is a triumph, but what about his project for the country?', *The Guardian*, 26 September 1996.
69 Peter Riddell, 'Look for the Blair necessities', *The Times*, 7 July 1994.
70 'Labour's awkward one-man band', *The Economist*, 28 September 1996.
71 Gould, *The Unfinished Revolution*, p. 240.
72 Gould, *The Unfinished Revolution*, p. 240.

73 In order to create a close partnership between the party and a new Labour govern-ment, a series of proposals were announced in January 1997. They included radical changes in the composition of the NEC, a three-year rolling review of the party pro-gramme, the establishment of a Joint Policy Committee drawn from the cabinet and the NEC, and the expansion of the National Policy Forum. The NEC was rescheduled to meet every two months instead of every month, and its committee structure was set to be replaced by a series of task forces. The intention of the plan was to end the NEC's formal monopoly over policy-making and to prevent it from adopting the role of a watchdog over a Labour government.

74 Quoted in Paddy Ashdown, *The Ashdown Diaries: Volume One 1988-1997* (London: Penguin, 2000), p. 324.

75 Quoted in 'Eyes on the prize' (Tony Blair interviewed by Andrew Jaspan and Sarah Baxter), *The Observer*, 10 September 1995.

76 Quoted in an interview with Ian Hargreaves and Steve Richards, *New Statesman*, 5 July 1996.

77 Paul Anderson, 'Blair's plebiscite', *New Statesman*, 5 April 1996.

78 Donald Macintyre, 'His course is set for a historic mission', *Independent*, 30 December 1995.

79 Quoted in Stephen Castle, 'Blair plays safe and sceptical', *Independent on Sunday*, 20 April 1997.

80 Quoted in Jonathan Freedland and Michael White, 'Major launches bitter attack on Blair', *The Guardian*, 30 April 1997.

81 Quoted in Freedland and White, 'Major launches bitter attack on Blair'.

82 John Major, 'Conservatives have served the many, not the few', *The Independent*, 16 April 1997.

83 Major, 'Conservatives have served the many, not the few'.

84 Quoted in Stephen Bates and Michael White, 'The merchants of doom', *The Guardian*, 22 April 1997.

85 Quoted in Freedland and White, 'Major launches bitter attack on Blair'.

86 Quoted in Anthony Bevins, 'Major launches crusade to save constitution', *The Independent*, 15 February 1997.

87 Quoted in Freedland and White, 'Major launches bitter attack on Blair'.

8 Conclusion

During the course of British parliamentary politics, there have always been leaders of political parties who have clashed openly, persistently and personally with other leaders. Likewise, the prospect of conclusive electoral outcomes to leadership competition has been an ever-present feature of the British system. The adversary culture of the party tradition has ensured that leaders and aspiring leaders confront one another both across parties and also within them. In one sense, the period examined in this study is, therefore, well within the grain of these traditions. In another, and arguably more significant sense, the interaction between John Major and Tony Blair marked a quite exceptional set of conditions. These not only revealed a range of insights into the intensifying dynamics of modern leadership politics, but also demonstrated the developmental trends in the processes of leadership contention.

The circumstances of this encounter were extraordinary. The Conservative party, which had established a hegemony status, became subject to a prolonged political crisis. As the properties of the hegemony became increasingly and retrospectively associated with a model of heroic leadership, the crisis became synonymous with a crisis over leadership and with John Major's leadership in particular. Just as the Conservatives departed from their customary discipline and cohesion on the subject of leadership, so the Labour party underwent a similarly dramatic metamorphosis. It dispensed with its traditional suspicions and inhibitions relating to leadership and became transformed into a spectacular embodiment of a leader-centred organisation. The combined effect of these developments was a 'struggle for power between John Major and Tony Blair' that had 'all the makings of an unrivalled personal battle'.[1] But it amounted to much more than this. These two leaders and their respective parties were locked into a collision course that acted as both an expression and a catalyst for the public projection of personal leadership and for the penetration of leadership issues into the conduct of British politics. The high stakes and high risks that permeated this conflict were a reflection of the role, the status and the ramifying potential of leadership within the priorities and investments of the respective parties. In examining the varied nature of this complex development at such a pivotal period, a number of conclusions offer themselves for consideration. They come in the form of strands that can be elicited from the analysis and which warrant individual comment and appraisal.

Leadership as a public commodity

The first strand relates to what can be termed the structure of public discussion upon leadership in contemporary British politics. This structure relates to the extensive scale and deepening intensity of leadership-centred comment and analysis in the review of political issues and party performance. The plight of the Conservative government during this period was quickly and unalterably characterised as a leadership crisis – i.e. a crisis not simply symbolised by the figurehead of a party leader, but one defined and explained by reference to John Major as an individual with personal failings and intrinsic flaws. Party leaders have increasingly stretched away from their organisational bases partly as a consequence of the dominance of the visual media but also because they are encouraged to do so by parties needing to compete effectively in an electorate with rising levels of voter dealignment and political scepticism. The disadvantage of such a development for leaders is one of high exposure and commensurate accountability when the public debate on leadership turns against them. John Major's chronic condition provided a classic example of the way that political and governmental problems can be refracted through the lens of a leadership discourse that can turn multiple complexities into simple dimensions.

Leaders and other senior participants and close observers of the political process may complain that what is conveyed to the public and what is received by it is not the real measure of leadership. This is shaped and extended behind the scenes amidst the political elites and is experienced at close quarters only within party and government hierarchies. The public only has access to partial impressions. Nevertheless, these perceptions, however inaccurate or unfair, constitute a considerable force upon a leader. It is a factor that conditions the status and leverage of leaders within political structures. Public impressions have a pivotal resonance to leaders. The medium of popular perception is continually fuelled by media reporting on the behaviour, reactions, choices, decisions, performances and appraisals of leaders. A vast hinterland of opinion polling and survey analysis supports the drumbeat of leadership news values. Leaders are now expected not only to perform in public but also to maintain a continual engagement with the public – even being seen to achieve a position of leading the public *in* public.

An integral component of this dynamic is the inclusion of public estimation and assessment of leadership performances. Polling organisations pose a considerable variety of questions relating to leadership. They vary from general inquiries to specific items, from behavioural categories to personality components, and from reactions to positive statements to responses elicited from negative declarations. Some questions relate to the personal attributes of leaders in isolation from one another. A representative sample of the themes used for this purpose is given below:

Well-informed	Clever
Intelligent	Grasp of detail
Sincere	Sound judgement
Likable	Friendly
Appealing	Down to earth
Honest/ethical	Knows his own mind
Says what he believes	Persuasive
Will get things done	Competent
Experienced	Explains himself effectively
Compassionate	Tough
Hardworking	Vision
Understand problems	Patriotic
Trustworthy to do the right thing in a decision	Good in crisis

Other questions assess the extent to which the respondent feels a personal identity with the leader (e.g. 'shares my views'; 'cares about me'; 'understands people like me'). By the same token, respondents can be invited to share negative estimations of leaders (e.g. the extent to which they are seen as 'arrogant', 'abrasive', 'not well educated', 'indecisive', 'out of touch', 'inflexible', 'talks down to people'). While some polls are based upon segmented answers to individual leaders, others are openly comparative in nature. They call upon respondents to make judgements between leaders over their respective skills in the handling of different policy issues (e.g. the economy, health, education, transport, foreign policy), or in relation to a number of leadership attributes (e.g. 'Who comes closest to your views?' 'Who is more honest?' 'Who is more appealing?' 'Who offers stronger leadership?' 'Who has the best ideas?').

The data collected from the public responses to these types of questions are publicised and tracked over time to provide supportive evidence to news items and to create leadership-based news stories. Just as the depth of John Major's crisis could be gauged by comparison with the difficulties of previous prime ministers (Table 8.1), so the prime minister and the leader of the opposition could be measured against a selected set of individual attributes (Table 8.2).

More advanced depictions of leadership attributes have been generated for public consumption. For example, MORI used a form of multivariate analysis to produce 'perceptual maps' that helped to 'define the relative posi-

Table 8.1 John Major's poll position (June 1993) in relation to previous prime ministerial low points

---

PRIME MINISTERS' LOWEST POINTS

In 1938 Gallup first asked the question, 'Are you satisfied with the prime minister of the day?' Below is a league table of the lowest ratings experienced by every prime minister since that time.'

Winston Churchill	48%	Lowest: 48% Apr 1954 Previous high: 55% Highest after that: 56% (Oct 1953)
Sir Alec Douglas-Home	42%	Lowest: 42% Dec 1963 Previous high: 48% Highest after that: 48% (Aug 1964)
Sir Anthony Eden	41%	Lowest: 41% Apr 1956 Previous high: 73% Highest after that: 56% (Dec 1956)
Clement Attlee	37%	Lowest: 37% Sept 1948 Previous high: 66% Highest after that: 57% (May 1951)
James Callaghan	33%	Lowest: 33% Nov 1976 Previous high: 57% Highest after that: 59% (Oct 1977)
Neville Chamberlain	32%	Lowest: 32% May 1940 Previous high: 68% Left office
Edward Heath	31%	Lowest: 31% Jun 1971 Previous high: 45% Highest after that: 43% (Jun 1973)
Harold Macmillan	30%	Lowest: 30% Oct 1957 Previous high: 54% Highest after that: 79% (May 1960)
Harold Wilson	27%	Lowest: 27% May 1968 Previous high: 69% Highest after that: 51% (Jun 1970)
Margaret Thatcher	23%	Lowest: 23% Apr 1990 Previous high: 53% Highest after that: 33% (Sep 1990)
John Major	21%	Lowest: 21% Jun 1993 Previous high: 59% (Feb 1991) Highest after that: ?

Source: Gallup/*Daily Telegraph* (4 June 1993)

Table 8.2 Tony Blair and John Major: comparative ratings (%)

Q: Which of the following apply to the two leaders?

	John Major	Tony Blair
A strong leader	10	26
You can believe what he says	13	14
In touch with ordinary people	10	32
A good image for Britain abroad	15	16
Likeable	27	31
He has lots of good ideas	8	23
Right leader to take Britain into the 21st century	6	16
Prisoner of divisions in his own party	40	12

Source: NOP/*Sunday Times* (10 May 1996)

tions of the three party leaders on attributes both positive and negative which people in focus groups'[2] reported as being significant. The results allowed each leader to be positioned in relation to the clusters of attributes to which they had a relatively closer association than the other leaders (Figure 8.1).

Such analysis could reveal over time how attributes could both change and become entrenched (Figure 8.2). A comparison between the patterns of leadership image in 1995 and 1996, for example, reveals that John Major remained rooted with negative associations such as being 'out of touch', 'narrow minded' and 'inflexible'. By contrast, Tony Blair's image had benefited largely at Paddy Ashdown's expense. Blair had established a closer correlation with a number of positive leadership attributes (i.e. 'understands world problems', 'sound judgement', 'personality' and 'honesty').

In spite of the sophistication of such analyses, they can neither determine the relationship between one attribute and another, nor assign a higher leadership value to one set of characteristics over another. What these measures, and other simpler rankings, reveal is the volatile nature of the leadership market. This is shown not just in relation to public attitudes to changing leadership but also to shifting emphases attached to different attributes. The polls continually track leaders on their public performance and on their relationship to the contemporary public attitudes towards political leadership. As John Major discovered, the critical attention given to him, his parliamentary party and his personal record was unremitting. It adversely affected his political base in the government, the party and the House of Commons. A symbiosis of decline rapidly gathered pace in which Major's authority as leader and prime minister

Figure 8.1 Leader image (February 1995)

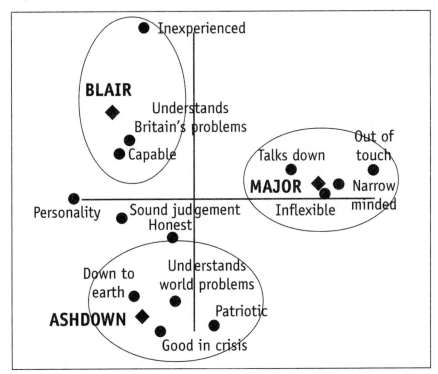

Source: MORI/*Times*

was persistently subverted by sceptics, rivals and critics, who exploited for personal gain the leadership question and the public's response to it. As Tony Blair was fêted for his leadership qualities, John Major became mired in a pubic domain of interpretive hostility, cross-cutting advice, demands to 'get a grip' and attempted relaunches. It was clear that political leadership had become more than a medium of political engagement and a forum of public theatre; it had become an instrument of populist participation and a category of political evaluation in its own right.

The volume of resources directed to the personalised projection and clash of leaderships bore testimony to the salience of the leadership dimension on both sides. The prolonged and intense nature of this concentrated competition for leadership credentials further deepened the matrix of public engagement with the precepts, language and symbolism of the theme. The period of the Major premiership was supposed to mark the end of dramatic leadership as an issue. Instead, it fostered a dramatic revival of interest in the properties and functions of leadership, and in its location and value. Although it drew upon

Figure 8.2 Leader image (October 1996)

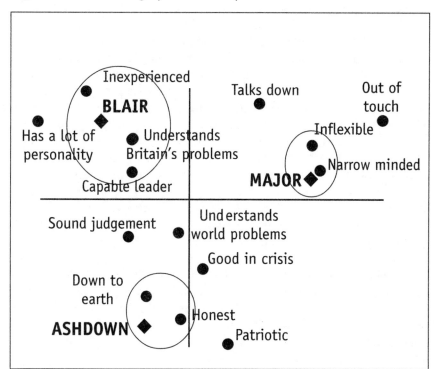

Source: MORI/*Times*

and developed themes that were associated with the Thatcher era, the framework of public discourse on leadership far surpassed the pattern of the 1980s both in terms of sustained interest and critical analysis.

The professionalisation of leadership

The second strand of discernible developments to be drawn from the cumulative process of the Major–Blair conflict is the growing professionalisation of leadership. The rise of the career politician at Westminster has been widely recognised as a characteristic feature of contemporary British politics.[3] Increasingly, MPs enter Westminster after having worked their way through an apprenticeship in cognate occupations (e.g. management, trade union administration, political research, the law, university lecturing, journalism, media programming and production). Once in parliament, they are totally committed to a long-term future in the House of Commons and beyond. As the number of independent 'outsiders' and amateur generalists has declined, so the intake of specialised professional politicians has grown to the extent of generating anxieties over whether they now 'inhabit a private intellectual and social world'[4] with a resultant 'narrowing of focus within Parliament'.[5]

Leaders have come to reflect these developments. They are now drawn exclusively from this cohort. More significantly, they apply the drive and the ethics of full-time specialisation to the task of leadership. In effect, political leaders are not only professional politicians in leadership positions; they are professional leaders who have to dedicate themselves to the continual pursuit of gaining advantages and avoiding failures in relation to other leaders. Such are the expectations assigned to leaders and such is the intensity of the public and media gaze upon them, that leaders have to remain restlessly attentive at all times in order to project and to protect their leaderships both singly and collectively. John Major and Tony Blair exemplified the total commitment to leadership priorities that is now a requirement of party dynamics.

Leaders are more than obsessive MPs, or striving politicians. They are obsessive and striving leaders whose energies and skills have had to undergo a qualitative shift to fulfill leadership roles to the point of exhaustive mono-mania. They will be monitored and judged on nothing less. In these conditions the gap between a leader and his or her colleagues in parliament is in one way less than it used to be when leaders were normally drawn from a definable and distinct governing class. But in every other respect, the gap between leaders and non-leaders has widened under the gravitational force of high leadership exposure, concentrated media investment, 24-hour news cycles, increasingly independent voters and the guiding imperative of leaders to establish their claims to public leadership. Leaders now have to maintain a constant engagement with the public. They have to personify their parties' interest in public issues and popular concerns. Leaders have to market their parties by marketing themselves and their ability to provide national leadership and effective governance. Leaders are responsible to their parties for providing the kind of highly visible leadership that takes them away from the party home base. By the same token, the enormous investment that parties make in their leaders affords them wide discretion to respond quickly and effectively to movements in public opinion. Given it is the leaders who are now the main agents of brand differentiation in a context of non-ideological politics and given the constant need for leaders to cultivate their parties' identities, then it becomes evident that the modern phenomenon of the 'permanent election' is driven more than anything else by the agendas of professionalised leadership.

Successive failures by Labour to return to government prompted extreme measures to be taken to correct the imbalance. Most dramatic was the establishment of the party's communications headquarters at Millbank. The hi-tech nature of the research, polling and media processing facilities was not only the chief instrument of the Blairite project but also a monument to New Labour's professionalism. Tony Blair's leverage and authority as a leader selected by an electoral college was strongly augmented by this highly sophisticated centre of public connection. Through private polling, focus groups and professional analysis, Millbank traced, tracked and assimilated every pulse of public opinion. Despite the advantages of incumbency John Major was seen to be wholly unable to compete with Tony Blair at this level of leadership influence and campaigning capacity. As Labour's leader-centred challenge to the Conservatives achieved unprecedented levels of organisational competence, the transition from leader of the opposition to prime minister was almost seamless. Blair had already proved himself to be fit for the premiership by his organisational achievement in taking over the Labour party and inaugurating a publicity machine of matchless quality. So emphatic and conclusive was Blair's success in having vindicated his claim to Number 10 through sheer political professionalism that both he and the party were fearful that Labour would suffer from 'reverse incumbency' – i.e. that the public would become so accustomed to Labour being depicted as a government in waiting that it would actually come to be seen as a *de facto* government. As a result, critical attention would shift away from the Conservative government's evident failures towards the possible flaws of the opposition.

Such was the gross disparity in the perceived levels of leadership competence between the two main parties that after the election the Conservatives immediately responded to New Labour's triumph with a radical restructuring of the party and a repositioning of the leadership within it. Labour in turn reacted to the need to remain vigilant on the issue of the leadership and its interface with the public. Number 10 swiftly established a new centralised regime of news management, media relations and government information designed to ensure that the Blair government would not succumb to the same afflictions that disorientated the Major administration. Critics complained that under Blair, government had become equated with campaigning. To the leadership, this did not necessarily amount to a criticism. Labour strategists were simply seeking to apply the professional standards of the campaign to the conduct of government.

Battling for leadership criteria

The framework of leadership competition provides the third strand of analysis to emerge from the Major–Blair confrontation. The relationship between leadership styles, predicaments and personality and the tactics of countering leadership claims were addressed in Chapter 7. It is appropriate at this point to note that the competition for leadership involves a complex and subtle set of dynamics that can change with time, situation and interpretation. The same features or characteristics of a leadership can be construed as constituting evidence of substantially different conditions and values, depending upon the shifting categories of leadership norms. The battle for leadership is in many respects a battle for the controlling influence over the leadership debate. This debate amounts to a continual contest over the varied interpretations and relative priorities of different leadership attributes in the shaping of the empirical and normative standards of contemporary leadership.

John Major epitomised the problems that a leader can confront when the tide of contested standards turns against the person in the leadership position. As we have seen in this study, Major marketed himself as the antidote to Margaret Thatcher. After a period when Thatcher had overreached herself and antagon-ised many of her colleagues by her heavy handed and imperious manner, Major sought to mark her departure by championing a consensus-based leadership. Major had personally witnessed Margaret Thatcher's increasing isolation in the premiership and was aware how this had made her vulnerable to leaks, divisions and dissent. By reviving what he considered to be the classic cabinet format of collegiate decision-making and collective responsibility, the new prime minister hoped to inaugurate a more open and collaborative govern-ment. Studies showed that Major was less active, less assertive and more collect-ivist in his approach to the cabinet.[6] This modus operandi typified his entire outlook to the task of leadership and its relationship to his own personality.

Major saw himself as a thoroughly ordinary person, but one who demon-strated the virtues of the prosaic amidst the political exotica of invective and intransigence: 'I wanted to show that it was possible to be prime minister and remain a human being, just like the fifty-five million other human beings in the country, but with an exceptional job.'[7] It was instructive that at this time the prime minister revealed Stanley Baldwin as one of his political heroes. He admired the 'capacity of Baldwin to still a nation that was socially adrift' which to Major was 'a very great gift and a very great skill'.[8] Baldwin's cultivated style of soothing reassurance and fireside radio chats found 'their echo in John Major's homely ordinariness and love of cricket'.[9] At the outset of his premier-ship, Major had been highly persuasive of the way that such a leadership could provide a sound anchorage to party and country. In October 1991, for example, Alan Cochrane and Peter Dobbie celebrated Major's calm and assimilative approach to leadership. They approved of the way that open debate was construed as a sign of prime ministerial strength.

> One senior cabinet minister last week described him as 'the chairman of the board', someone who is recognised as a boss who has the confidence to allow his colleagues to fire off their opinions in cabinet at will – even if they be diametrically opposed to his own. Gone, but not forgotten, are the leaks and divisions of Thatcher cabinet. Gone, but not forgotten, are the insults, real as well as imagined, which Thatcher heaped on senior colleagues.[10]

After the grandeur of Margaret Thatcher, John Major offered a different kind of connection to the public. Sir Robin Day recognised not only the difference but the value of the difference '[H]e has negative charisma. He is an ordinary man in an extraordinary position. That rather appeals to people because they can identify with him.'[11] Major succeeded in appealing to a vast constituency of aspiration. His well-publicised background together with his visibility as a prime minister, unaffected by being prime minister, made his example a much more tangible measure of life's possibilities than that provided by Mrs Thatcher and by Conservative party doctrines. He showed every indication of being able to disarm his opponents with a populism of common-sense attitudes and real-life accounts of social mobility. To the Conservatives, it was essential that their exceptional leader should continue to be portrayed as an outstandingly ordinary person.

And yet within two years, Major had become the object of scornful derision and political denigration. He was now castigated for being ordinary in an exceptional position and for inducing extraordinary failures because of who he was and where he served. Ambition was seen to have surpassed ability. Major was widely regarded to have been tragically promoted beyond his natural level. Most crucially, the prime minister had lost the battle over the criteria and standards of leadership interpretation. His style of leadership was now interpreted as a sign of weakness rather than strength. Cabinet conflicts were no longer portrayed as positive signs of a mature leadership; they were now assumed to be indicators of factionalism and a chronic lack of leadership. Major was generally viewed as having an 'almost touching naiveté concerning consensus. He seemed genuinely to believe that a discursive style of decision-making committed ministers to policy.'[12] When this equation no longer held, the Prime Minister had little notion of how to recreate the harmony of the 1991–92 period: 'Major confused the desire to be a team-builder with an ability to be one.'[13]

The prime minister had failed on his own criteria of leadership. Moreover, he had also been unsuccessful in maintaining the salience of his preferred approach to leadership within the spheres of professional estimation and public opinion. In essence, he had managed neither to sustain his own leadership standard, nor to protect its integrity as a valued type. As a consequence, Major had made himself highly vulnerable in the political struggle over what constitutes leadership and over who could best provide it. This conflict is a ceaseless struggle that is centred upon the delegitimisation and displacement of established leaders. John Major's catastrophic collapse in this competition over the analytical and evaluative priorities of leadership throws into high relief the continual need for a leader to maintain a pivotal position in this highly reactive political dimension. Major did not merely lose his leadership; he lost control over how that leadership was defined and interpreted.

John Major's considered reflections on his diminishing fortunes in the premiership are particularly revealing in this context. He makes it clear that he felt ill served by the contributions made, both implicitly and explicitly, by his predecessor to the leadership issue. In his view, these references to an idealised past defined by strong leadership made him far more vulnerable to the Blair surge than would otherwise have been the case. Major was acutely aware that the advantages of incumbency did not always extend to the requirements of leadership competition. He was envious of Margaret Thatcher who had been in opposition before becoming prime minister: 'She followed a disastrous Labour decade, and was able to boldly attack her inheritance. I had to talk up my inheritance, while moving with a minimum of fuss to correct my own party's mistakes.'[14] He was also sensitive to the advantages enjoyed by Tony Blair for the same reason.

> Only now years later, is it possible to understand how much was lost because I came into Number 10 from *government*, without my own programme settled rather than from *opposition*, where my priorities would have been prepared and ready for action. The speed at which the incoming Labour government was able to act in 1997 illustrates the point: their plans were ready to roll, giving an impression of dynamism … I did not enjoy the luxury of working up my own programme at leisure. It had to be done at speed and amidst the frenzy of government.[15]

And yet in having recounted the numerous advantages in developing a leadership profile in opposition, Major asserted that he was temperamentally unsuited to the 'special art'[16] of opposition. It was difficult enough to deal with a leader of the opposition like Tony Blair who was prodigiously lucky and who had stolen the Conservatives' clothes in policy. But Major's problems were compounded by the distraction of his own undisciplined party.

Major was quite unable to fathom why the Conservatives were not assisting their own prime minister in the battle over leadership credentials. As a consequence, self-pity and a sense of fatalism were never far beneath the surface. This is clearly discernible in Major's own description of dealing with cabinet indiscipline: 'In February [1995] I wearily instructed cabinet once more to end the "speculation and debate" over the single currency. In my heart, I knew the words would have little effect, and as expected, off-the-record briefing on the subject continued.'[17] Once out of office, Major regretted that he had 'rarely found his authentic voice in politics'.[18] In retrospect, he felt that he had been 'too conservative, too conventional. Too safe, too often. Too defensive. Too reactive'.[19] In his view, he had a 'rough-and-ready decency' and he 'should have advocated it more often and made a virtue of it'.[20] Even this strategy would probably not have turned the tide. Major was irreversibly beached upon a visibly outmoded and discredited brand of leadership. Like

Margaret Thatcher, he had been instrumental in creating the conditions in which his vision of leadership was no longer consistent with the changing patterns of leadership norms and expectations.

Another dimension of this strand of leadership competition is provided by the impulse towards mutual security. In spite of the confrontational enmity that exists between leaders competing for the premiership, there is also a level of interdependency and with it an impulse towards stability. Parties and leaders invest prodigious resources into the establishment and marketing of their own leaderships. However, they also commit comparable levels of time and energy to the targeting of opposition leaders and their claims to national leadership. The extended juxtaposition of the two main party leaders can reach a state of near symbiosis in which the meaning and relevance of each leader's credentials come to rely on the presence of the other leader. In essence, each leader is portrayed as being the solution to the problem of the other leader. A leader may subject another leader to every variety of condemnation and vilification, but such assaults are not normally designed to precipitate a change of leadership.

A rapid and unforeseen leadership change is more disruptive to the other party than it is to the party making the alteration. Just as Labour was suddenly disorientated by the dramatic departure of Margaret Thatcher in 1990, so the Conservatives were caught wholly off balance by the events surrounding the death of John Smith. Accordingly, the Labour leadership was acutely anxious when John Major triggered a leadership contest in 1995. 'The Blairite project presupposed Major's continuance in office'[21] and, therefore, it was essential that the Labour leadership calibrate its reactions to give as much assistance as possible to the prime minister, but not to the extent of making it appear that Major was Labour's preferred candidate. Blair was concerned that a Conservative party led by Michael Heseltine would not only be harder to beat, but would badly disrupt Labour's planning and strategy. The Labour party as a whole was conspicuously quiet during the contest. It is widely believed in Conservative circles that Blair gave Major such an easy ride in the last Prime Minister's Questions before the ballot, that the prime minister was able to give an able and witty performance in front of his electorate. Blair also wrote an article for *The Times* in which he recounted the standard indictment of the government, but qualified it by a strategically understated, yet highly significant, acknowledgement of John Major's value as a political leader. He concluded that even though the Conservatives were 'divided beyond repair', their plight was at least moderated by the presence of John Major: 'With the possible exception of the Prime Minister, nobody is capable of closing the gap between the two wings which are fast becoming two parties.'[22]

The end result of the contest was precisely what Tony Blair would have preferred as the optimum outcome: namely a weakened John Major but one whose security of tenure had been confirmed until the General Election. The leader of the opposition therefore was 'the long term gainer from the leadership contest.'[23] Once Major was re-elected to the leadership, Blair was immediately able to revert to the standard strategy. The relief that his quarry had survived was palpable:

> [T]he result is that whatever changes are made to the Cabinet, and whatever presentational changes are made, that drift and that lack of direction will simply continue. They opened the lid with the leadership election. They peered inside and were sufficiently horrified to slam the lid back on again. But those divisions are there and heaven only knows what type of government we'll get from now on.[24]

The episode served to reinforce the importance that is attached to maintaining the integrity of the context within which leaders compete against one another. Even though both the Conservative and Labour parties now approve of the free market principle, where leadership competition is concerned there remains a marked aversion in the leadership market to any instability in the form of new products and rebranding exercises.

The Thatcher–Blair nexus

The final strand that warrants individual recognition is the symbolic and substantive connection between Margaret Thatcher and Tony Blair. The linkage provided not only a continuous subtext to the Major–Blair competition but also a key point of reference by which both leaders could be perceived and assessed. In different ways, Major and Blair used Thatcher in the creation and projection of their leadership identities. In Major's case, he used the Thatcher experience in a critical context, in order to establish himself as a counterweight to his predecessor. More significantly, it was Blair who made approving references to Thatcher and who sought to establish her as a standard of leadership against which both he and Major could be judged. At the same time that John Major was intent upon removing Thatcher from the matrix of leadership competition, Tony Blair was using his position to reinstate her and to draw on her record as a model of leadership that should be emulated rather than denounced. The prime minister wanted to restore the status and prestige of 'transactional leadership' where the emphasis lay upon political exchange, effective brokerage and negotiated settlements. Blair, on the other hand, was determined to adopt Thatcher's characteristic style of 'transformative leadership', which sought to alter the customary profile of political attachments both by energising participants to an appreciation of new objectives and by fostering high levels of collective purpose to achieve them.[25]

Some of Tony Blair's conspicuous attachment to Margaret Thatcher was attributed to political expediency. The figure and record of Thatcher had become a useful device by which to embarrass the prime minister and to create further disturbance within the Conservative party. On the other hand, there is little doubt that Tony Blair personally admired Margaret Thatcher for the way she combined a radical programme with the driving energy to achieve it. Blair also held a programme to renew Britain and, like Thatcher, was personally disposed to lead from the front with the same clarity and conviction that she had shown in the 1980s. It was recognised within New Labour that Margaret Thatcher had had a 'clear set of goals' and had worked to 'make everything (and everyone) conform to these priorities'.[26] Now Blair had a personal agenda and like Mrs Thatcher he was 'impatient when others [did] not have the courage or imagination to go along with him'.[27] Blair did not demur from the suggestive associations that these assertions produced. The *Sunday Telegraph*, for example, acknowledged that Blair was a 'student of Lady Thatcher'.[28] He was described as admiring 'her vigorous prosecution of a clear point of view',[29] which the paper recognised was in stark contrast to John Major style of leadership. By contrast, Blair was depicted as being as resolutely geared to the leadership role as Margaret Thatcher had been in the past. Martin Jacques observed the shift to Thatcher appreciation within New Labour, which in itself was a mark of Blair's leadership:

> Blair's constant point of reference is Margaret Thatcher. He admires her radicalism, her sheer courage and determination, and much of what she did. Blair was the first Labour leader to recognise that many of the changes of the eighties – globalisation, privatisation, the redefinition of the state, the growth of individualism – were both inevitable and desirable.[30]

Philip Gould strongly supported this linkage. Survey research and focus group evidence showed that strong leadership was widely approved by the public: 'They want politicians who are tough, honest and courageous, and who govern with principle. That is why they respected Margaret Thatcher and in the end lost faith in John Major. The public want leaders who lead, they want governments that tough it out.'[31]

The Thatcherite parallel was not merely appropriated for political effect. It was actively cultivated with the woman herself. Blair afforded her public respect; asked for and accepted her guidance; and gave full recognition to her achievements. Although Thatcher 'was dying, politically', John Rentoul describes how Blair 'kept her alive'[32] at the very time that John Major wanted to bury her: 'Her gratitude and pride at Blair's seeking her advice, combined with her irritation at the pygmy succession in her own party, made her easy prey for an opportunist of instinctive political genius. In contrast to John Major's sullen resentment at her back-seat driving, Blair put her in the front seat and politely listened to her directions – while steering the vehicle where he willed.'[33]

Blair's campaign to lead the Labour party was peppered with references, veiled or otherwise, to Margaret Thatcher leadership qualities. His drive for the premiership was similarly characterised by constant allusions to the claim that Britain was 'crying out for strong leadership and clear distinction'.[34] In government, the memory of Major's shambolic administration and the way it became so vulnerable to unfavourable comparisons with the Thatcher era remained a powerful conditioning factor.

This construction of recent history deeply affected the governing style of the Blair premiership. The overriding consideration in key decision-making was that the new prime minister should not look weak. For example, in 1997 Blair was faced with his first backbench revolt. The highly contentious issue relating to the cancellation of projected additional payments to single parents on social security provoked a powerful parliamentary protest. According to Andrew Rawnsley, this action was perceived in Number 10 as 'a virility test' for Blair – 'a challenge to his toughness'.[35] The model of Margaret Thatcher and the memory of John Major's dysfunctional government were shown to have been internalised as conditioned reflexes: 'If the choice was between being seen as weak and dithering or harsh and unbending, then he would choose to be seen as Margaret Thatcher rather than John Major. The cut was going to proceed.'[36] Margaret Thatcher's once notorious vices had been metamorphosed into legendary virtues in the crucible of Major's dissolution. John Major had come to the premiership determined to provide an antidote to Margaret Thatcher. But ultimately, it was Tony Blair who sensed that the more important antidote was the one that would counteract the leadership of the Major administration and replace it with something identifiably similar to the Thatcher design.

Margaret Thatcher's reinstatement as a leader of legendary focus and formidable drive, combined with Tony Blair's transfiguration of the Labour party into an electoral machine capable of winning two successive landslides, has had a significant aggregate effect upon British politics. In essence, it has established a culture of leadership within the conventions and strategies of political conduct. While Margaret Thatcher already has a mythic status in this dimension, Tony Blair will acquire similarly iconic properties either before leaving office, or shortly afterwards. He will have demonstrated that Thatcher was not an aberrant feature of exceptional circumstances, so much as the expression of a set of leadership dynamics that he himself extended to an even higher level of personalisation and projection.

Notwithstanding the extent to which Thatcher and Blair can be wholly construed as representing a continuity of systemic forces, the sheer scale of their political success ensures that they will constitute a gold standard for party planning and leadership aspiration well into the foreseeable future. Both leaders will become part of a largely undifferentiated model of leadership achievement, in which political and electoral success will be characterised and explained by reference to leadership-centred categories and virtues. Leaders operating in a post-Blair political environment, along with party strategists, political planners and market researchers will seek to emulate the Thatcher-Blair model. At the same time, leadership aspirants will press the case for their candidacies by claims that they would be better able than their competitors to satisfy the criteria of such a model. Incumbents and challengers will have to accustom themselves not merely to demonstrating leadership of a party, but to establishing and maintaining a controlling influence of the leadership issue that now runs through British politics. The joint legacy of Thatcher and Blair, therefore, will ensure that the high-profile nature of leadership presentation will remain intensely competitive, as leaders and contenders seek to unlock the established potential of the British system for leader-led political advances.

The present study has sought to show that the pivotal period in this emphatic and deepening process of leadership politics coincided with the administrations of John Major. The extent to which Thatcher's successor was personally culpable for the Conservative party's disarray and subsequent electoral collapse is open to question. What is indisputable is that Major came not only to be associated with weak leadership but to be indelibly equated with a prolonged and chronic leadership crisis that became the defining condition of his government. Many complex issues and developments were reduced – often inaccurately and unfairly – to the personal inadequacies of the prime minister. Ironically, for a highly pragmatic politician who valued conciliation and consensus above all else, Major became the centrepiece of internecine factionalism and sectarian strife within his own party. To the extent that Major sought to invest his leadership with the imprimatur of his own personal experiences and qualities, so the disabling effects of his government's specta-cular deterioration attached themselves to him in the form of individual failure. As a consequence, John Major's style of leadership and its perceived effects remain, and will continue to be, a powerful conditioning factor to future leadership conduct. Today's leaders and their replacements will look as much to Major as to Blair for guidance in the construction and maintenance of their claims to leadership credentials. The compulsion to avoid any repetition of Major's dysfunctional governments will continue to complement the more seductive appeal of emulating Blair's achievements in turning the leadership issue to his own long-term political advantage.

At the end of his parliamentary career in 2001, John Major looked back upon his premiership and remained mystified by how his style had come to be criticised and rejected as ineffectual: 'I tried to revive the essence of genuine cabinet government in the early Nineties, only to be told by those who pronounce on such things that this was not strong leadership: strong leaders apparently make up their minds before any debate and do not draw on collective wisdom.'[37] Major resolutely continued to believe that his brand of leadership had its merits over that of his predecessor and especially over the style of his of the Blair government: 'My approach – listening, considering, cajoling and then deciding – although possibly old-fashioned, was more in the tradition of democratic government than the imposition of views pre-determined in discussion with advisers rather than with elected colleagues in cabinet.'[38] Implicit in Major's comment was a hope that the philosophy and value of his leadership would come to be recognised in the future. The contemporary dynamics of leadership competition, together with the deterrent effect of John Major's own notorious premiership, suggest that the wait will be a very long one.

Paradoxically in the present climate, Major's brand of non-controversial pragmatism would be highly controversial in its inhibition upon the development and outreach of leadership. His rejection of transformative leadership would not be regarded as conciliatory, so much as inflammatory in dispensing with such a valuable instrument of mobilisation. To imitate Major's professed lack of vision would be seen as rendering a leader blind to the possibilities of creating a new identity for a party in the post-ideological age. In effect, leadership, or at least the claim to leadership, is now a deeply rooted component of the political battle. As John Major discovered with Margaret Thatcher and then with Tony Blair, the problems of strong leadership are not resolved by its diminution but by its renewal and reconstitution.

Notes

1 'The will to win', *Sunday Times*, 13 October 1996.
2 Robert M. Worcester and Roger Mortimore, *Explaining Labour's Landslide* (London: Politico's, 1999), p. 50.
3 For example, see Anthony King, 'The Rise of the Career Politician in Britain and Its Consequences', *British Journal of Political Science*, vol. 2 no. 3 (July 1981), pp. 249–86; Peter Riddell, *Honest Opportunism: The Rise of the Career Politician* (London: Hamish Hamilton, 1993).
4 Riddell, *Honest Opportunism*, p. 28.
5 Riddell, *Honest Opportunism*, p. 26.
6 Martin Burch and Ian Holliday, *The British Cabinet* System (London: Prentice Hall/ Harvester Wheatsheaf, 1996), pp. 142–6.
7 John Major, *The Autobiography* (London: HarperCollins, 1999), p. 210.
8 Quoted in David Wastell, 'Why Mr Dull is my hero, by John Major', *Sunday Telegraph*, 3 November 1991.
9 'The models for Mr Major', *Sunday Telegraph*, 3 November 1991.
10 Alan Cochrane and Peter Dobbie, 'Now he's a king of hearts', *Mail on Sunday*, 13 October 1991.
11 Quoted in Barbara Amiel, 'The man who would be Major', *Sunday Times*, 29 March 1992.

12 Chris Brady, 'Collective Responsibility of the Cabinet: An Ethical, Constitutional or Managerial Tool?' *Parliamentary Affairs*, 52, no. 2 (April 1999), p. 222.

13 Brady, 'Collective Responsibility of the Cabinet: An Ethical, Constitutional or Managerial Tool?' p. 223.

14 Major, *The Autobiography*, p. 209.

15 Major, *The Autobiography*, p. 219.

16 Major, *The Autobiography*, p. 178.

17 Major, *The Autobiography*, p. 604.

18 Major, *The Autobiography*, p. xxi.

19 Major, *The Autobiography*, p. xxi.

20 Major, *The Autobiography*, p. xxii.

21 Hywel Williams, *Guilty Men: Conservative Decline and Fall 1992–1997* (London: Aurum, 1998), p. 120.

22 Tony Blair , 'Labour's better way', *The Times*, 30 June 1995.

23 Peter Riddell, 'Only Blair gains in the end', *The Times*, 7 July 1995.

24 Quoted in Stephen Goodwin, 'Opposition MPs cock-a-hoop at result they had hoped for', *The Independent*, 5 July 1995.

25 For a full examination of the distinction between these two different kinds of leadership, see James MacGregor Burns, *Leadership* (New York: Harper and Row, 1979), chs 1, 16, 17.

26 Peter Mandelson and Roger Liddle, *The Blair Revolution: Can New Labour Deliver?* (London: Faber and Faber, 1996), p. 236.

27 Mandelson and Liddle, *The Blair Revolution*, p. 238.

28 'A vote for change', *Sunday Telegraph*, 2 July 1995.

29 'A vote for change'.

30 Martin Jacques, 'His project for the party is a triumph, but what about his project for the country?' *The Guardian*, 26 September 1996.

31 Philip Gould, *The Unfinished Revolution: How the Modernisers Saved the Labour Party* (London: Little, Brown, 1998), p. 328.

32 John Rentoul, *Tony Blair: Prime Minister* (London: Little, Brown, 2001), p. 276.

33 Rentoul, *Tony Blair*, p. 276.

34 Tony Blair, 'Britain is crying out for strong leadership', *Daily Telegraph*, 8 December 1994.

35 Andrew Rawnsley, *Servants of the People: The Inside Story of New Labour* (London: Penguin, 2001), p. 113.

36 Rawnsley, *Servants of the People*, p. 114.

37 John Major, 'Goodbye (… and good riddance to Tony Blair's shameful attitude to Parliament)', *Mail on Sunday*, 4 March 2001.

38 Major, 'Goodbye (… and good riddance to Tony Blair's shameful attitude to Parliament)'.

Index